JASON T. KRUSE
WRITER, ARTIST, CREATOR

RAY MCINTYRE
COLORIST

PATRICK COYLE
LETTERING AND BOOK DESIGN

JOHN CASEY
LETTERING ASSISTANT

SHANNON ERIC DENTON
KOMIKWERKS, LLC.
BOOK PACKAGING

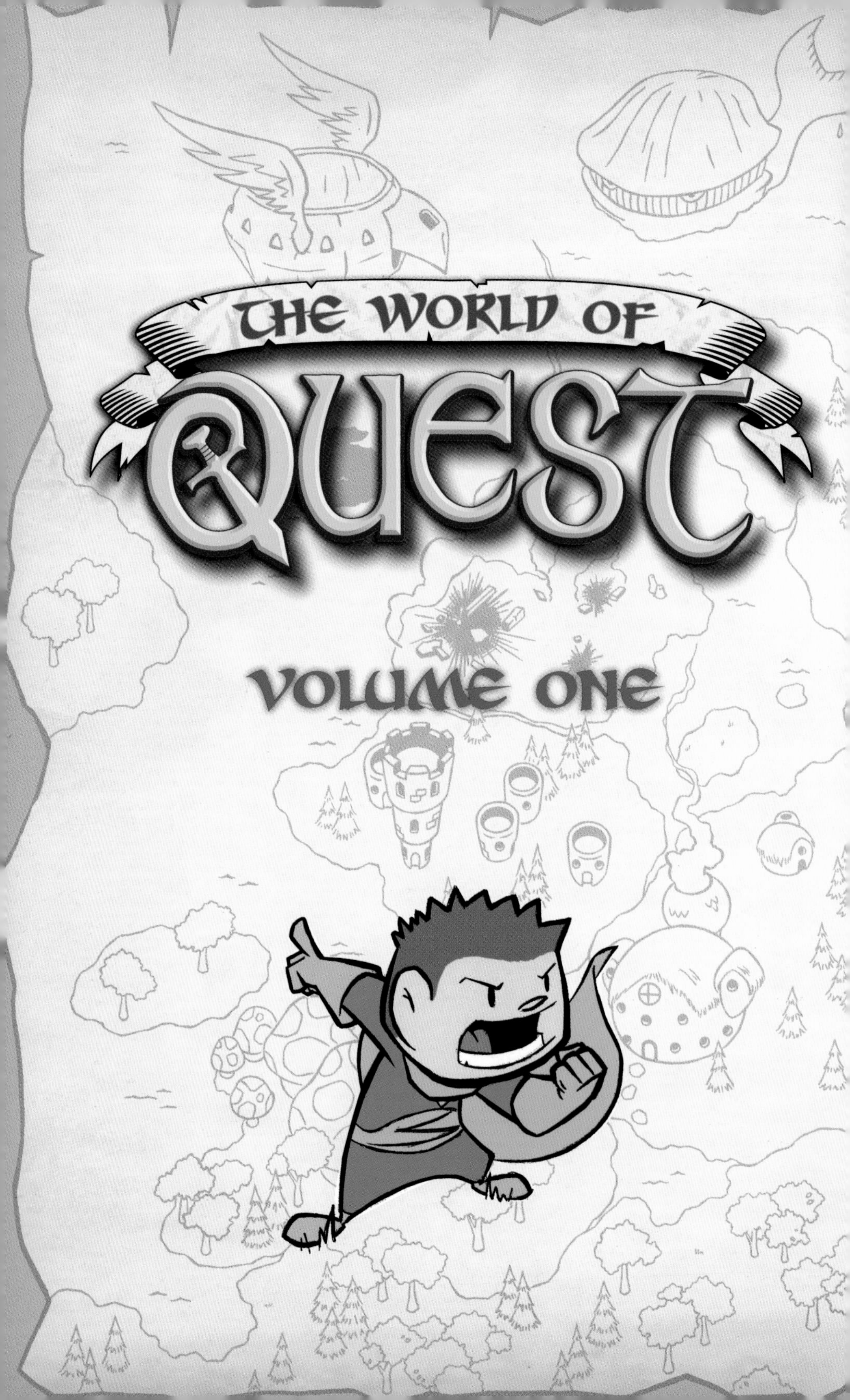
THE WORLD OF
QUEST
VOLUME ONE

CONTENTS

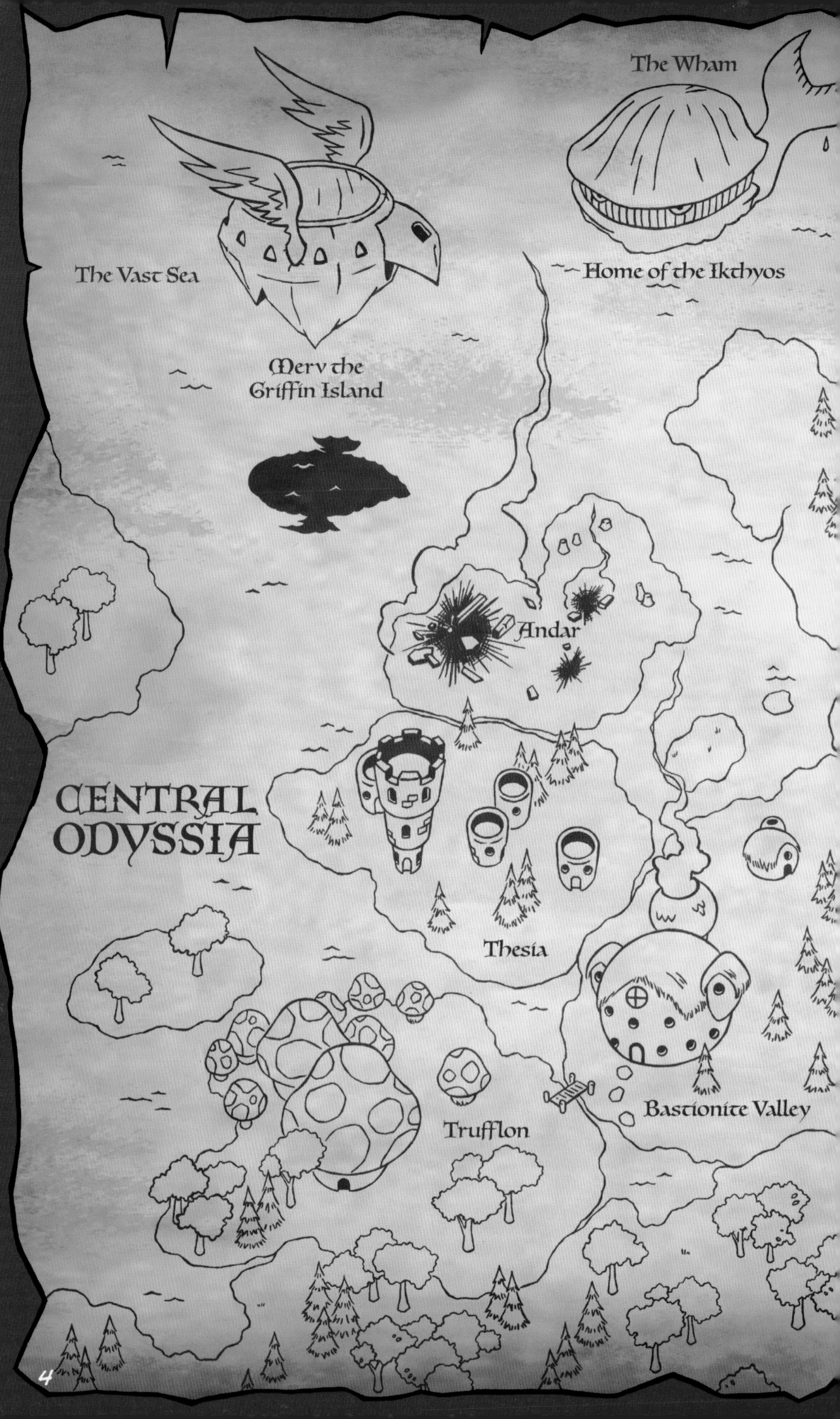
The Wham
The Vast Sea
Home of the Ikthyos
Merv the
Griffin Island
Andar
CENTRAL
ODYSSIA
Thesia
Bastionite Valley
Trufflon

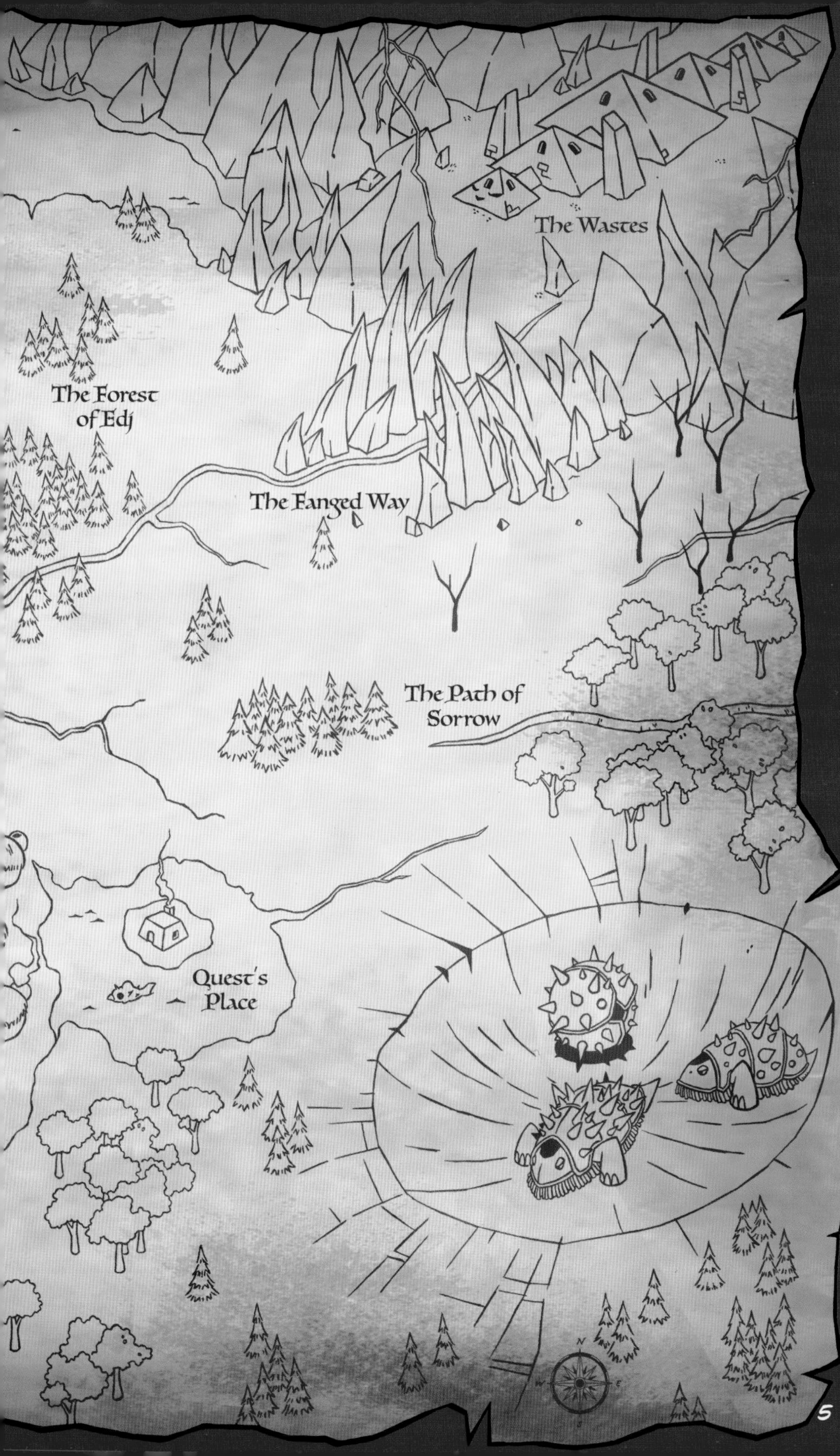

The Wastes
The Forest of Edj
The Fanged Way
The Path of Sorrow
Quest's Place
N
W
E
S

CHAPTER ONE
GETTING TO KNOW YOU...

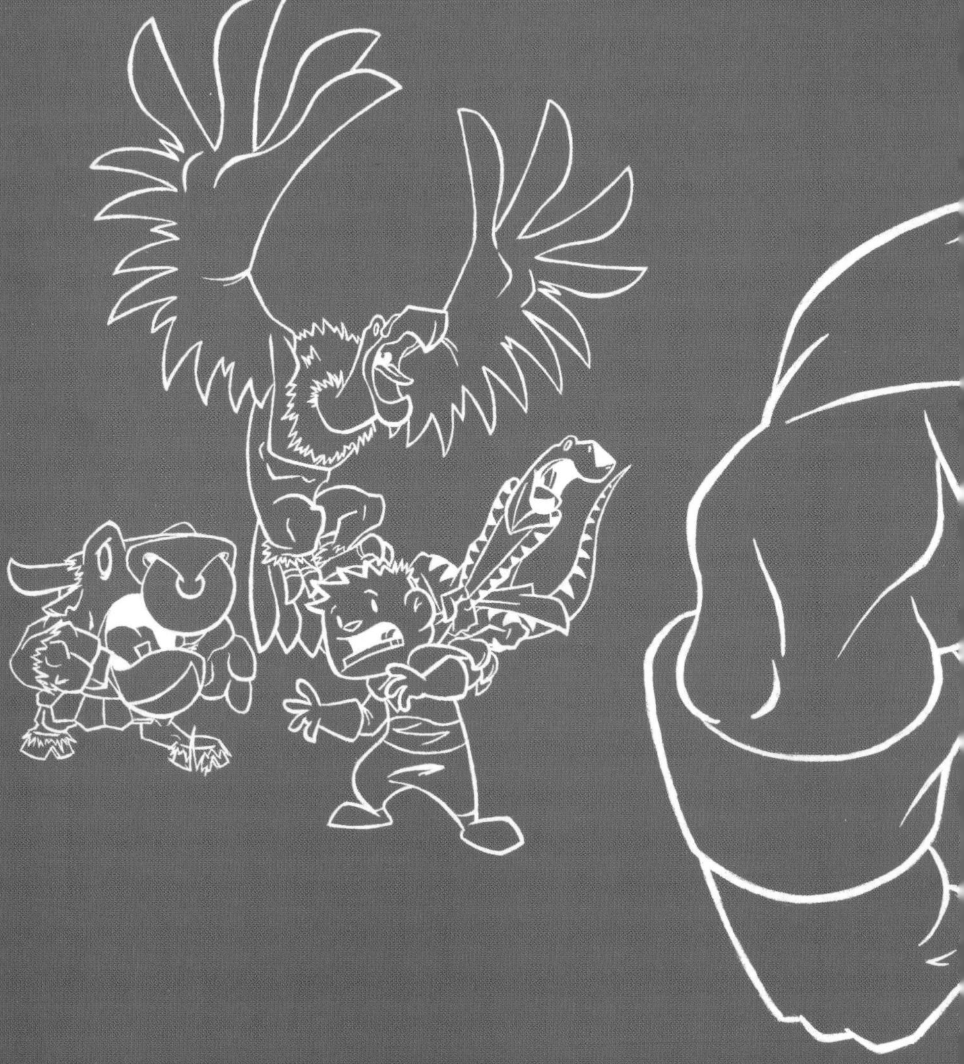

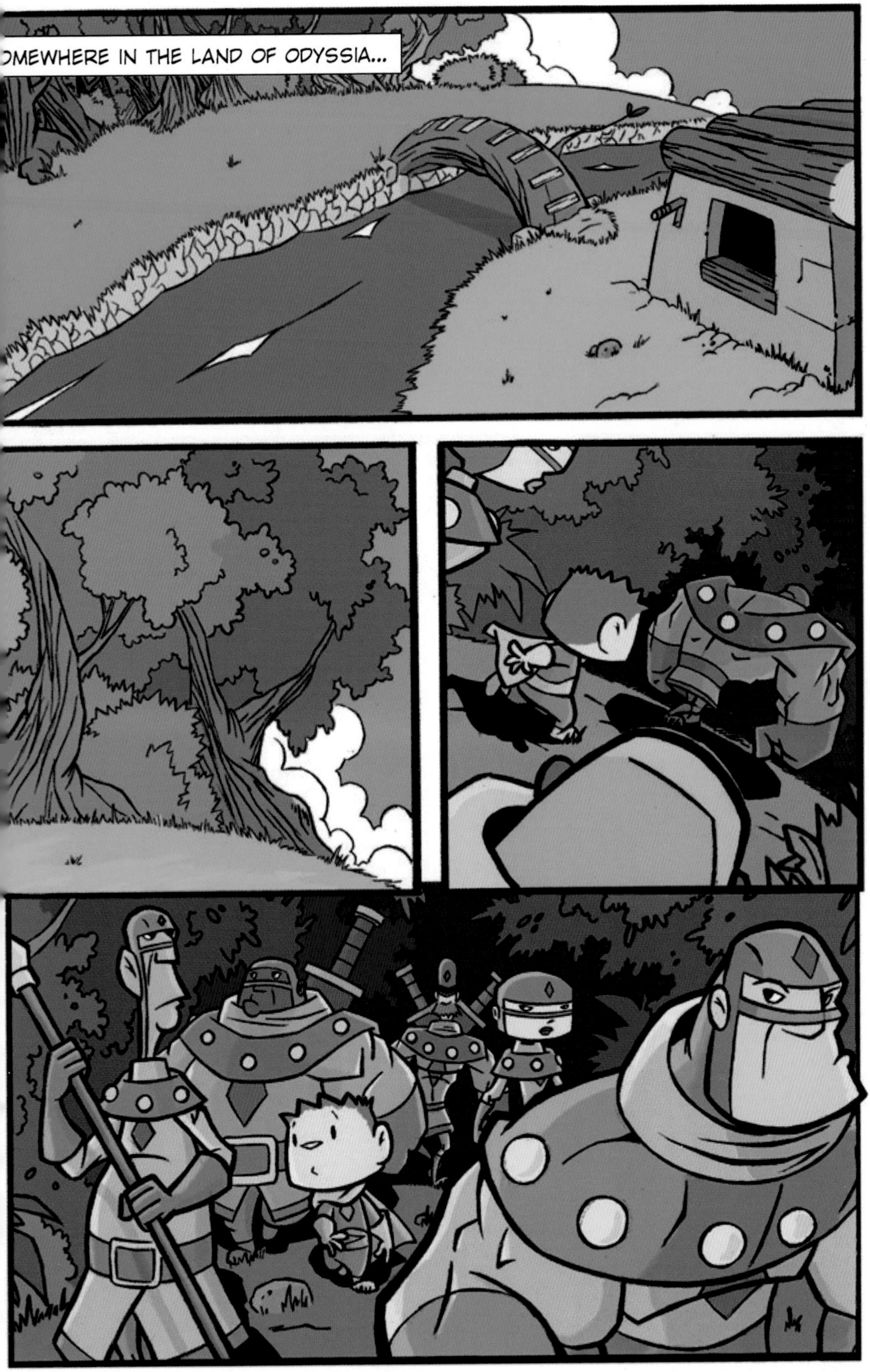
OMEWHERE IN THE LAND OF ODYSSIA...

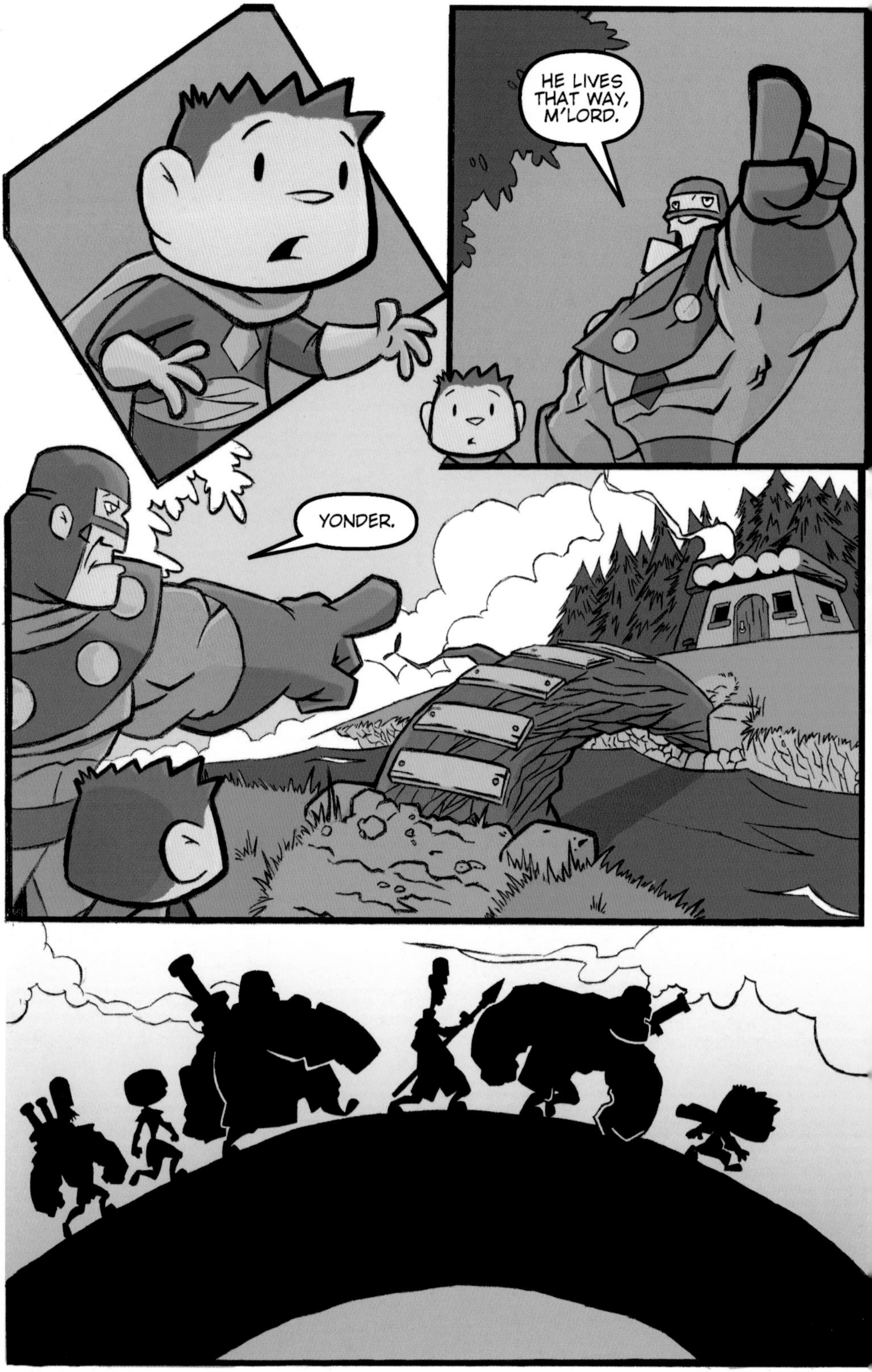
HE LIVES THAT WAY, M'LORD.
YONDER.

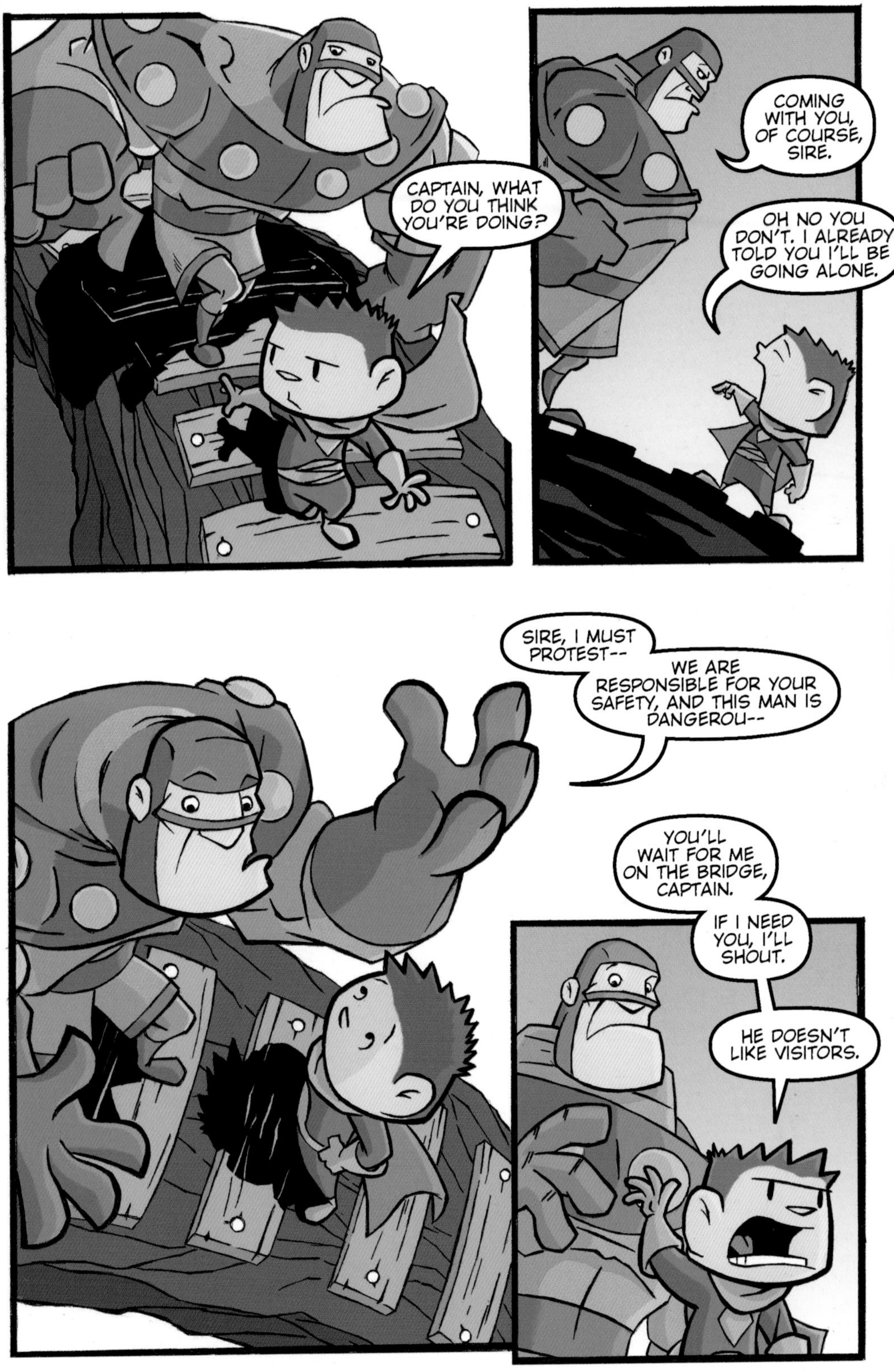
CAPTAIN, WHAT DO YOU THINK YOU'RE DOING?
COMING WITH YOU, OF COURSE, SIRE.
OH NO YOU DON'T. I ALREADY TOLD YOU I'LL BE GOING ALONE.
SIRE, I MUST PROTEST--
WE ARE RESPONSIBLE FOR YOUR SAFETY, AND THIS MAN IS DANGEROU--
YOU'LL WAIT FOR ME ON THE BRIDGE, CAPTAIN.
IF I NEED YOU, I'LL SHOUT.
HE DOESN'T LIKE VISITORS.

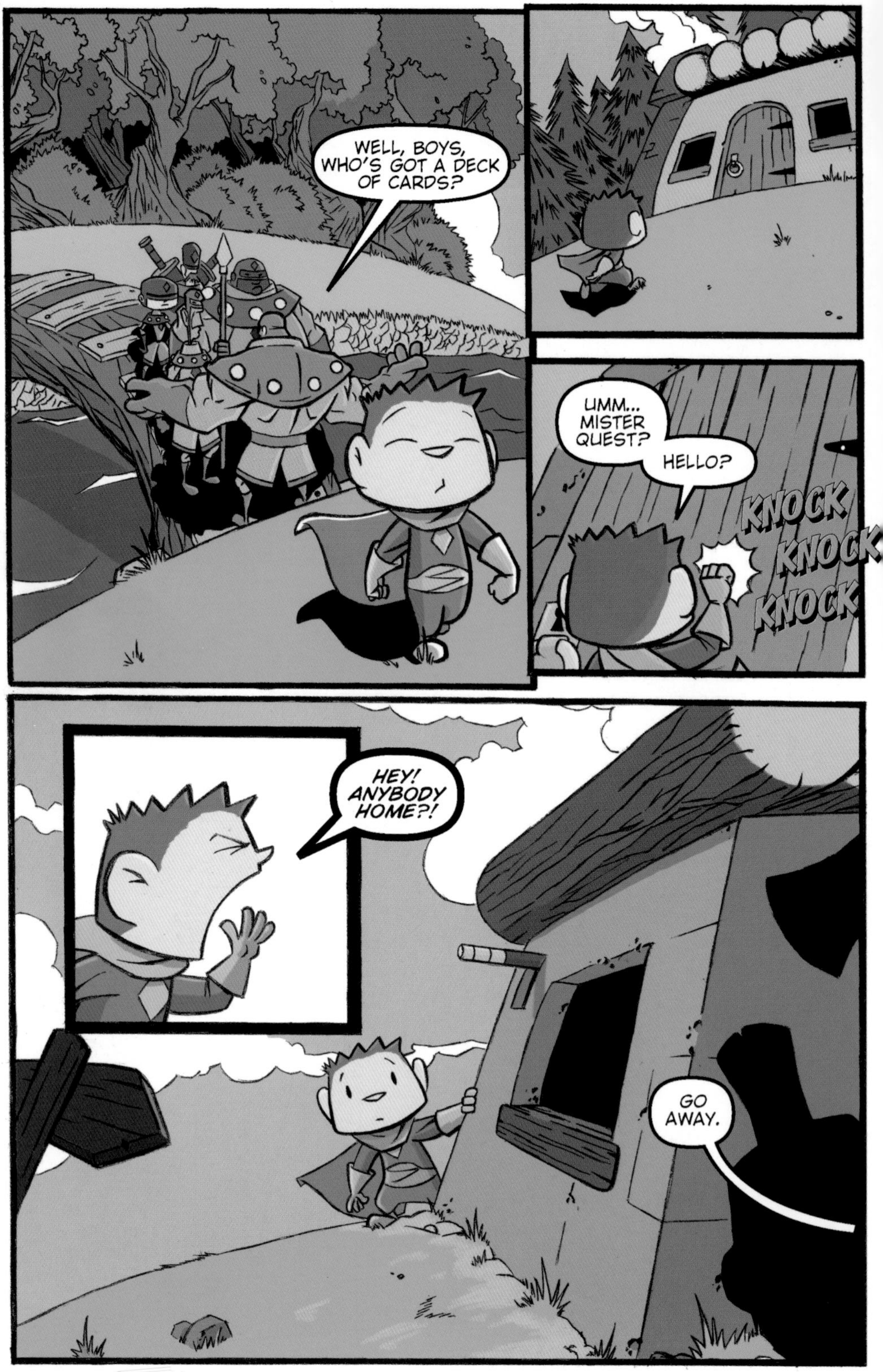
WELL, BOYS, WHO'S GOT A DECK OF CARDS?
UMM... MISTER QUEST?
HELLO?
KNOCK KNOCK KNOCK
HEY! ANYBODY HOME?!
GO AWAY.

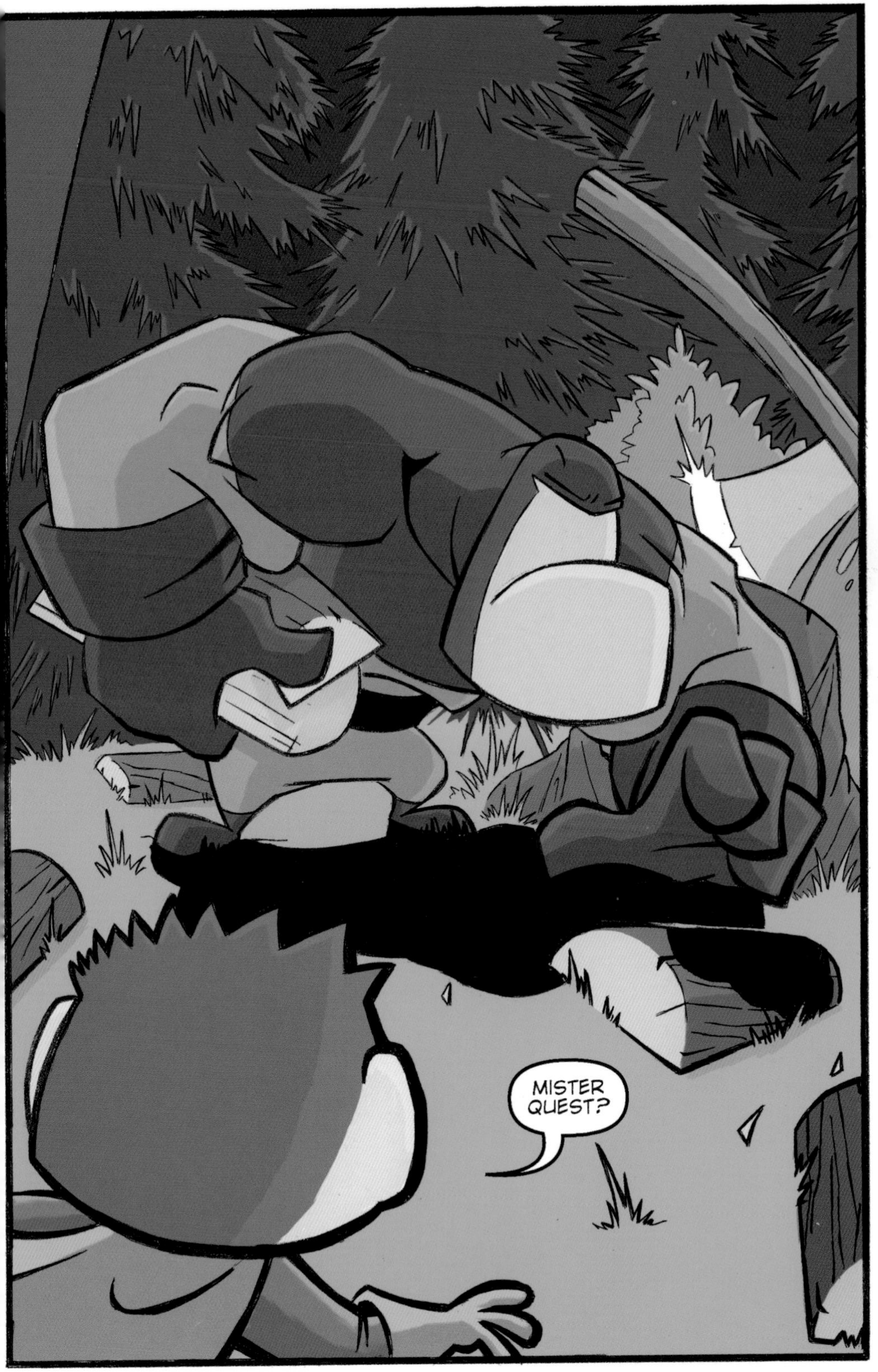
MISTER QUEST?

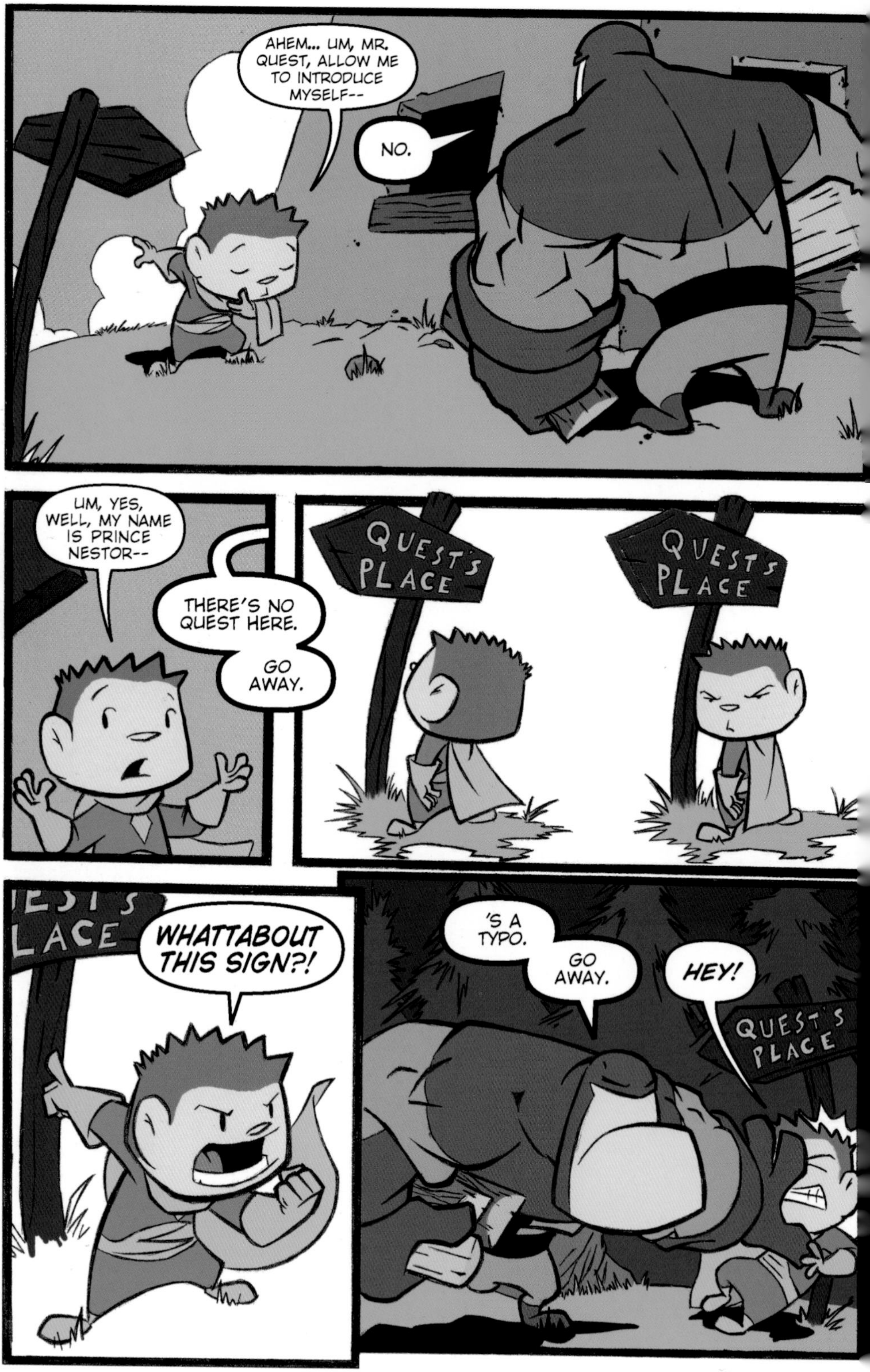
AHEM... UM, MR. QUEST, ALLOW ME TO INTRODUCE MYSELF--
NO.
UM, YES, WELL, MY NAME IS PRINCE NESTOR--
THERE'S NO QUEST HERE.
GO AWAY.
QUEST'S PLACE
QUEST'S PLACE
WHATTABOUT THIS SIGN?!
'S A TYPO.
GO AWAY.
HEY!
QUEST'S PLACE

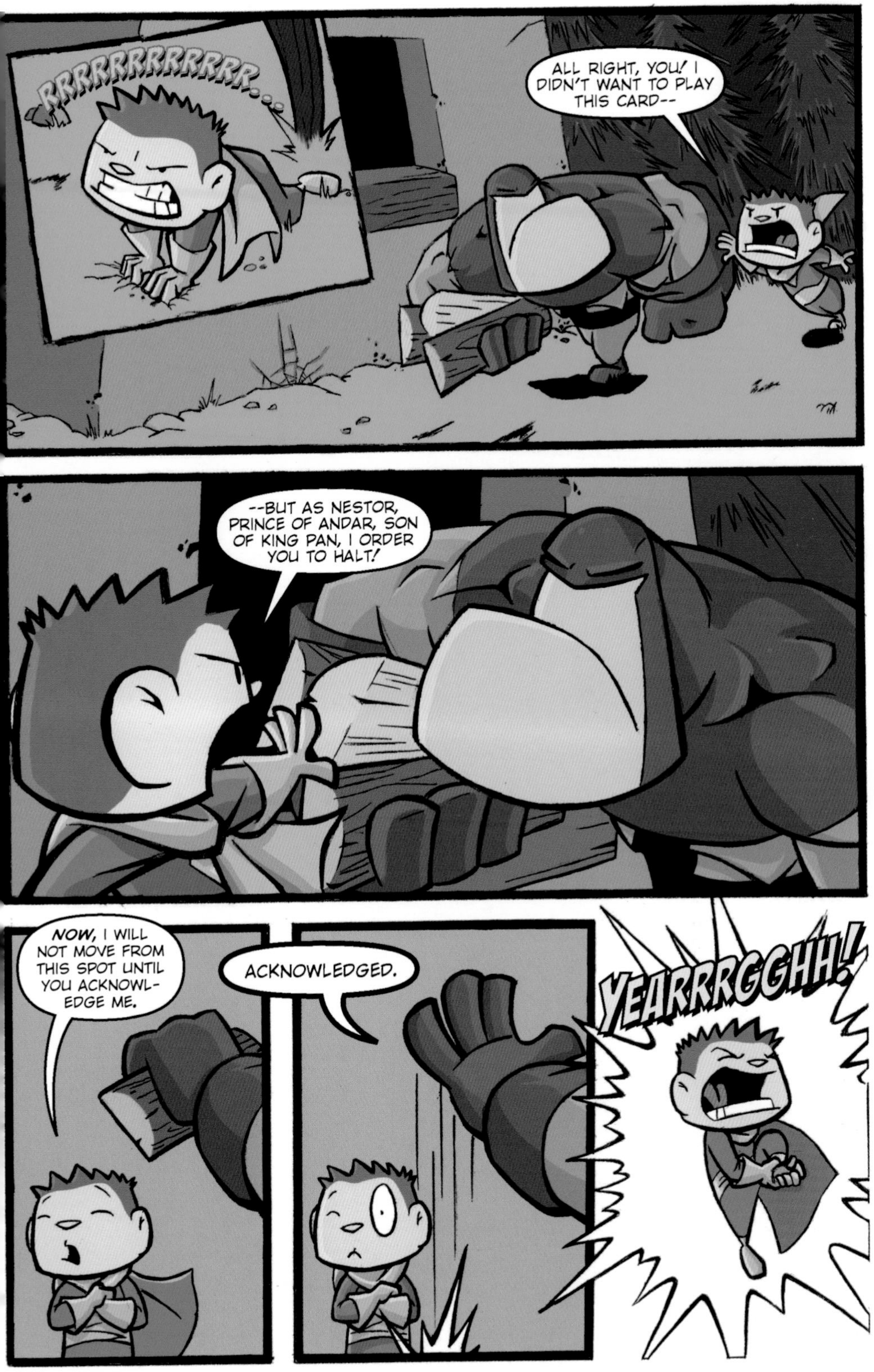
RRRRRRRRRRRRR...
ALL RIGHT, YOU! I DIDN'T WANT TO PLAY THIS CARD--
--BUT AS NESTOR, PRINCE OF ANDAR, SON OF KING PAN, I ORDER YOU TO HALT!
NOW, I WILL NOT MOVE FROM THIS SPOT UNTIL YOU ACKNOWL-EDGE ME.
ACKNOWLEDGED.
YEARRRGGHH!

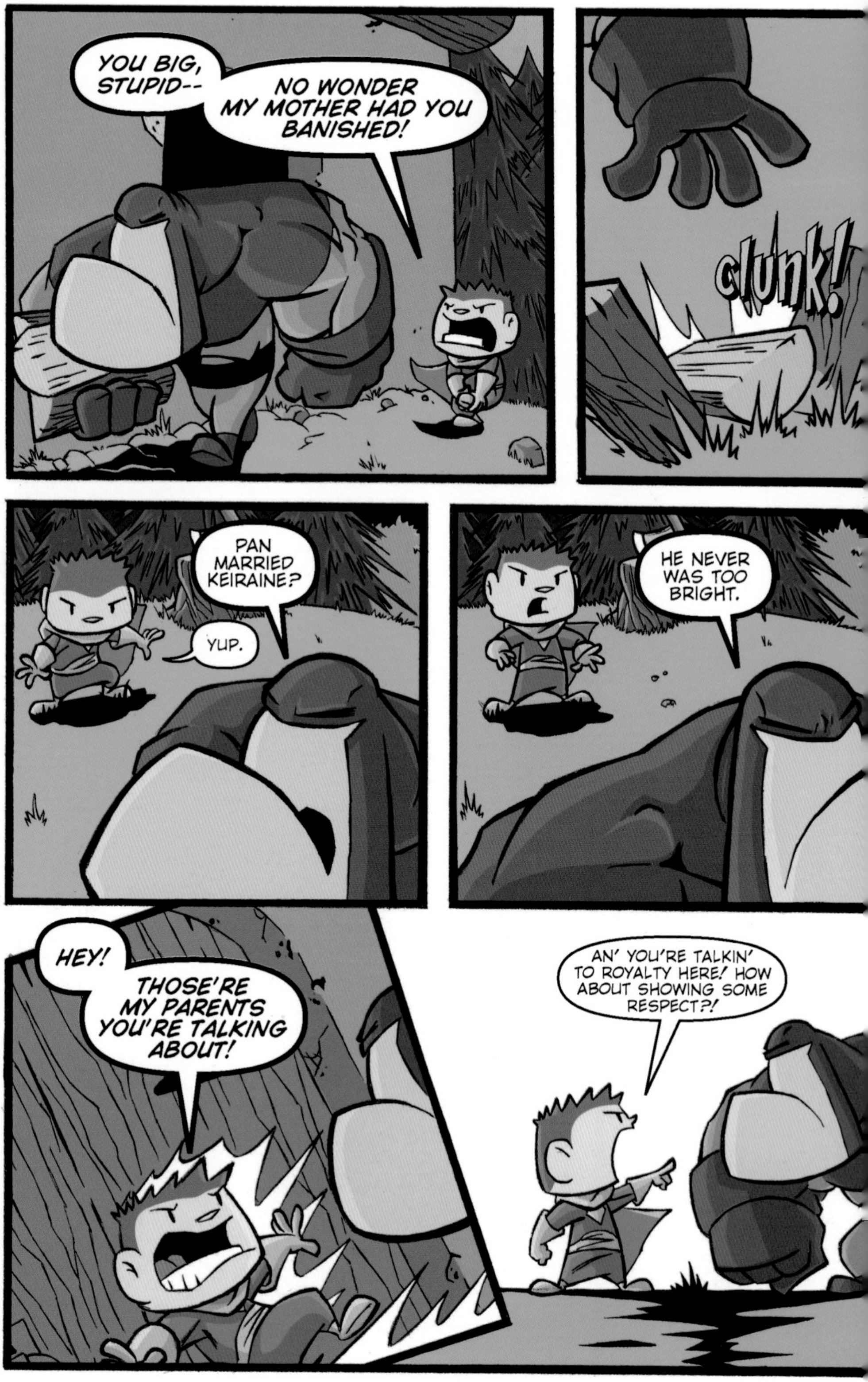
YOU BIG, STUPID--
NO WONDER MY MOTHER HAD YOU BANISHED!
CLUNK!
PAN MARRIED KEIRAINE?
YUP.
HE NEVER WAS TOO BRIGHT.
HEY!
THOSE'RE MY PARENTS YOU'RE TALKING ABOUT!
AN' YOU'RE TALKIN' TO ROYALTY HERE! HOW ABOUT SHOWING SOME RESPECT?!

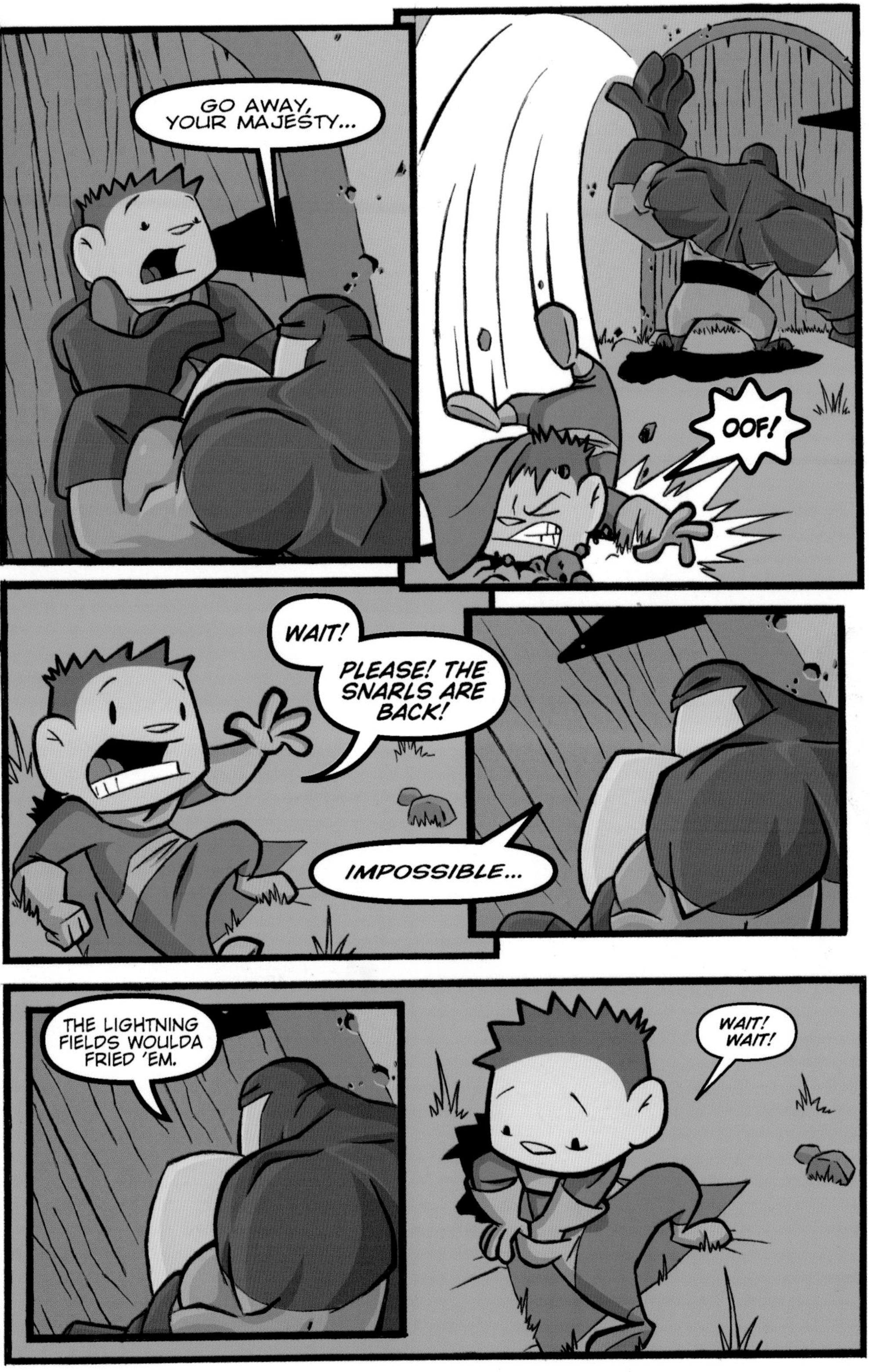
GO AWAY, YOUR MAJESTY...
OOF!
WAIT!
PLEASE! THE SNARLS ARE BACK!
IMPOSSIBLE...
THE LIGHTNING FIELDS WOULDA FRIED 'EM.
WAIT! WAIT!

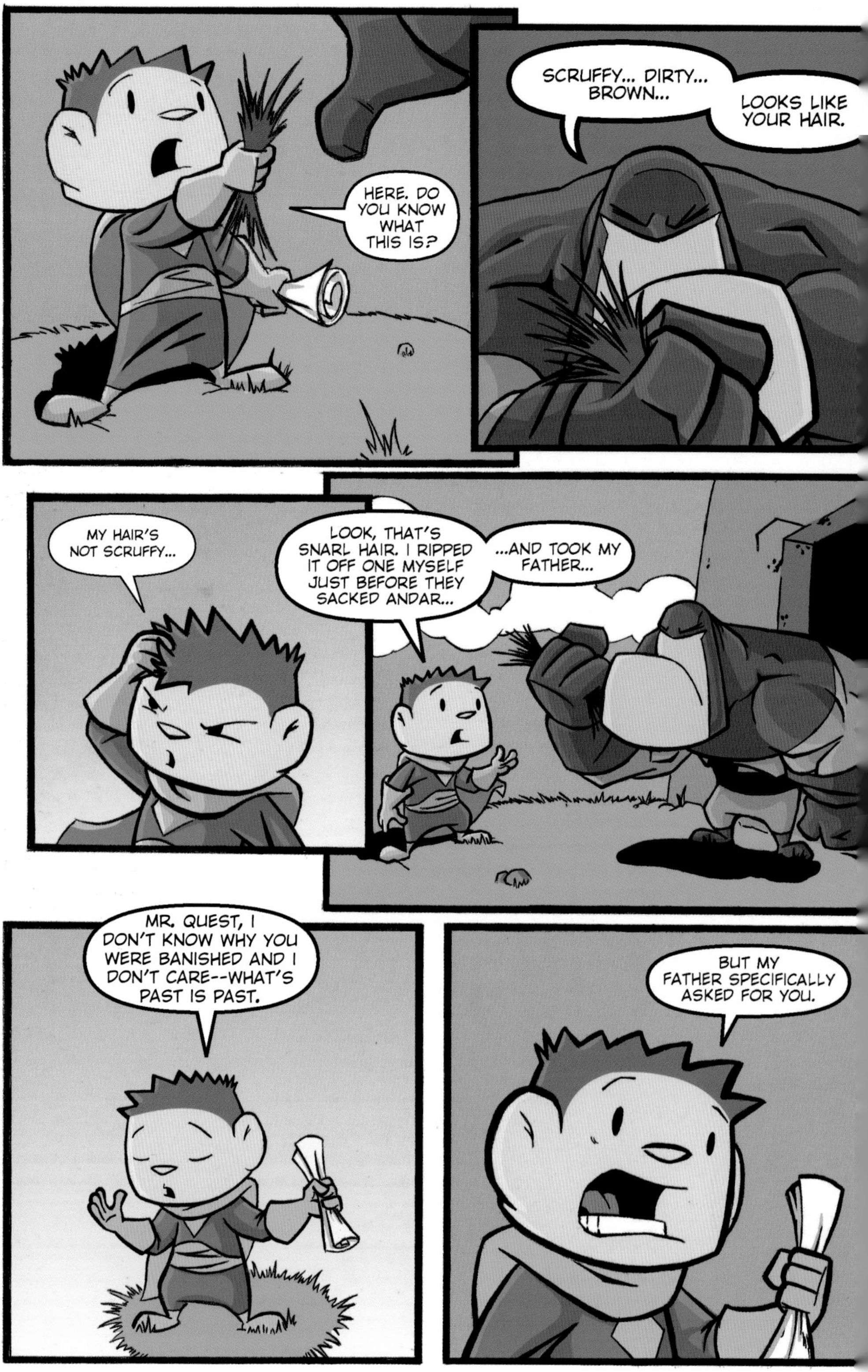
HERE. DO YOU KNOW WHAT THIS IS?
SCRUFFY... DIRTY... BROWN...
LOOKS LIKE YOUR HAIR.
MY HAIR'S NOT SCRUFFY...
LOOK, THAT'S SNARL HAIR. I RIPPED IT OFF ONE MYSELF JUST BEFORE THEY SACKED ANDAR...
...AND TOOK MY FATHER...
MR. QUEST, I DON'T KNOW WHY YOU WERE BANISHED AND I DON'T CARE--WHAT'S PAST IS PAST.
BUT MY FATHER SPECIFICALLY ASKED FOR YOU.

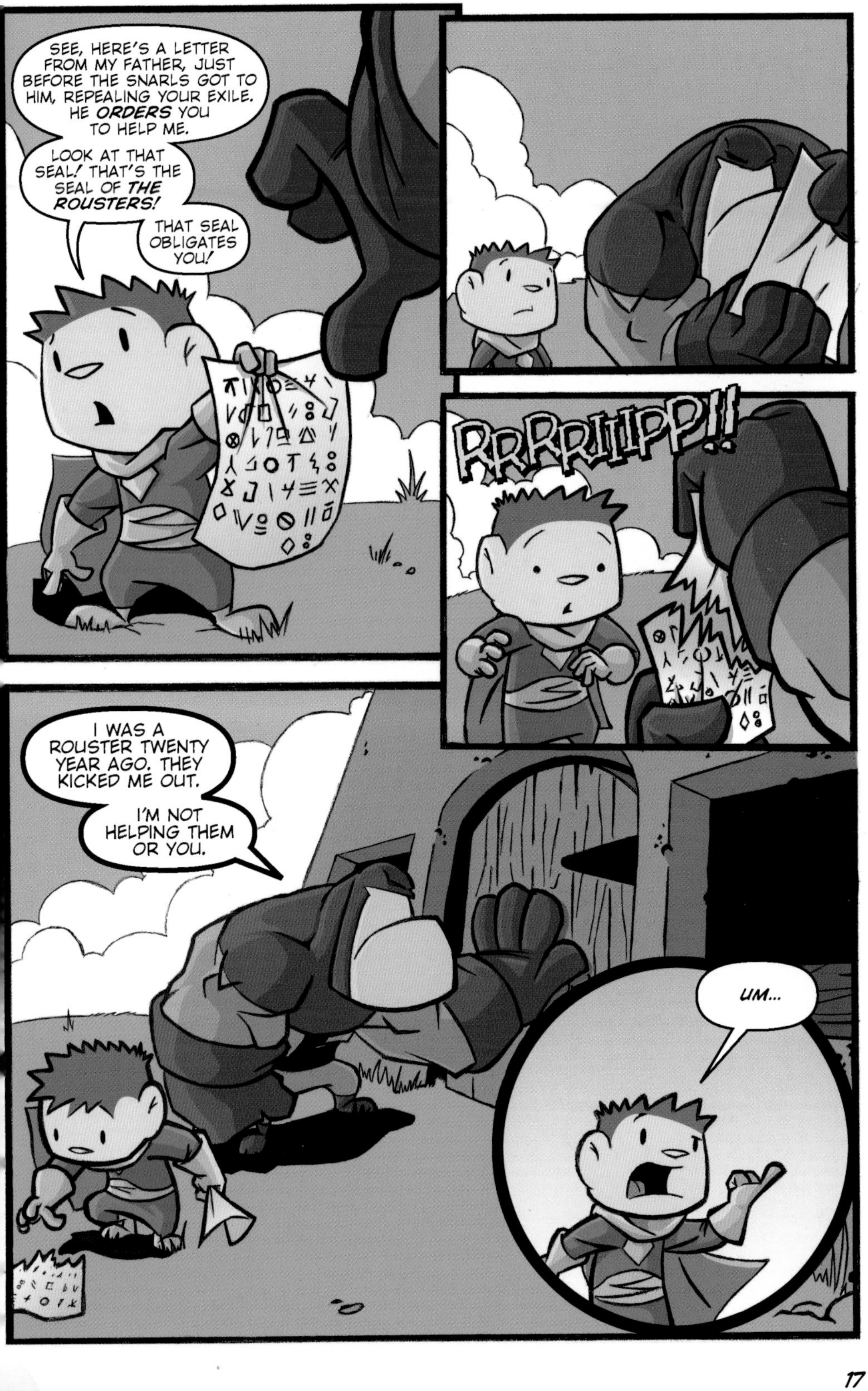
SEE, HERE'S A LETTER FROM MY FATHER, JUST BEFORE THE SNARLS GOT TO HIM, REPEALING YOUR EXILE. HE ORDERS YOU TO HELP ME.
LOOK AT THAT SEAL! THAT'S THE SEAL OF THE ROUSTERS!
THAT SEAL OBLIGATES YOU!
RRRRIIIPP!!
I WAS A ROUSTER TWENTY YEAR AGO. THEY KICKED ME OUT.
I'M NOT HELPING THEM OR YOU.
UM...

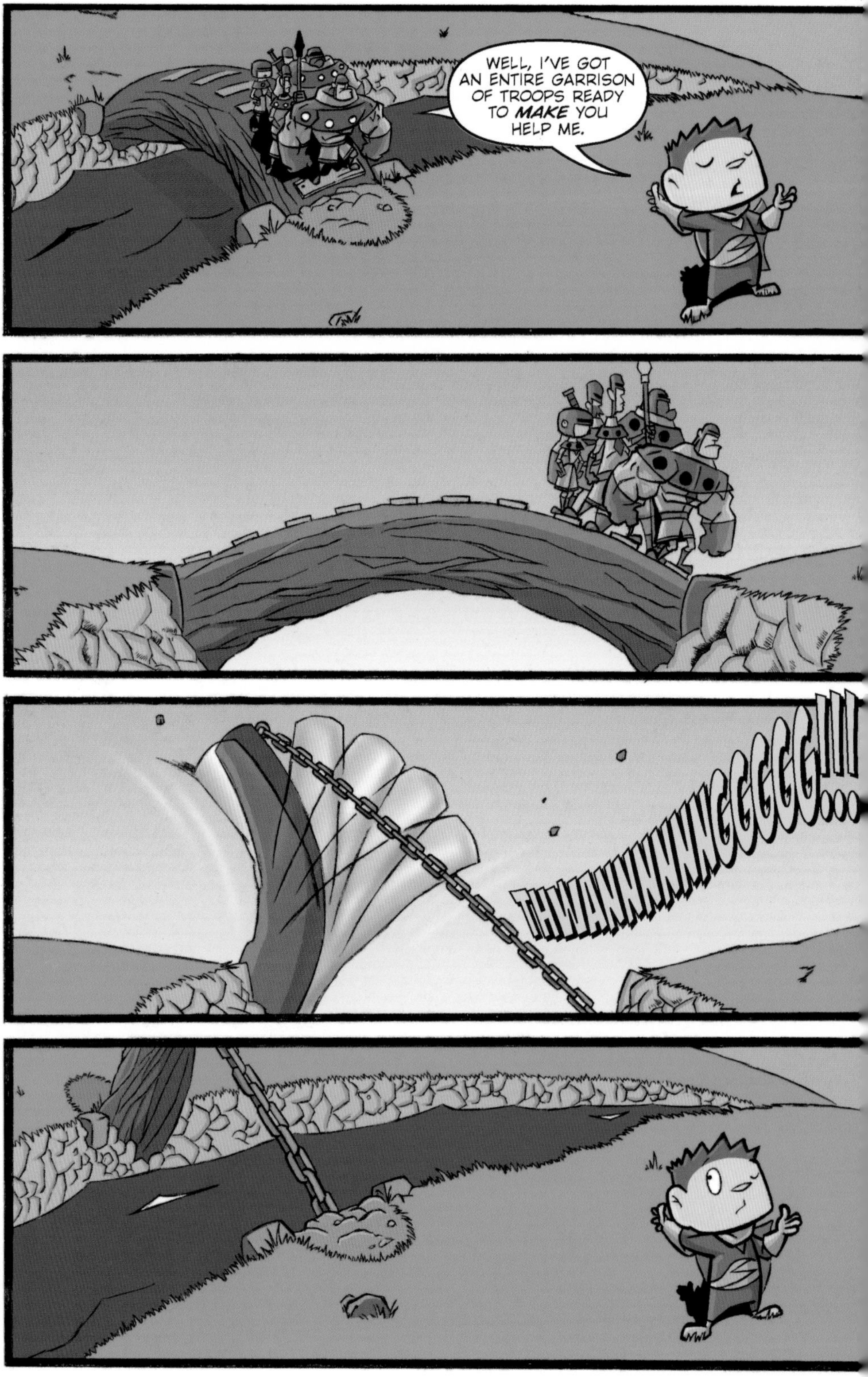
WELL, I'VE GOT AN ENTIRE GARRISON OF TROOPS READY TO MAKE YOU HELP ME.
THWANNNNNNGGGG!!!...

YOU... W-WOW... Y-YOU... C-COULD... Y-Y-YOU...
THEY'LL LAND IN THE TREES. HARMLESSLY... PROBABLY...
NOW GO AWAY.
BUT THE SNARLS...
I'M TOO OLD TO BE FIGHTING SNARLS. AND I WON'T.
FINE! GO AHEAD AND HIDE, YA COWARD!
NUTS...

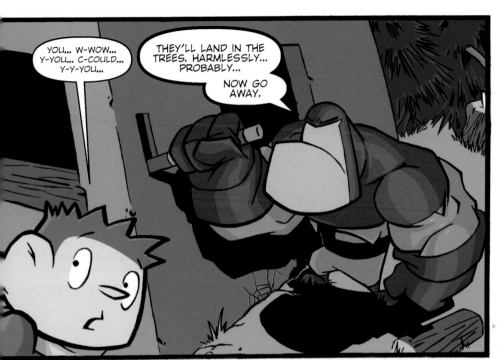

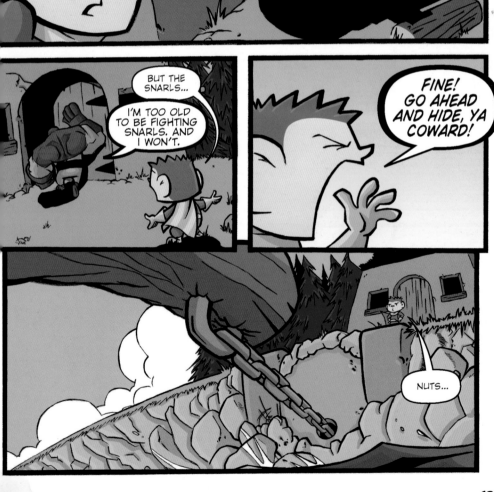

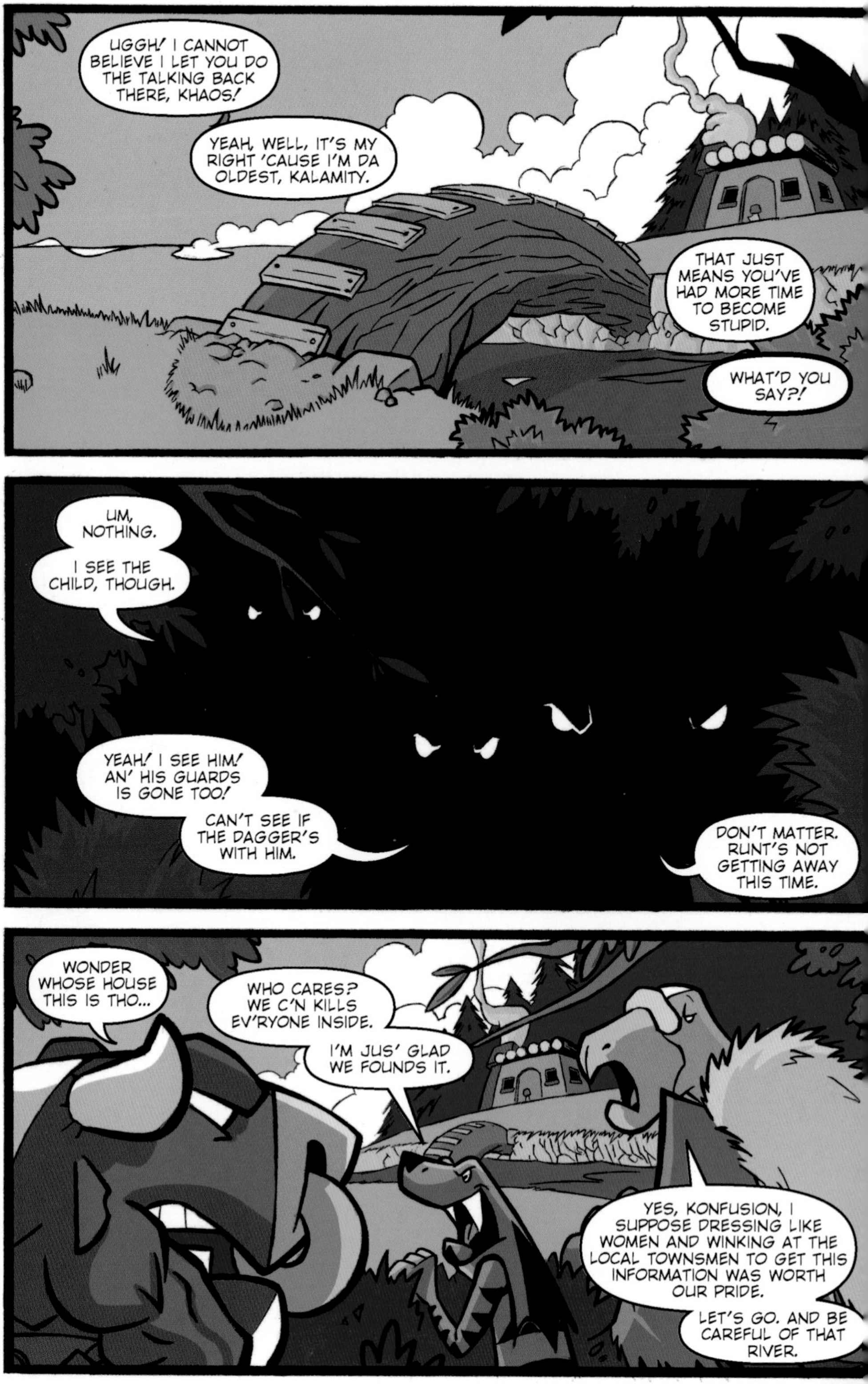
UGGH! I CANNOT BELIEVE I LET YOU DO THE TALKING BACK THERE, KHAOS!
YEAH, WELL, IT'S MY RIGHT 'CAUSE I'M DA OLDEST, KALAMITY.
THAT JUST MEANS YOU'VE HAD MORE TIME TO BECOME STUPID.
WHAT'D YOU SAY?!
UM, NOTHING.
I SEE THE CHILD, THOUGH.
YEAH! I SEE HIM! AN' HIS GUARDS IS GONE TOO!
CAN'T SEE IF THE DAGGER'S WITH HIM.
DON'T MATTER. RUNT'S NOT GETTING AWAY THIS TIME.
WONDER WHOSE HOUSE THIS IS THO...
WHO CARES? WE C'N KILLS EV'RYONE INSIDE.
I'M JUS' GLAD WE FOUNDS IT.
YES, KONFUSION, I SUPPOSE DRESSING LIKE WOMEN AND WINKING AT THE LOCAL TOWNSMEN TO GET THIS INFORMATION WAS WORTH OUR PRIDE.
LET'S GO. AND BE CAREFUL OF THAT RIVER.

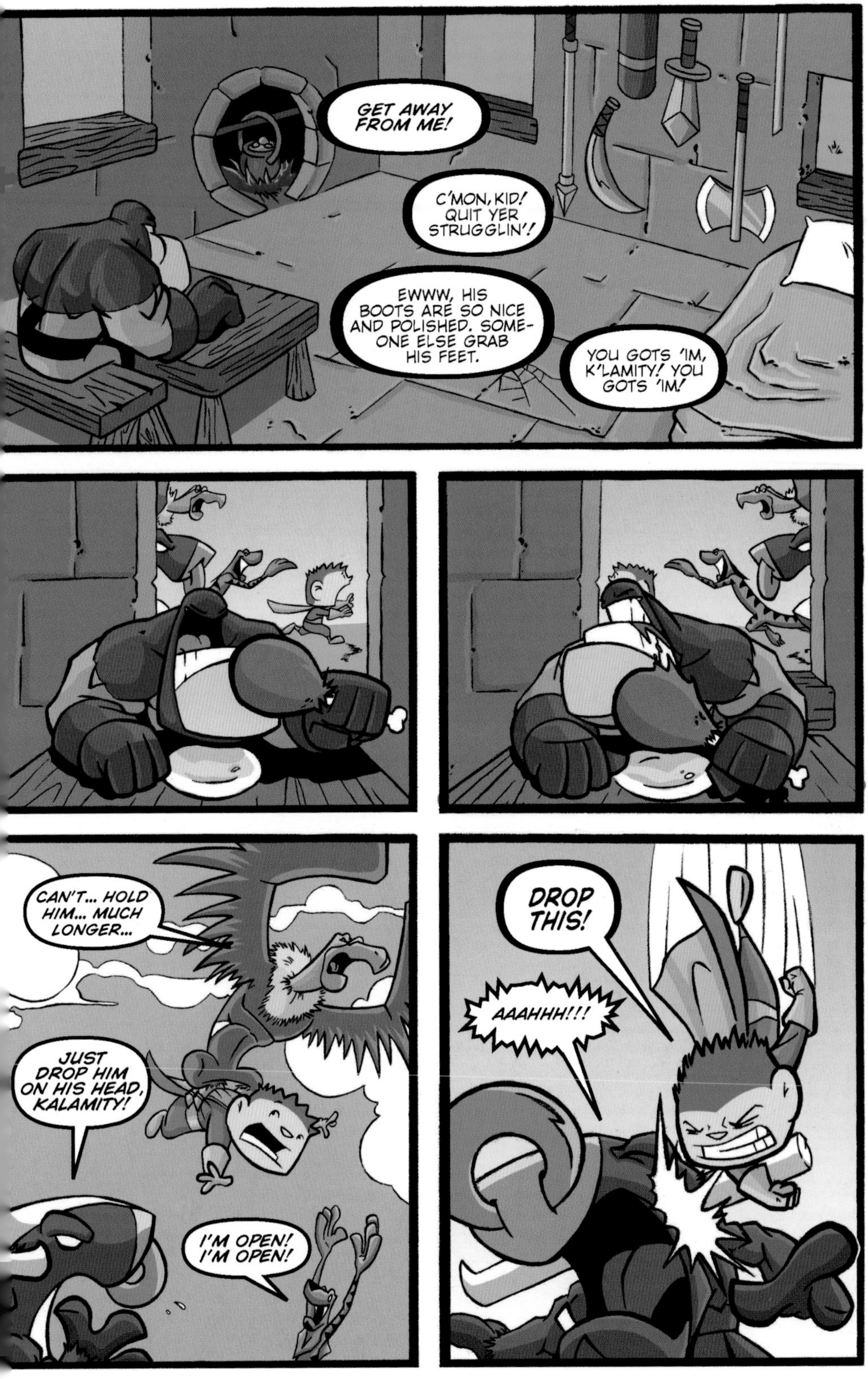

GET AWAY FROM ME!
C'MON, KID! QUIT YER STRUGGLIN'!
EWWW, HIS BOOTS ARE SO NICE AND POLISHED. SOME-ONE ELSE GRAB HIS FEET.
YOU GOTS 'IM, K'LAMITY! YOU GOTS 'IM!
CAN'T... HOLD HIM... MUCH LONGER...
JUST DROP HIM ON HIS HEAD, KALAMITY!
I'M OPEN! I'M OPEN!
DROP THIS!
AAAHHH!!!

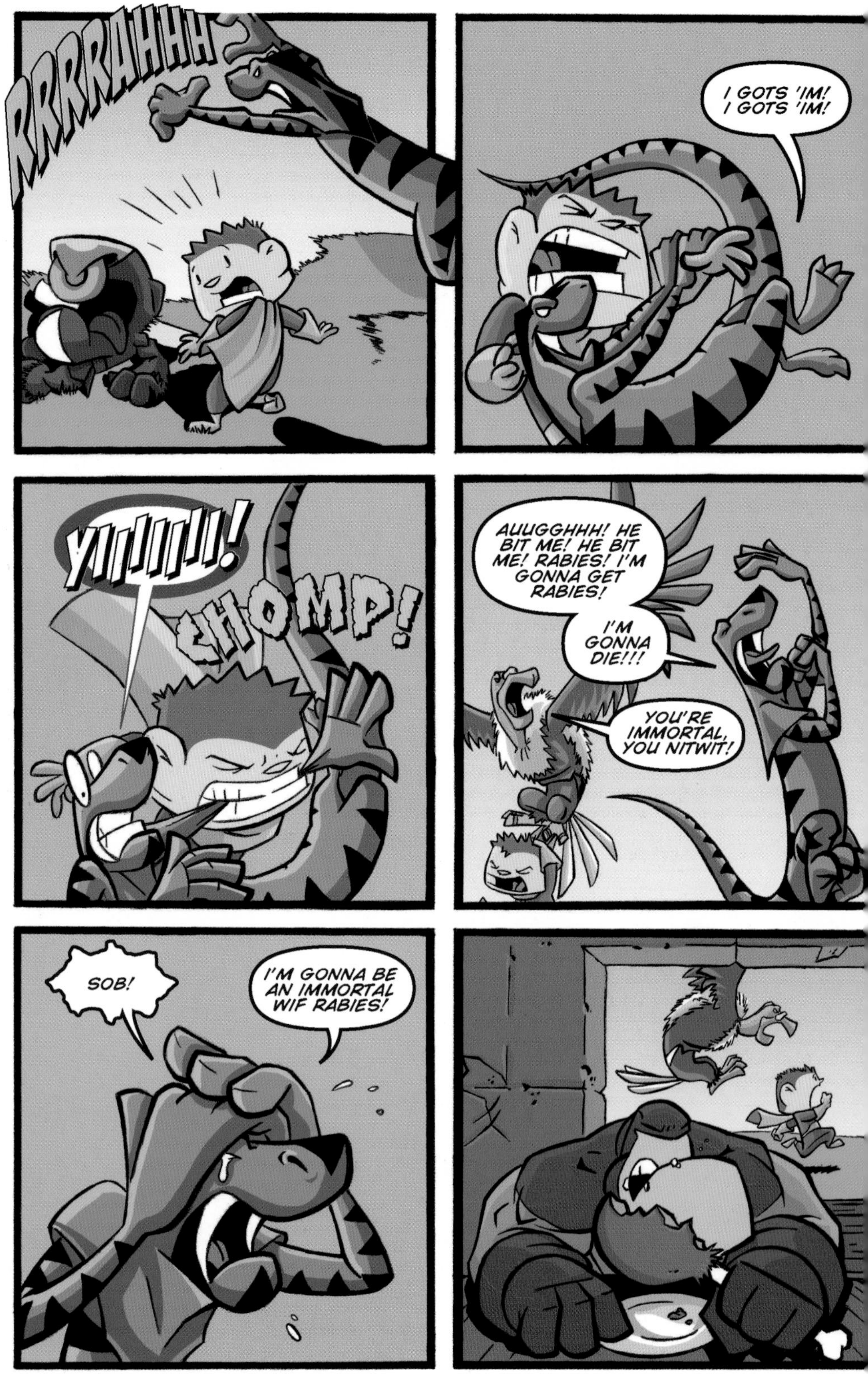
RRRAHHH
I GOTS 'IM! I GOTS 'IM!
YIIIIIII!
CHOMP!
AUUGGHHH! HE BIT ME! HE BIT ME! RABIES! I'M GONNA GET RABIES!
I'M GONNA DIE!!!
YOU'RE IMMORTAL, YOU NITWIT!
SOB!
I'M GONNA BE AN IMMORTAL WIF RABIES!

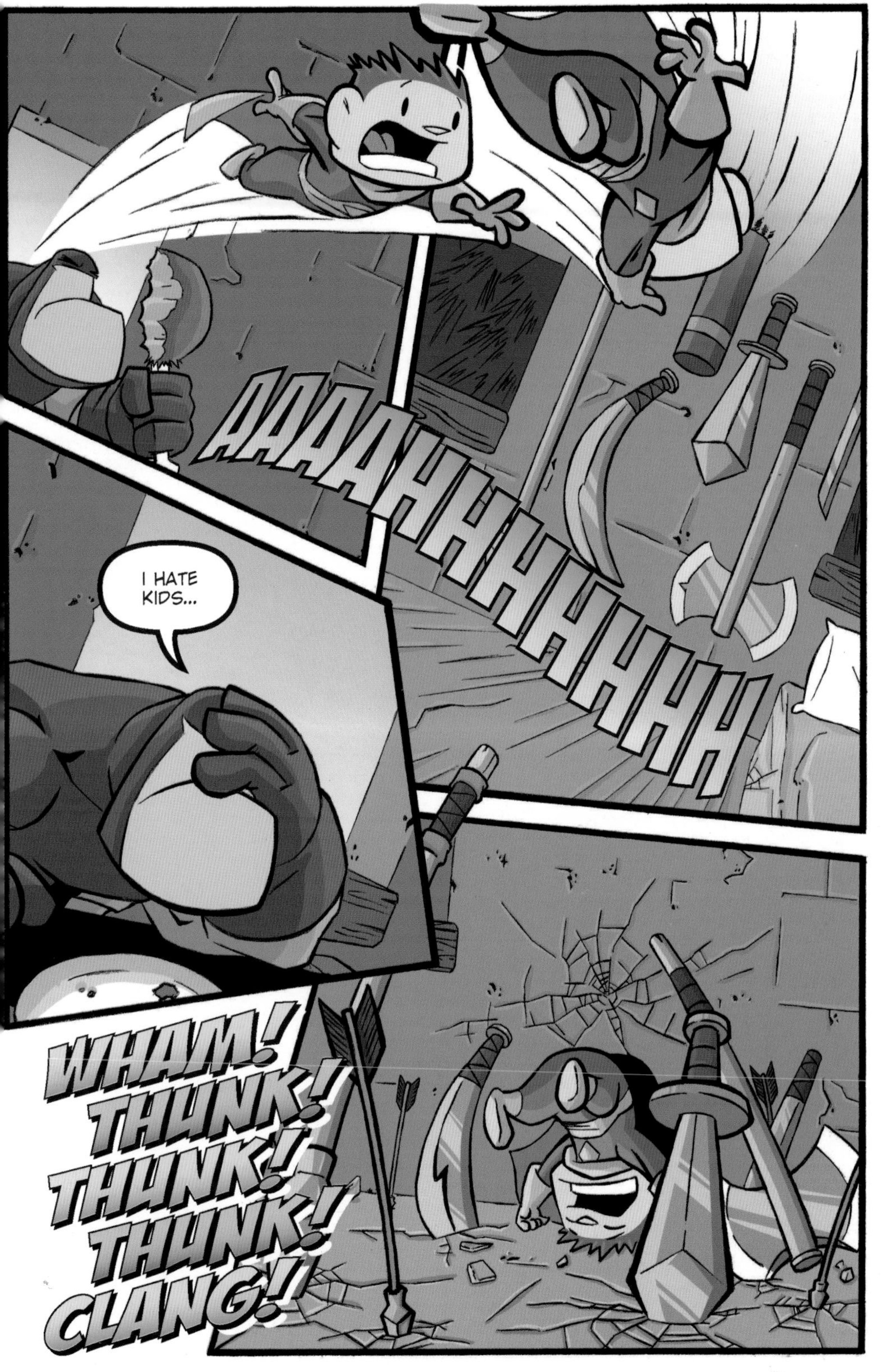
AAAAHHHHHHHHHH
I HATE KIDS...
WHAM! THUNK! THUNK! THUNK! CLANG!

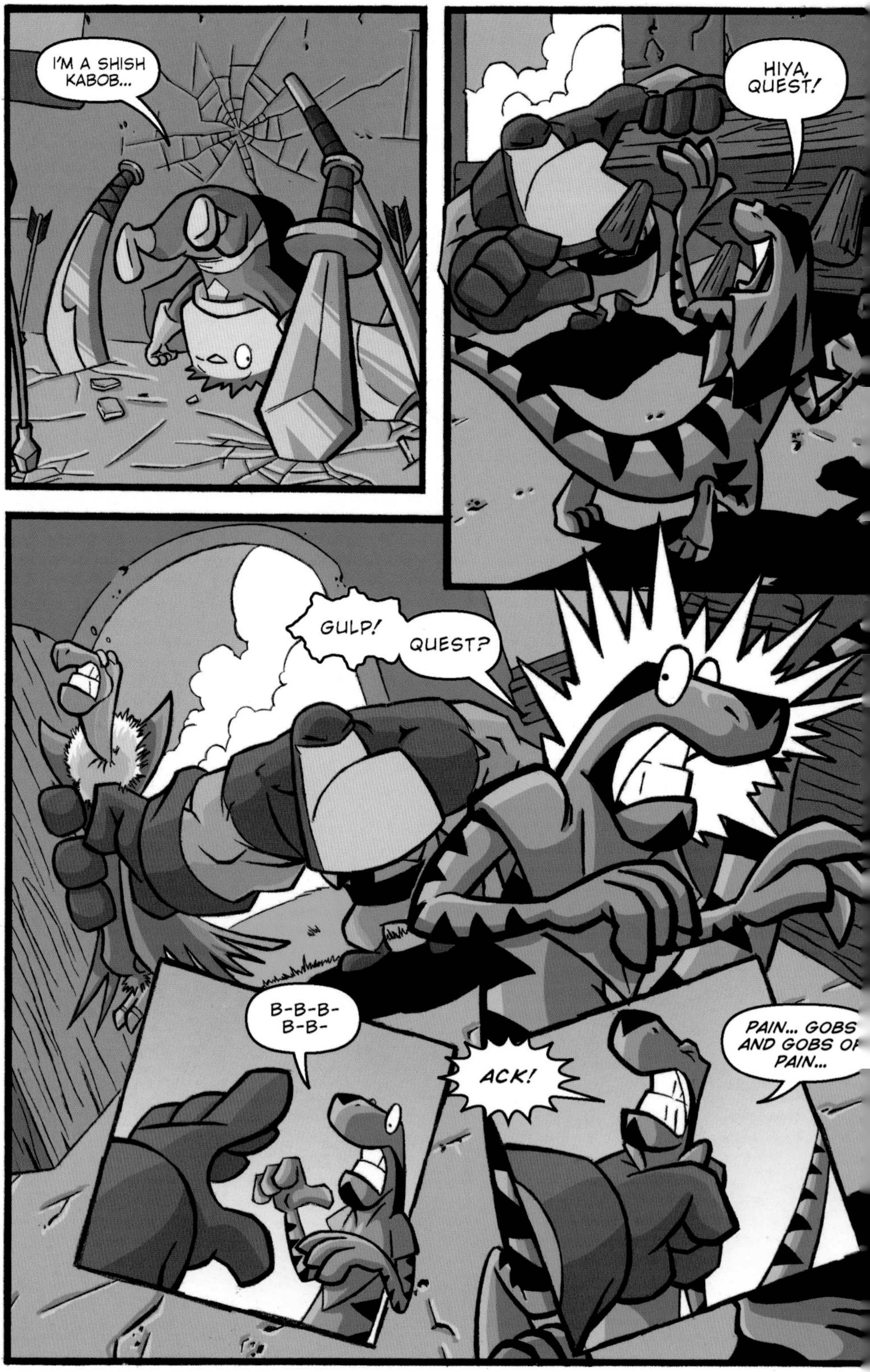
I'M A SHISH KABOB...
HIYA, QUEST!
GULP!
QUEST?
B-B-B-B-B-
ACK!
PAIN... GOBS AND GOBS OF PAIN...

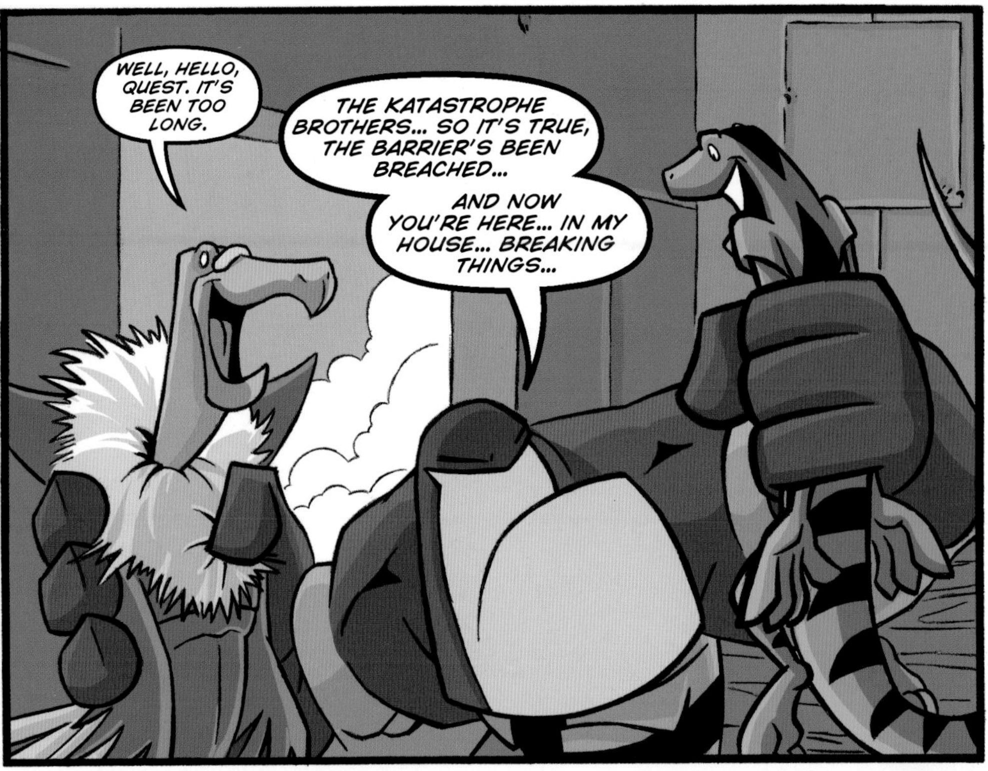
WELL, HELLO, QUEST. IT'S BEEN TOO LONG.
THE KATASTROPHE BROTHERS... SO IT'S TRUE, THE BARRIER'S BEEN BREACHED...
AND NOW YOU'RE HERE... IN MY HOUSE... BREAKING THINGS...

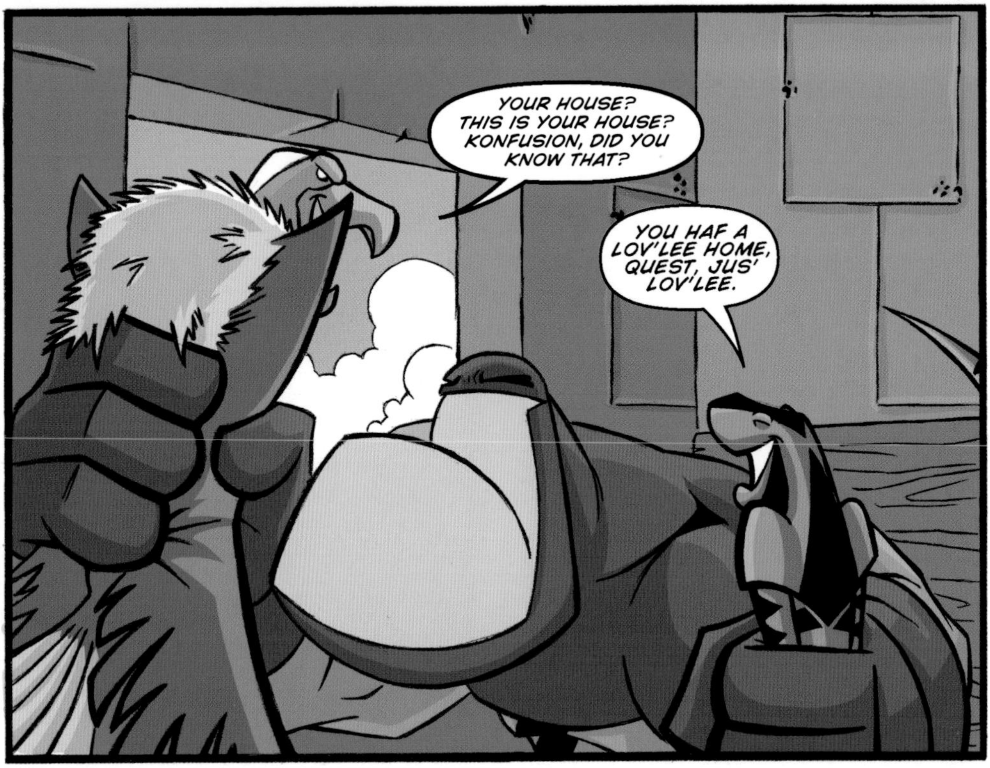
YOUR HOUSE? THIS IS YOUR HOUSE? KONFUSION, DID YOU KNOW THAT?
YOU HAF A LOV'LEE HOME, QUEST, JUS' LOV'LEE.

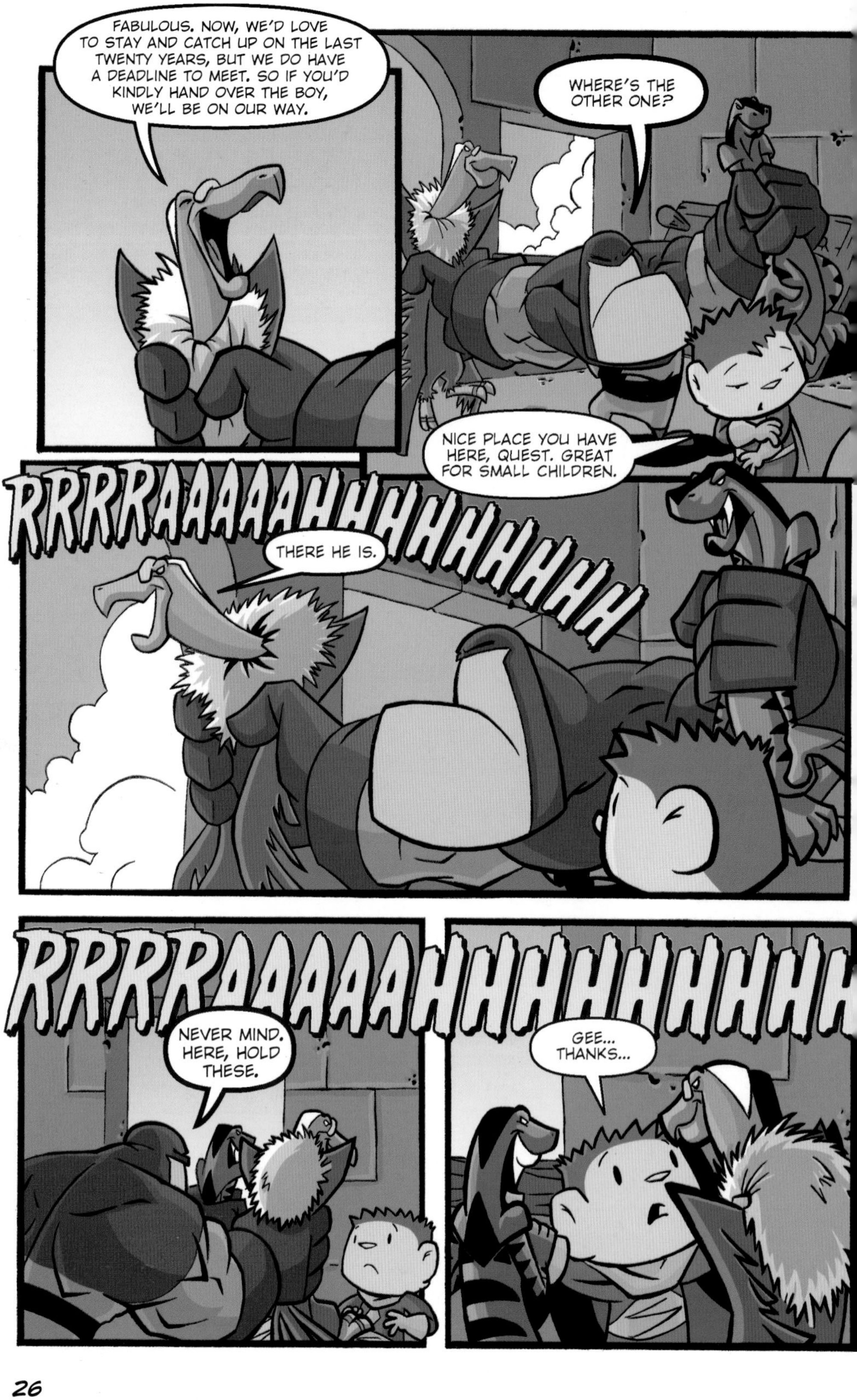
FABULOUS. NOW, WE'D LOVE TO STAY AND CATCH UP ON THE LAST TWENTY YEARS, BUT WE DO HAVE A DEADLINE TO MEET. SO IF YOU'D KINDLY HAND OVER THE BOY, WE'LL BE ON OUR WAY.
WHERE'S THE OTHER ONE?
NICE PLACE YOU HAVE HERE, QUEST. GREAT FOR SMALL CHILDREN.
RRRRAAAAAHHHHHHHHHH
THERE HE IS.
RRRRAAAAAHHHHHHHHHH
NEVER MIND. HERE, HOLD THESE.
GEE... THANKS...

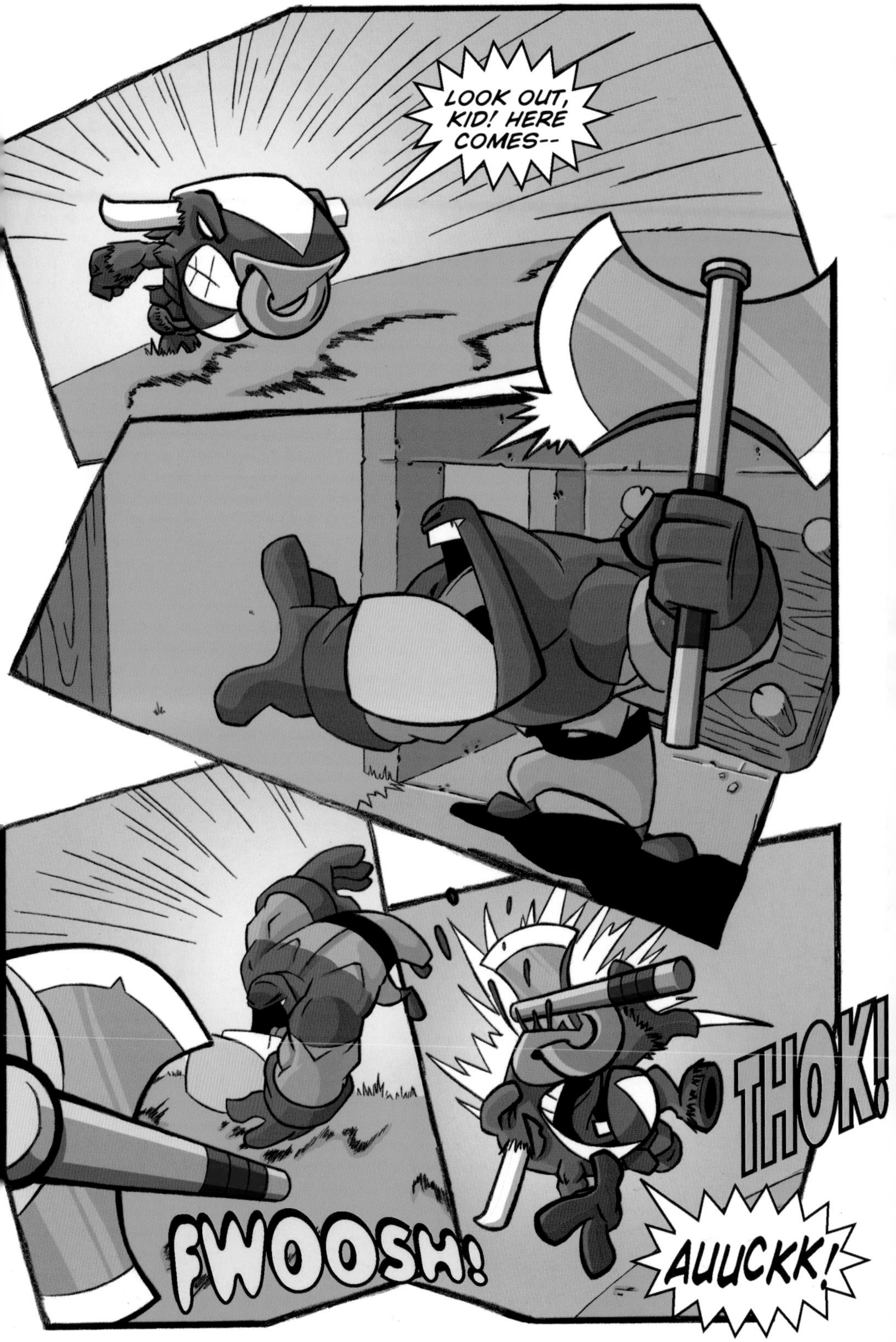
LOOK OUT, KID! HERE COMES--
FWOOSH!
THOK!
AUUCKK!

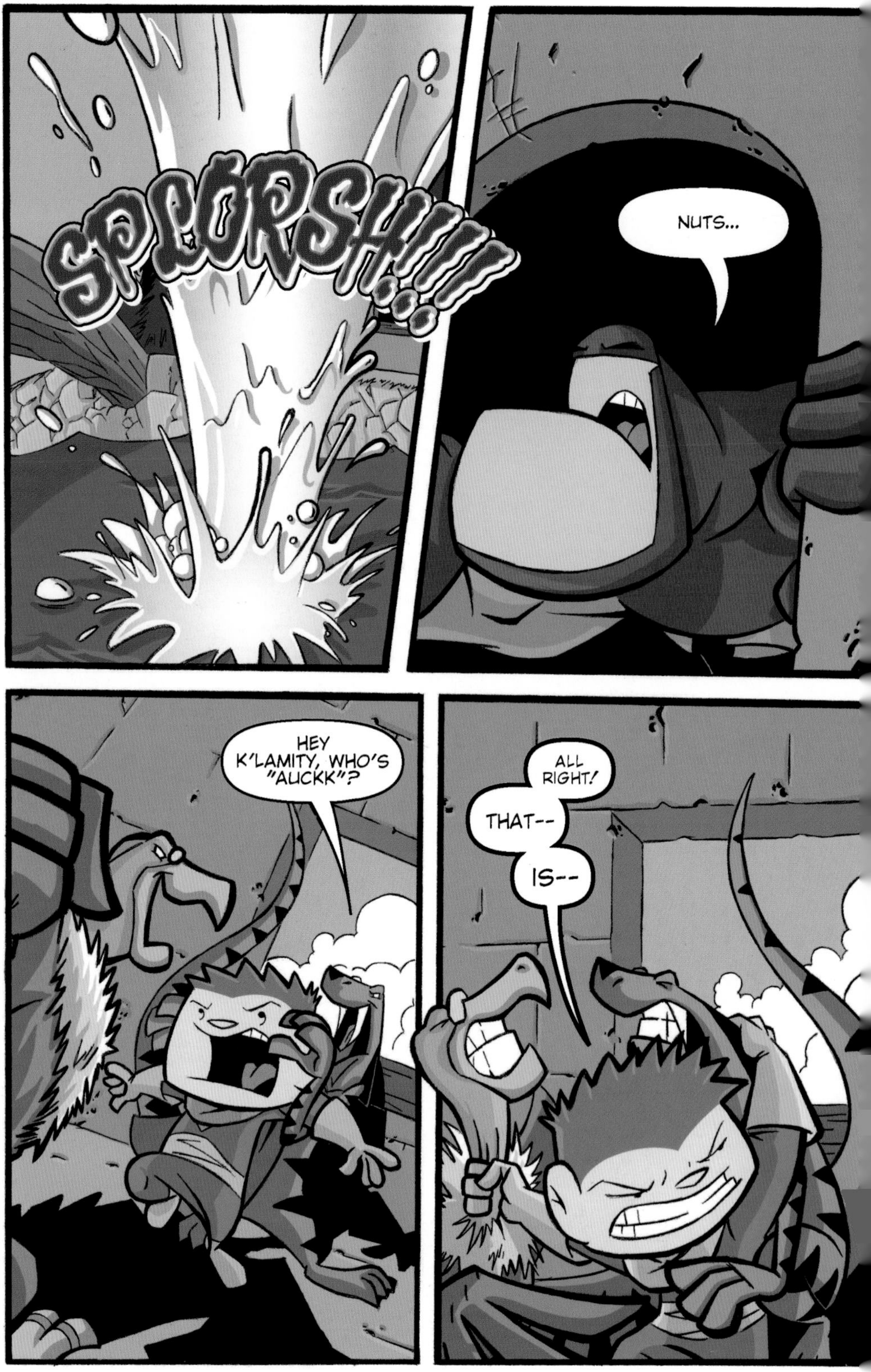
SPLORSH!!!
NUTS...
HEY K'LAMITY, WHO'S "AUCKK"?
ALL RIGHT!
THAT--
IS--

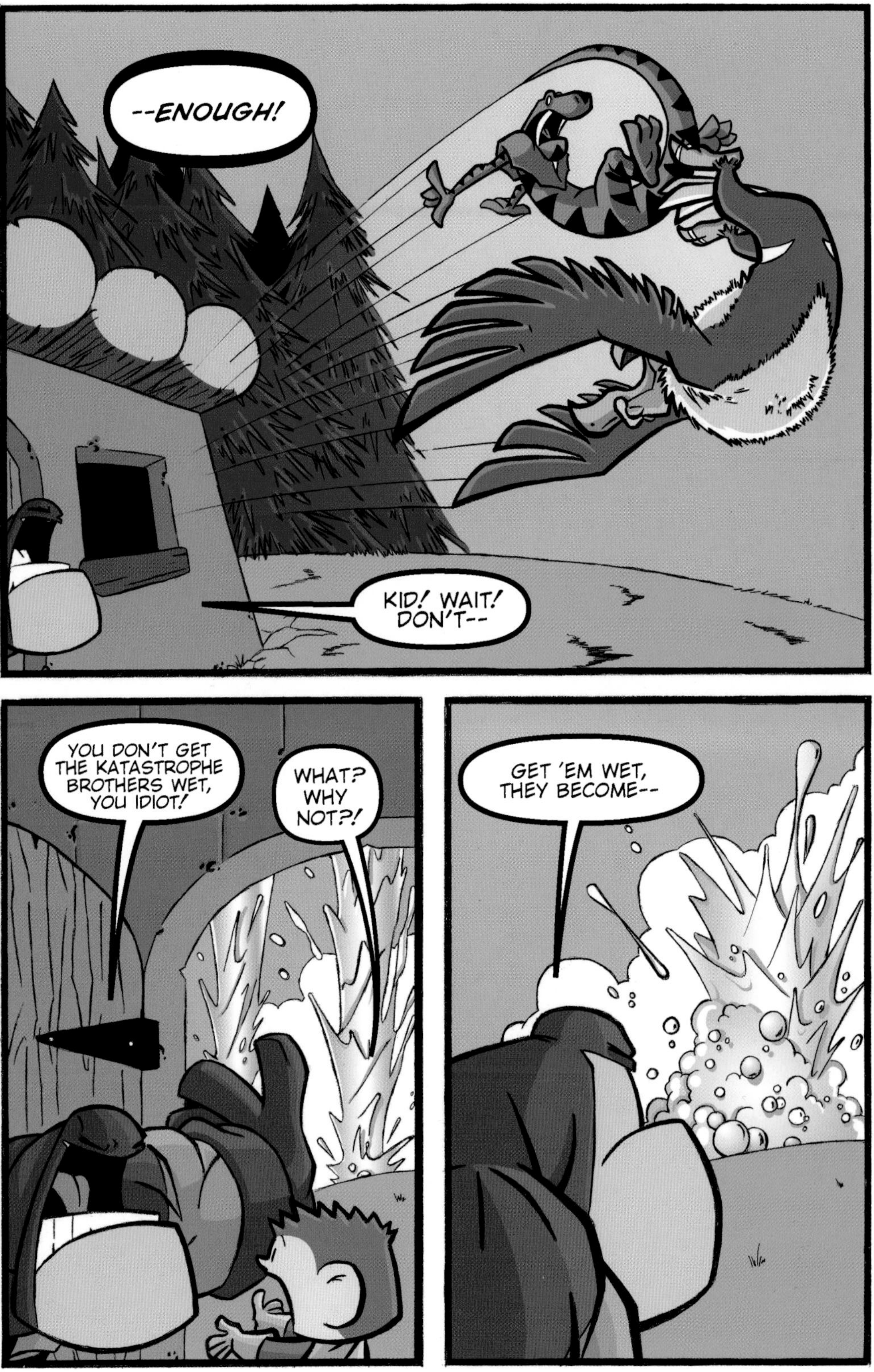
--ENOUGH!
KID! WAIT! DON'T--
YOU DON'T GET THE KATASTROPHE BROTHERS WET, YOU IDIOT!
WHAT? WHY NOT?!
GET 'EM WET, THEY BECOME--

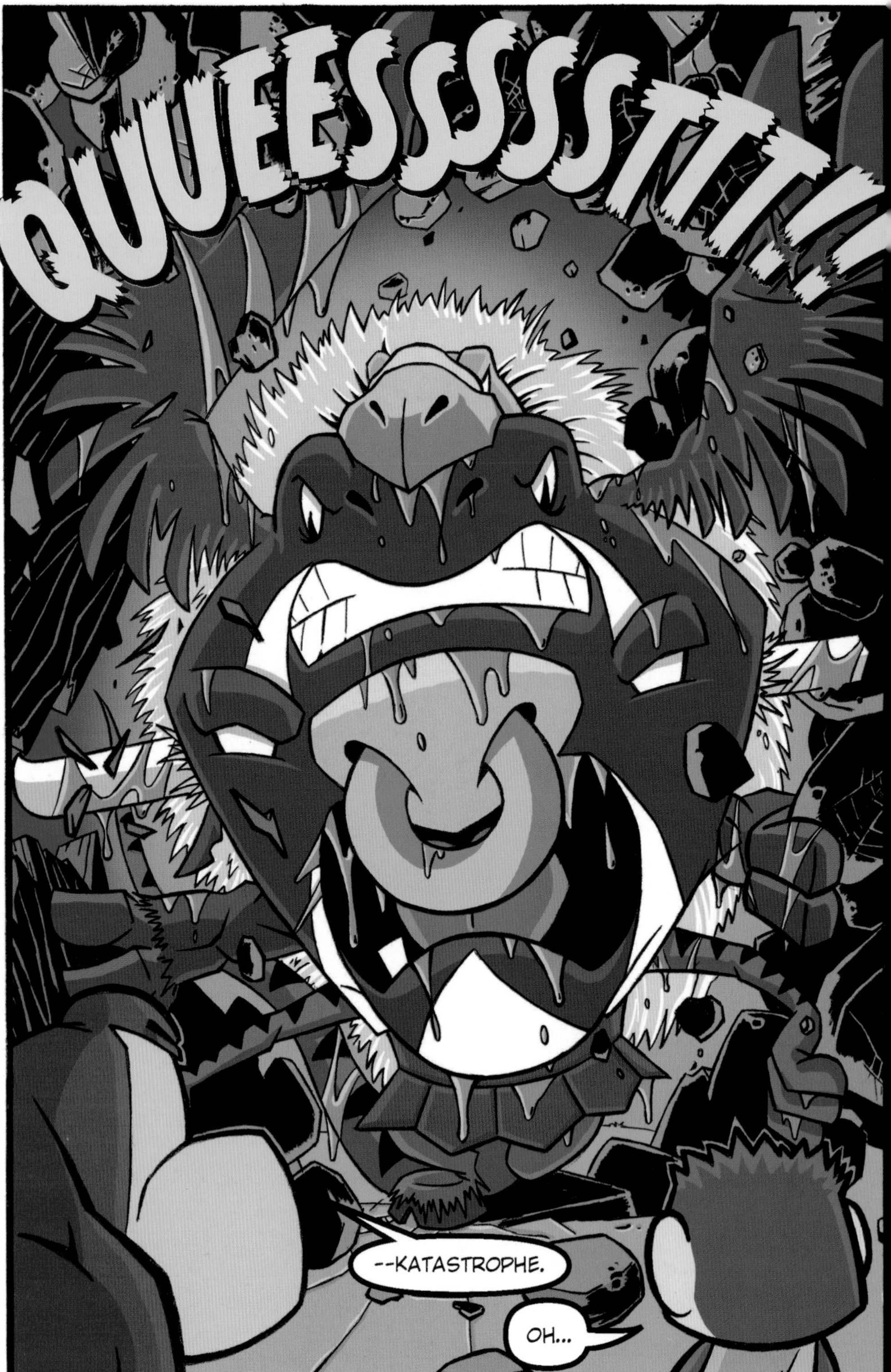
QUUEESSSSSSTTT!!
--KATASTROPHE.
OH...

CHAPTER TWO
STUCK IN THE MIDDLE WITH GOO...

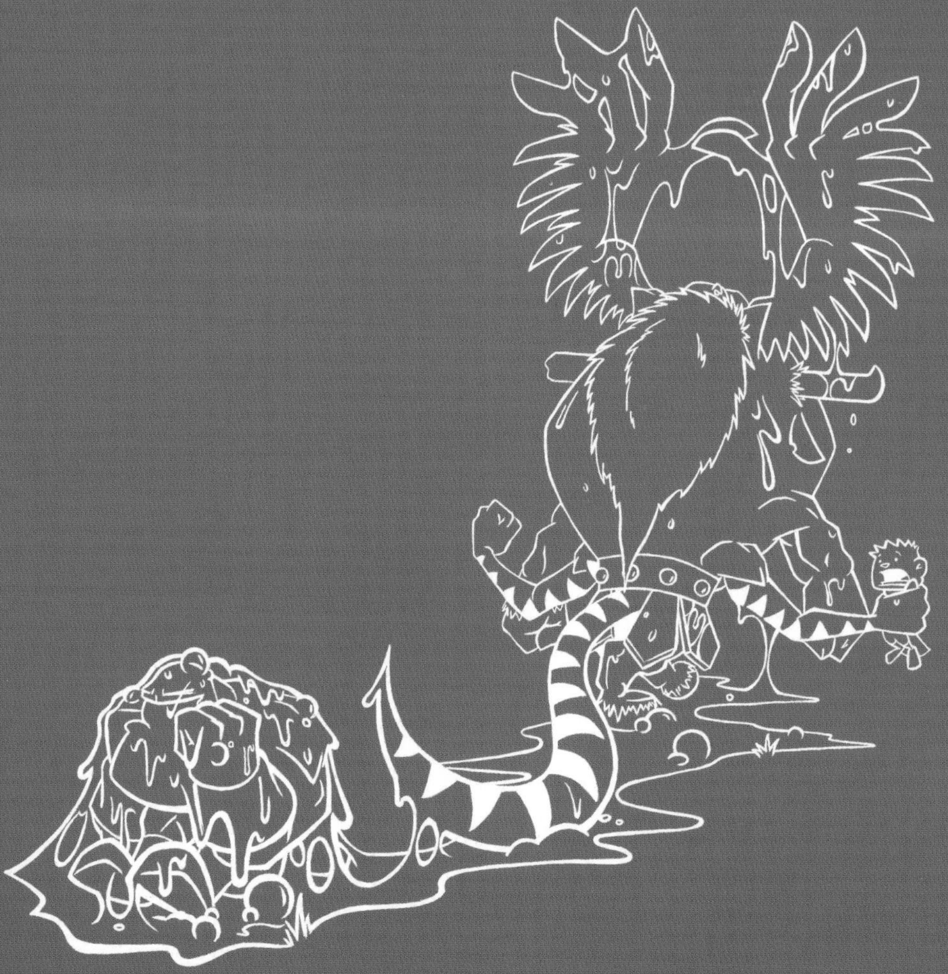

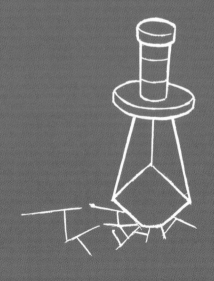

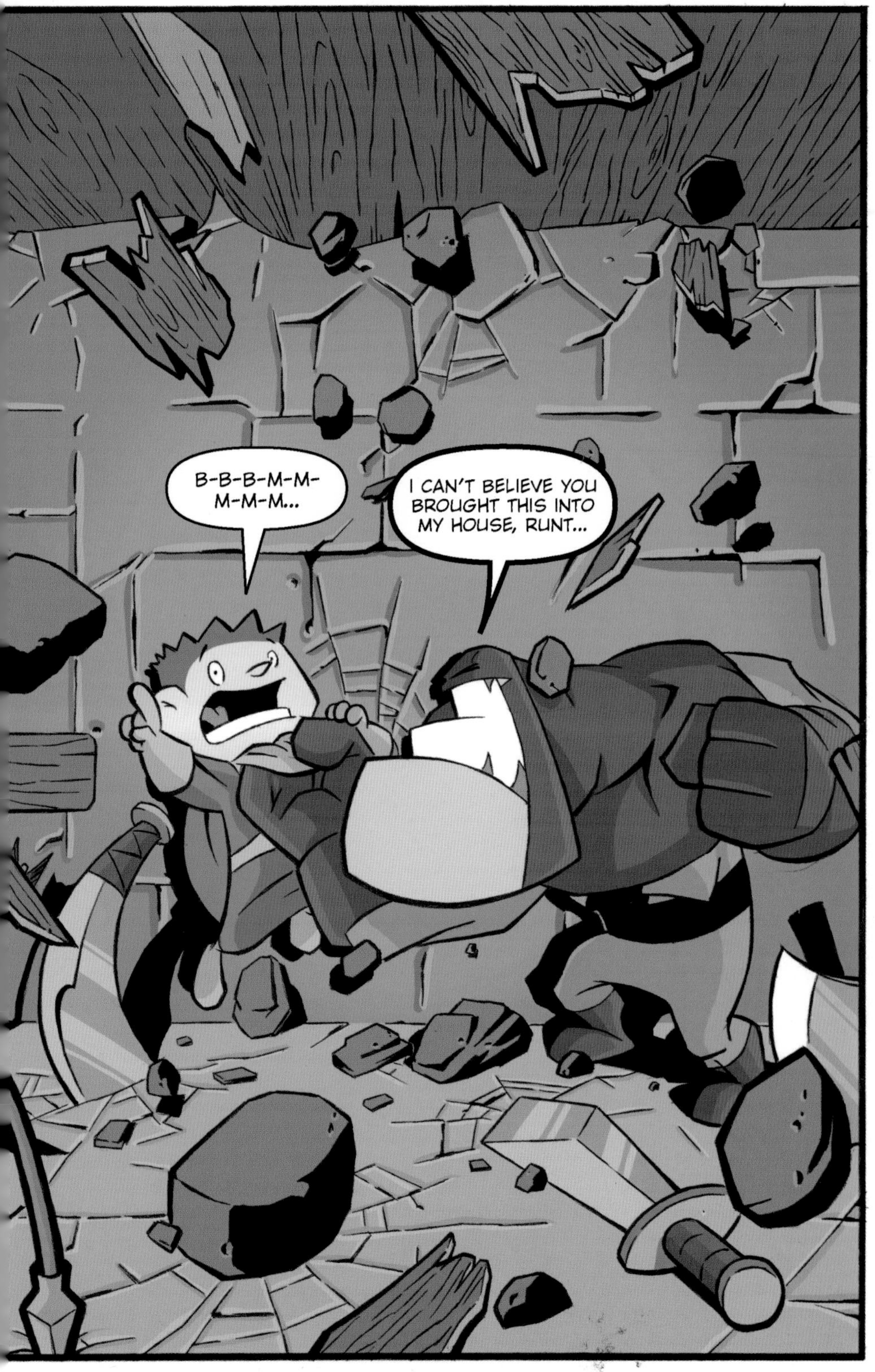
B-B-B-M-M-M-M-M...
I CAN'T BELIEVE YOU BROUGHT THIS INTO MY HOUSE, RUNT...

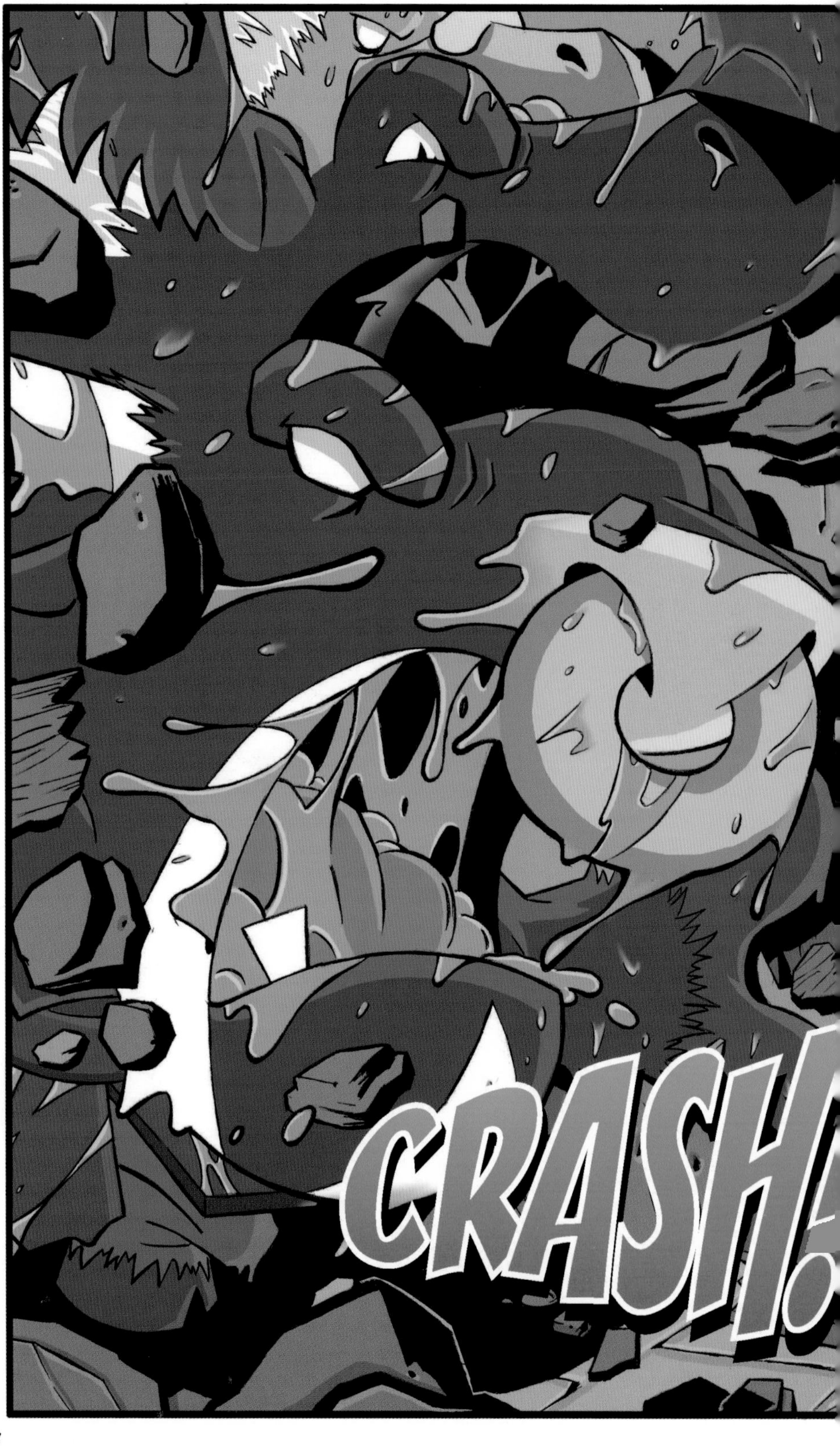
CRASH!

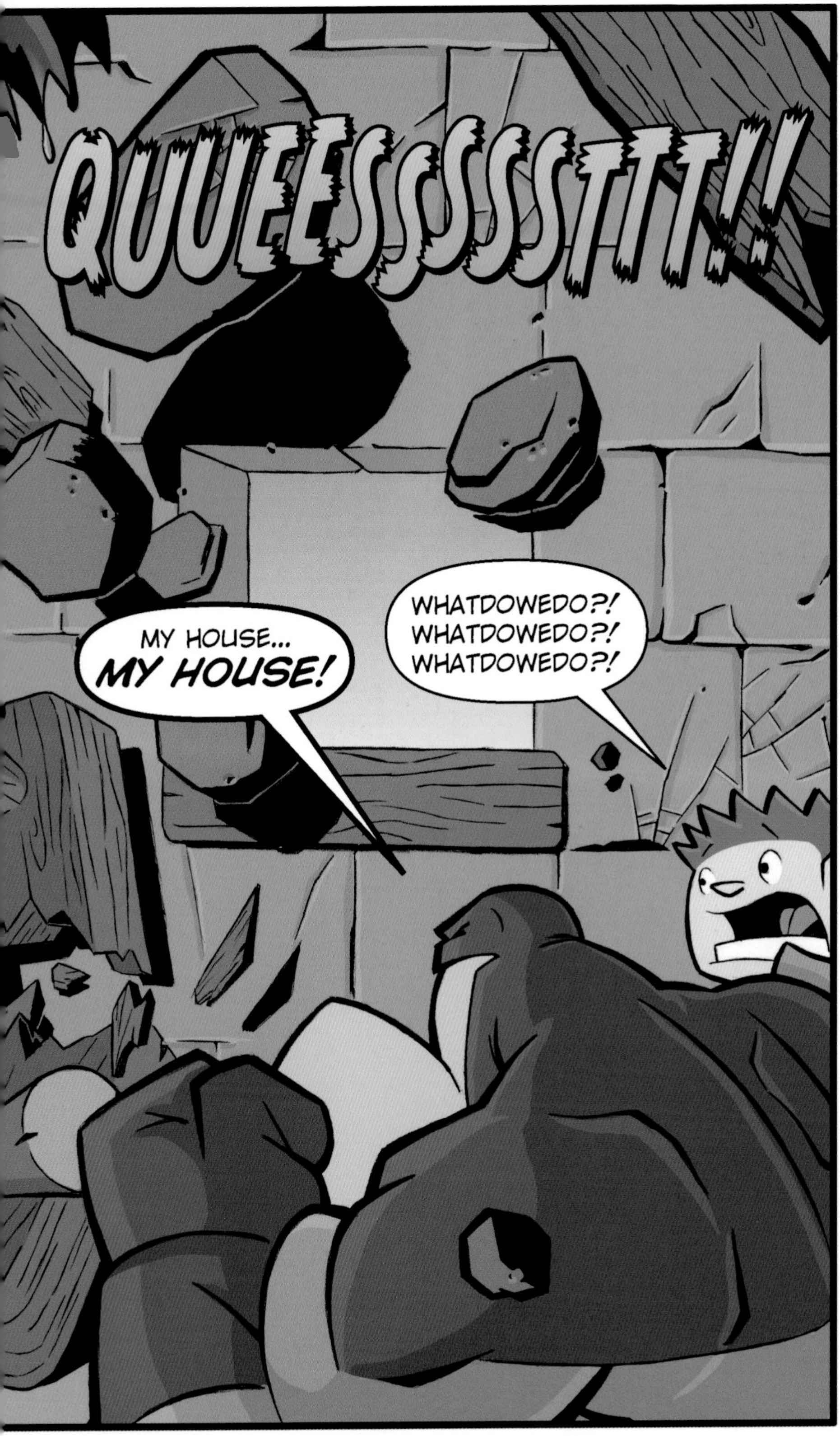
QUUEESSSSSSTTT!!
MY HOUSE... MY HOUSE!
WHATDOWEDO?! WHATDOWEDO?! WHATDOWEDO?!

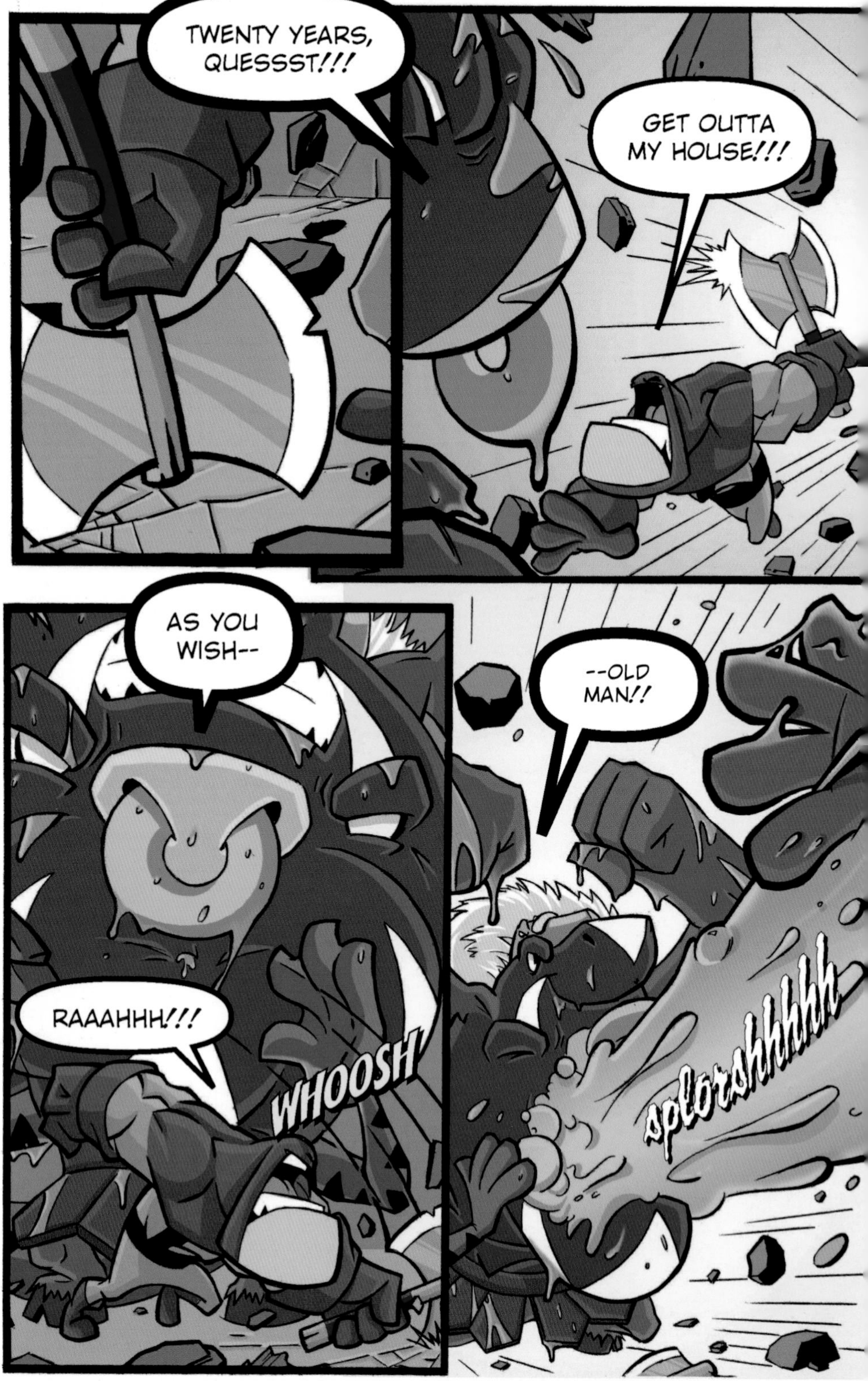
TWENTY YEARS, QUESSST!!!
GET OUTTA MY HOUSE!!!
AS YOU WISH--
--OLD MAN!!
RAAAHHH!!!
WHOOSH
splorshhhhh

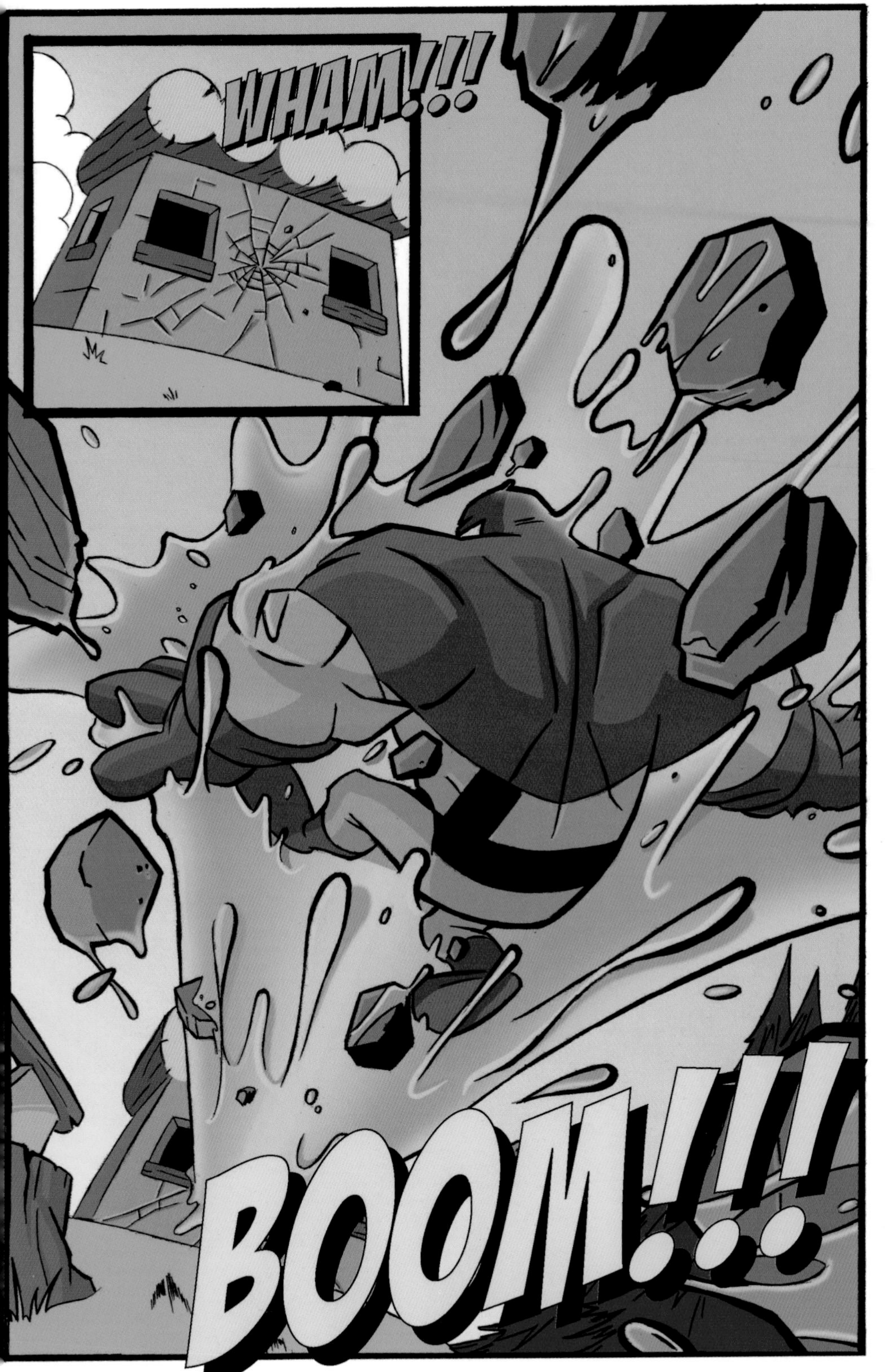
WHAM!!!
BOOM!!!

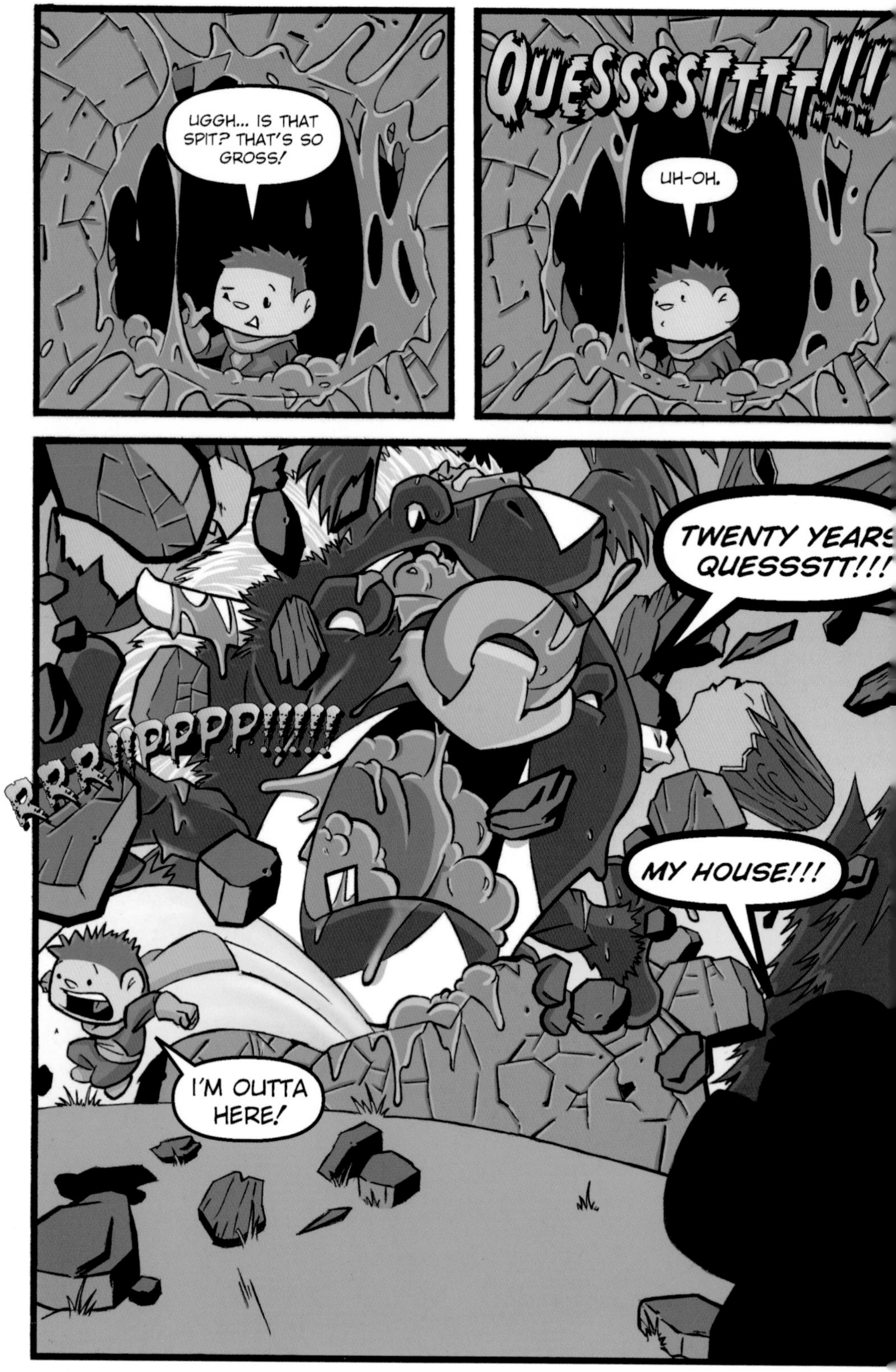
UGGH... IS THAT SPIT? THAT'S SO GROSS!
QUESSSSTTTT!!!
UH-OH.
TWENTY YEARS QUESSSTT!!!
RRRIIPPPP!!!!!
MY HOUSE!!!
I'M OUTTA HERE!

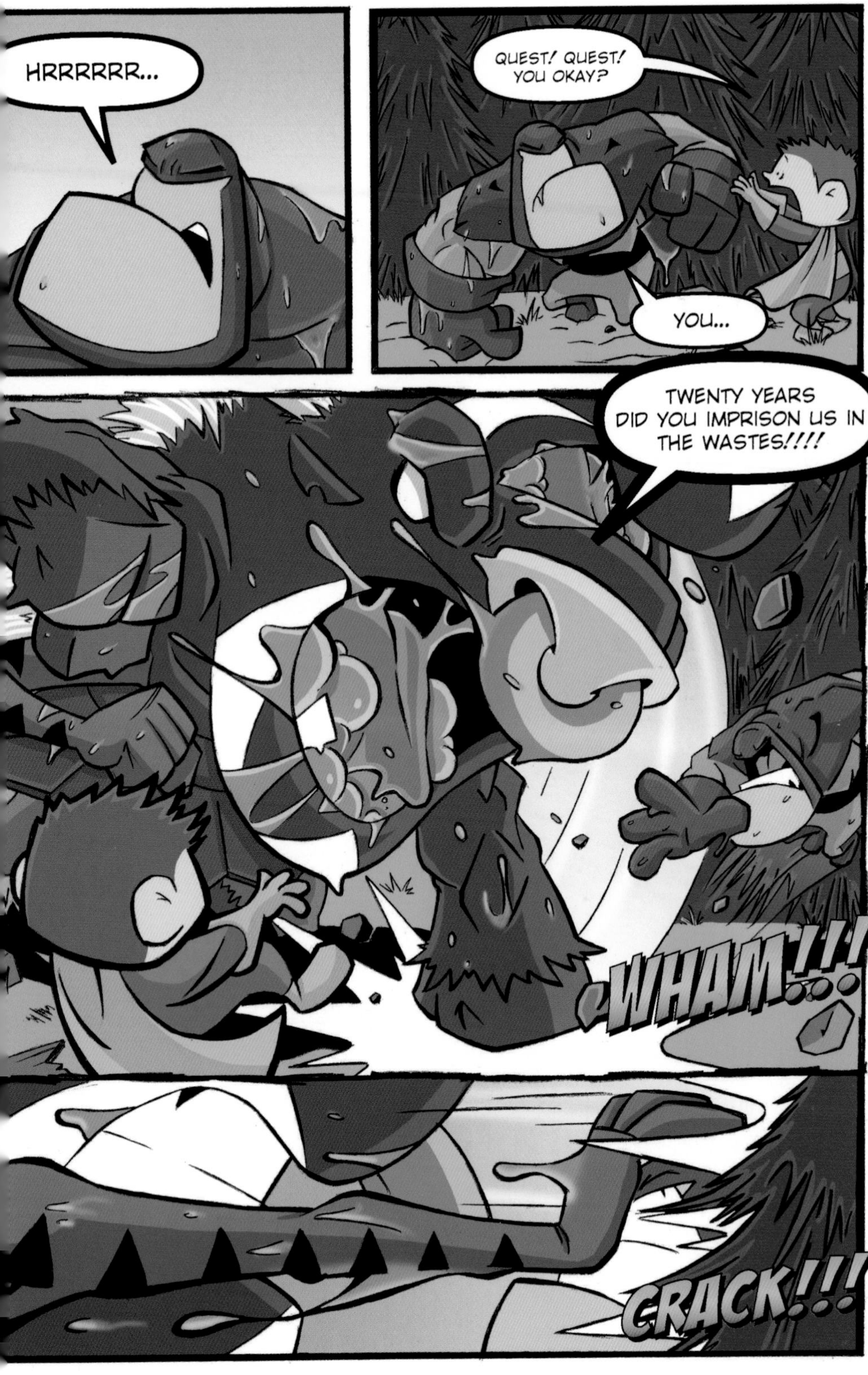
HRRRRRR...
QUEST! QUEST! YOU OKAY?
YOU...
TWENTY YEARS DID YOU IMPRISON US IN THE WASTES!!!!
WHAM!!!
CRACK!!!

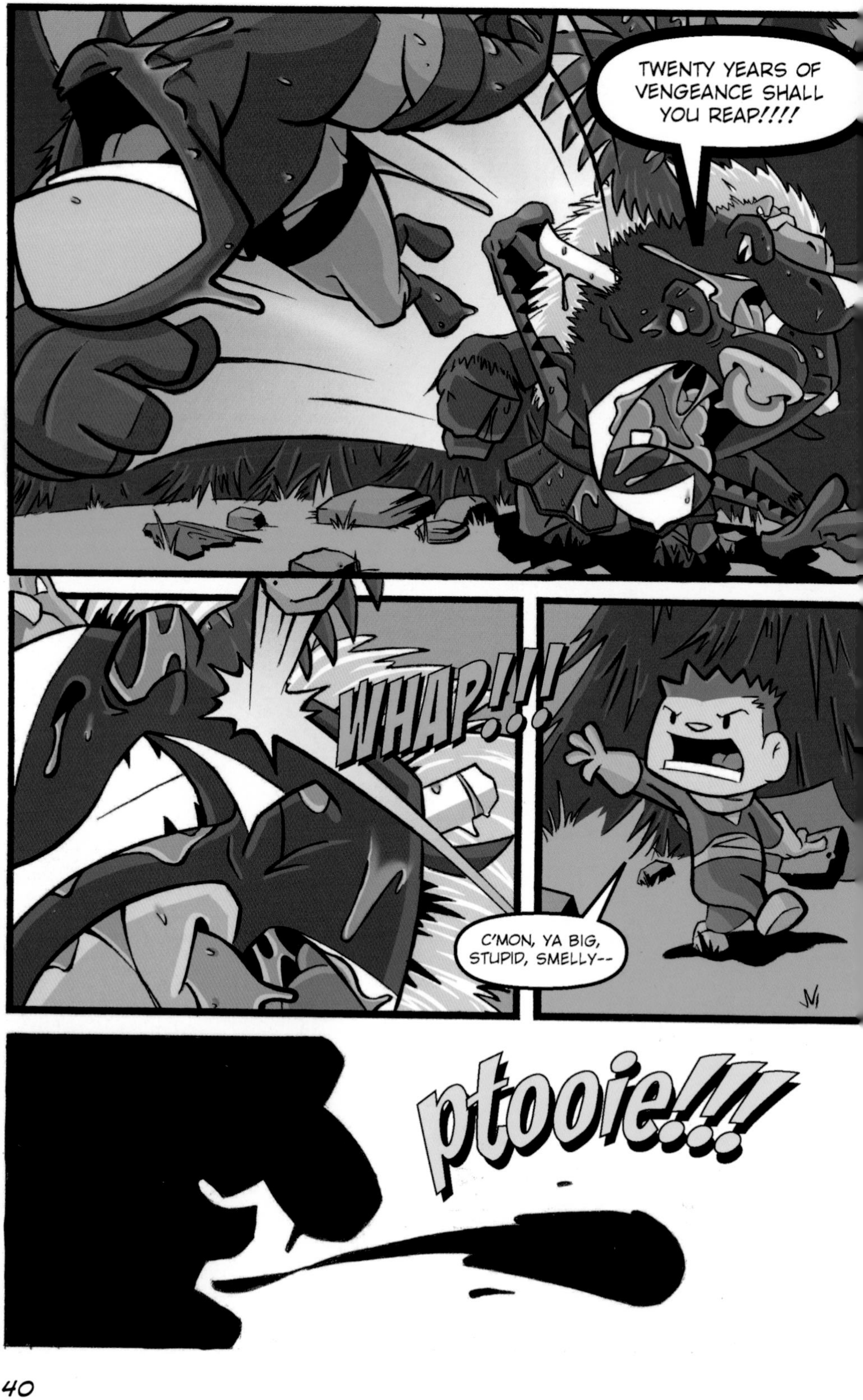
TWENTY YEARS OF VENGEANCE SHALL YOU REAP!!!!
WHAP!!!
C'MON, YA BIG, STUPID, SMELLY--
ptooie!!!

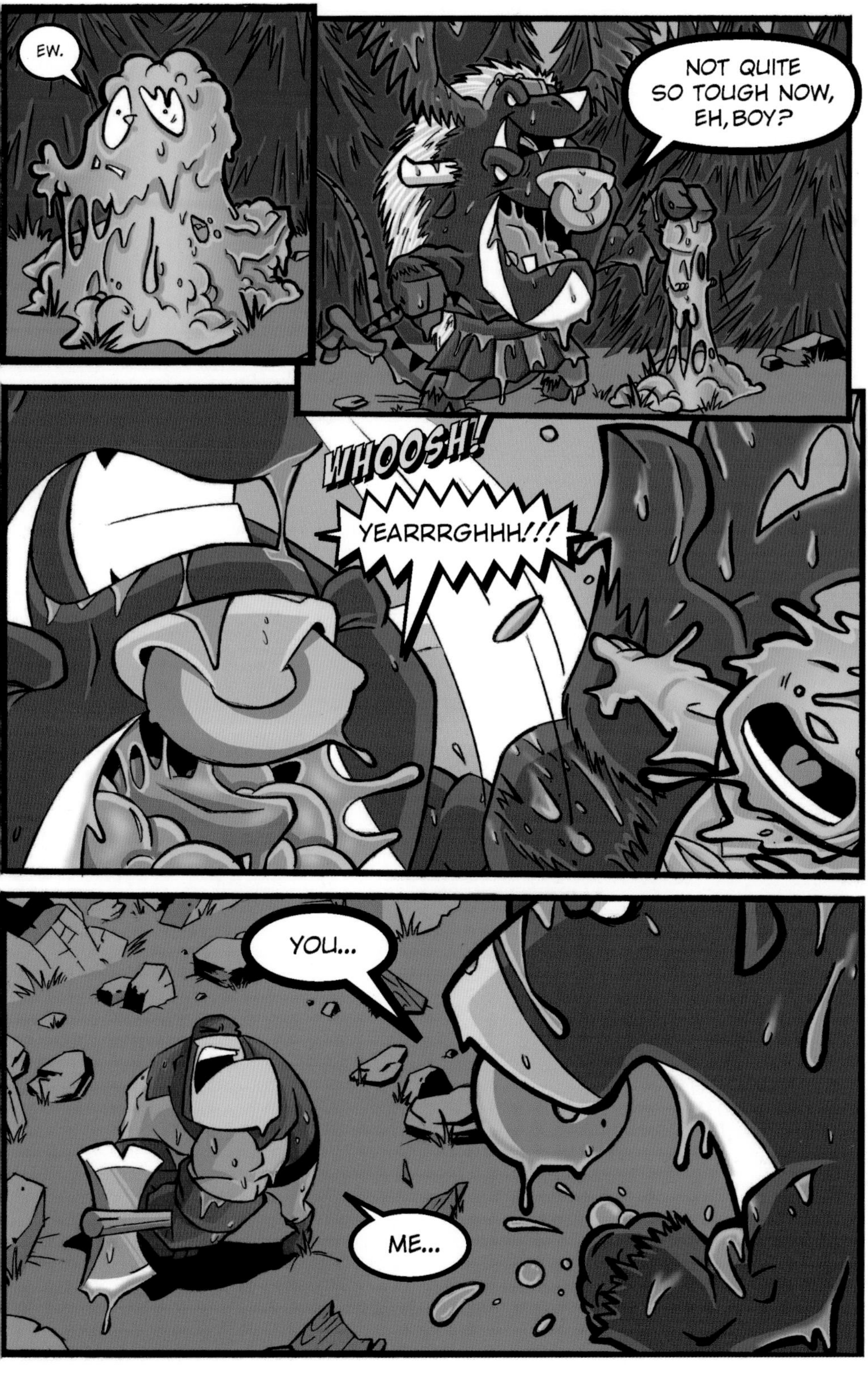
EW.
NOT QUITE SO TOUGH NOW, EH, BOY?
WHOOSH!
YEARRRGHHH!!!
YOU...
ME...

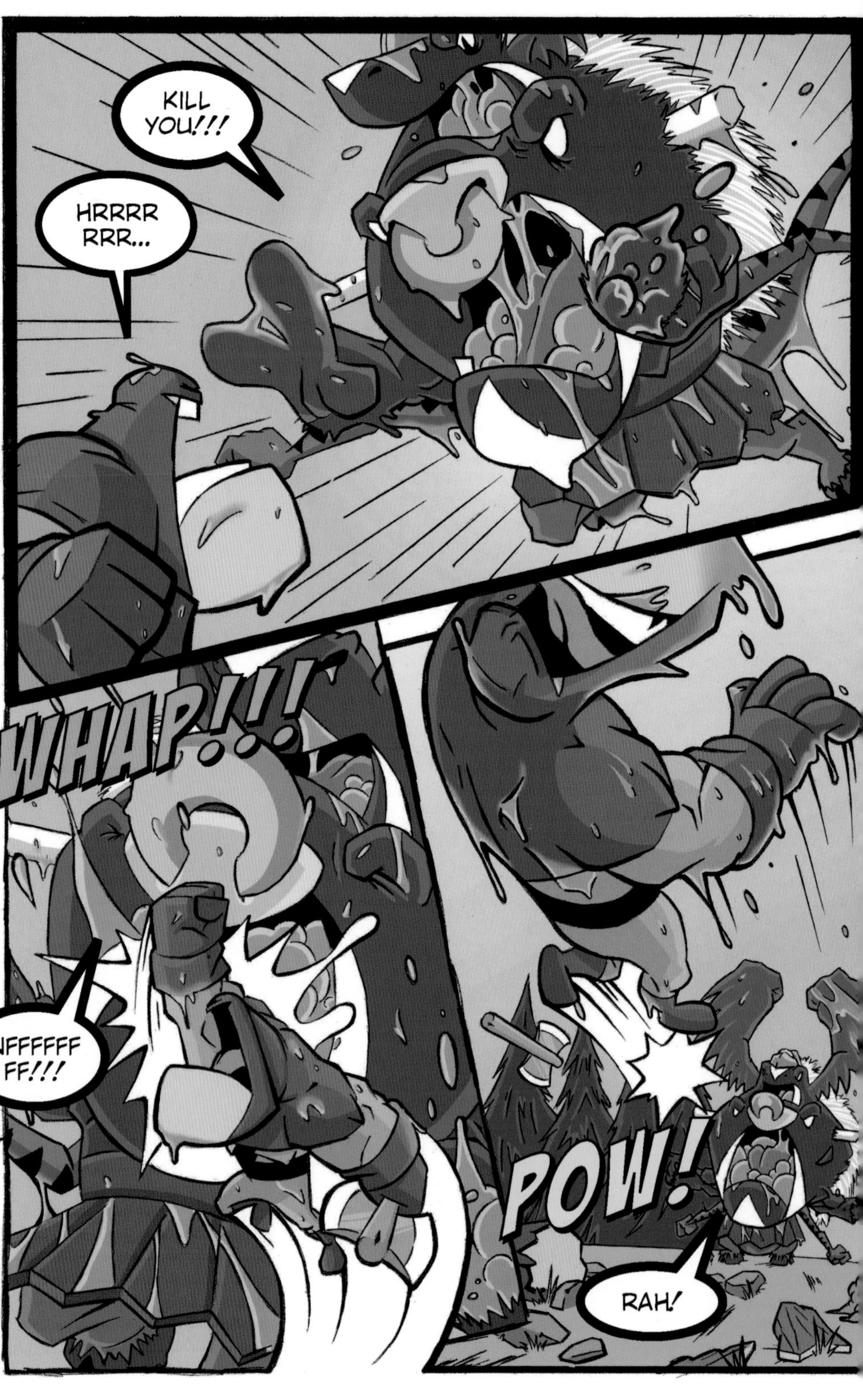
KILL YOU!!!
HRRRR RRR...
WHAP!!!
NFFFFFF FF!!!
POW!
RAH!

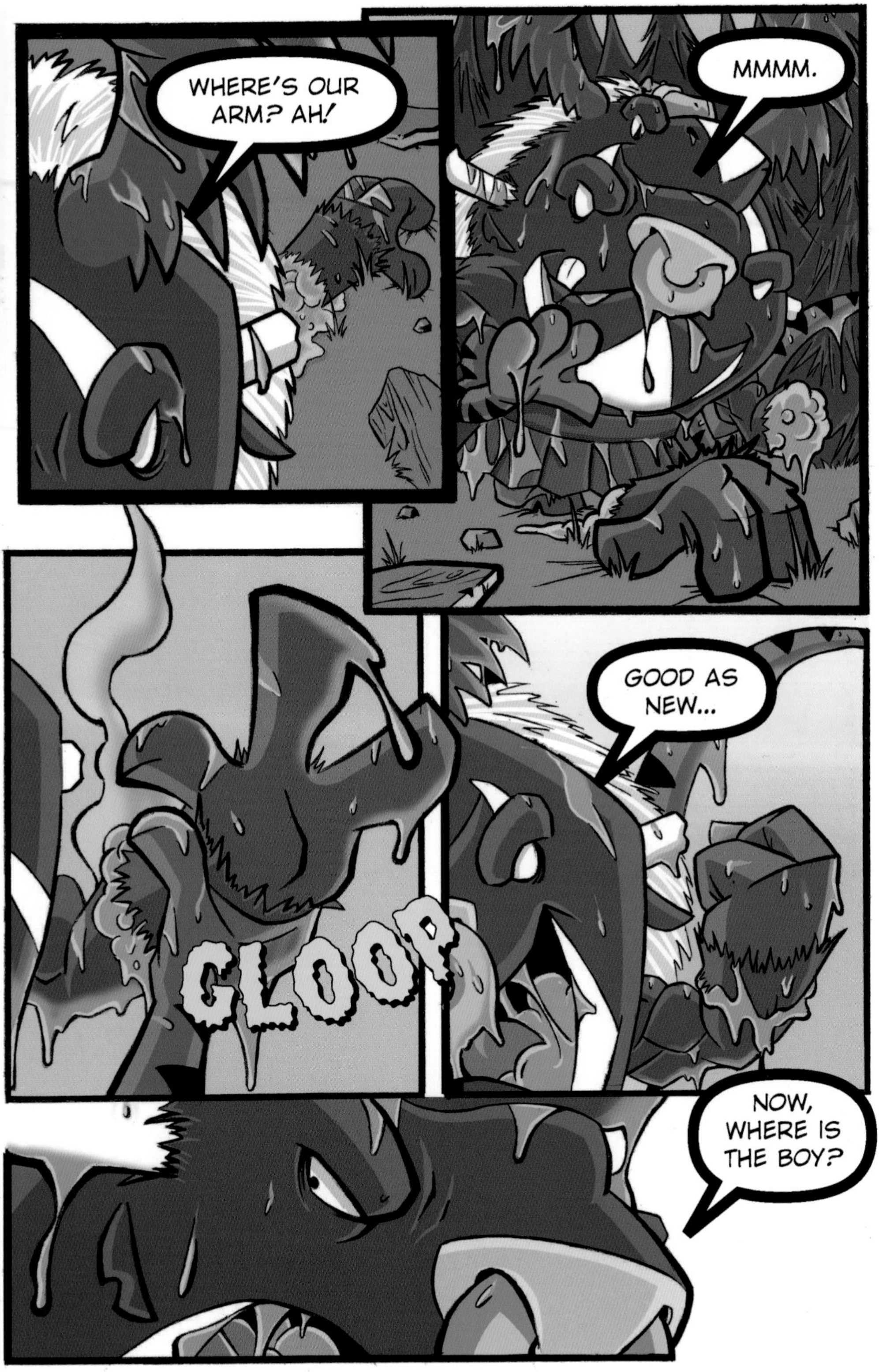
WHERE'S OUR ARM? AH!
MMMM.
GLOOP
GOOD AS NEW...
NOW, WHERE IS THE BOY?

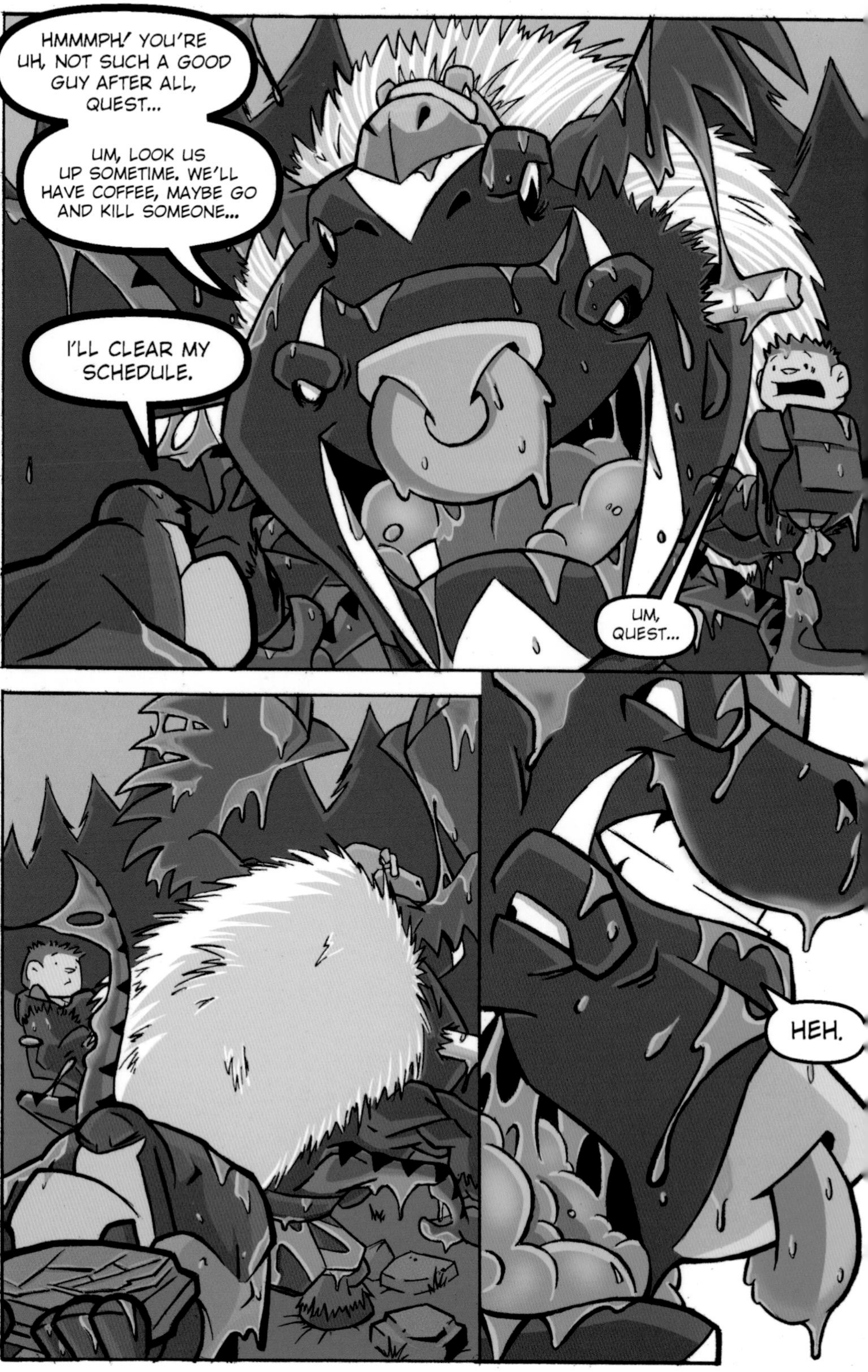
HMMMPH! YOU'RE UH, NOT SUCH A GOOD GUY AFTER ALL, QUEST...
UM, LOOK US UP SOMETIME. WE'LL HAVE COFFEE, MAYBE GO AND KILL SOMEONE...
I'LL CLEAR MY SCHEDULE.
UM, QUEST...
HEH.

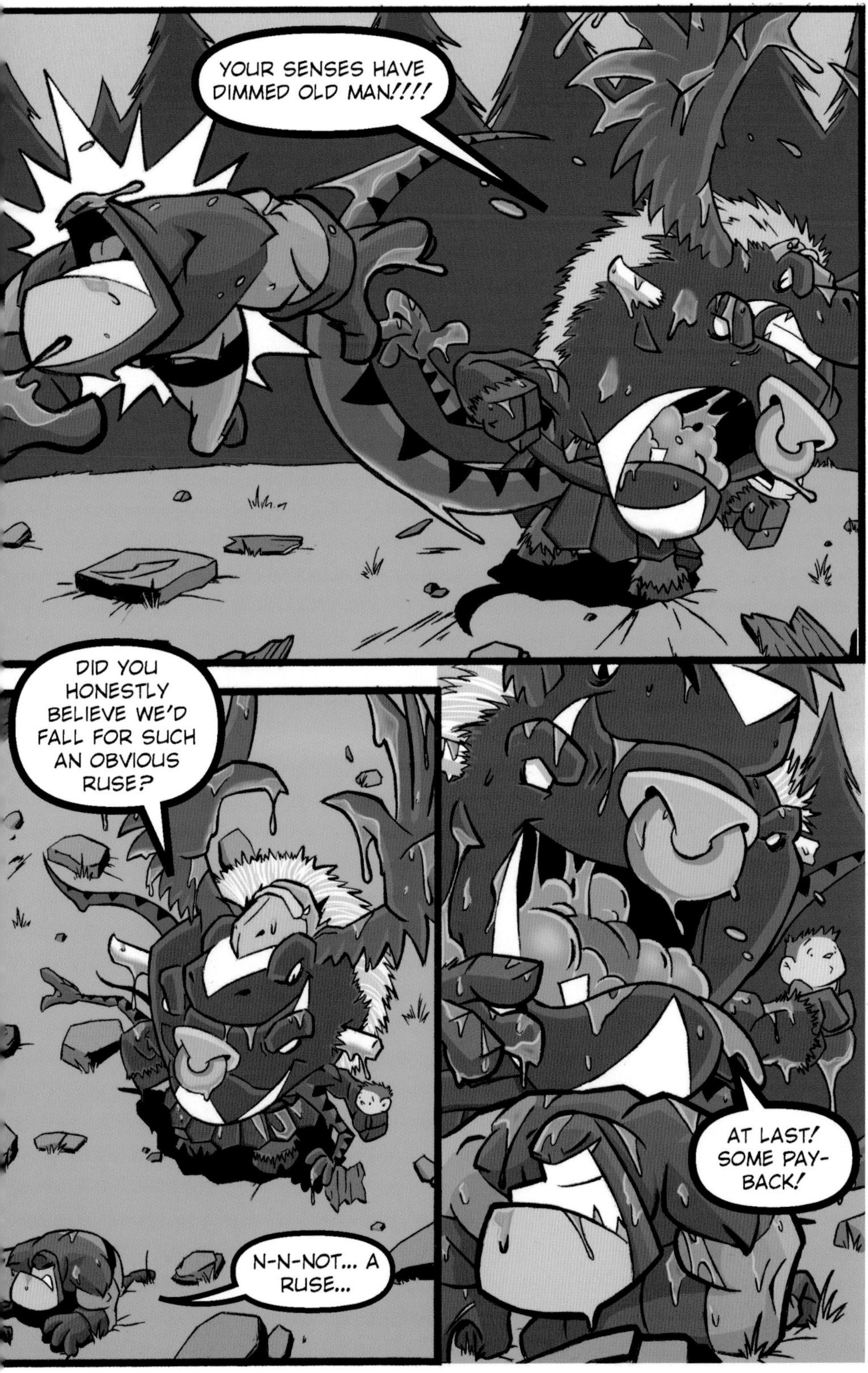
YOUR SENSES HAVE DIMMED OLD MAN!!!!
DID YOU HONESTLY BELIEVE WE'D FALL FOR SUCH AN OBVIOUS RUSE?
N-N-NOT... A RUSE...
AT LAST! SOME PAY-BACK!

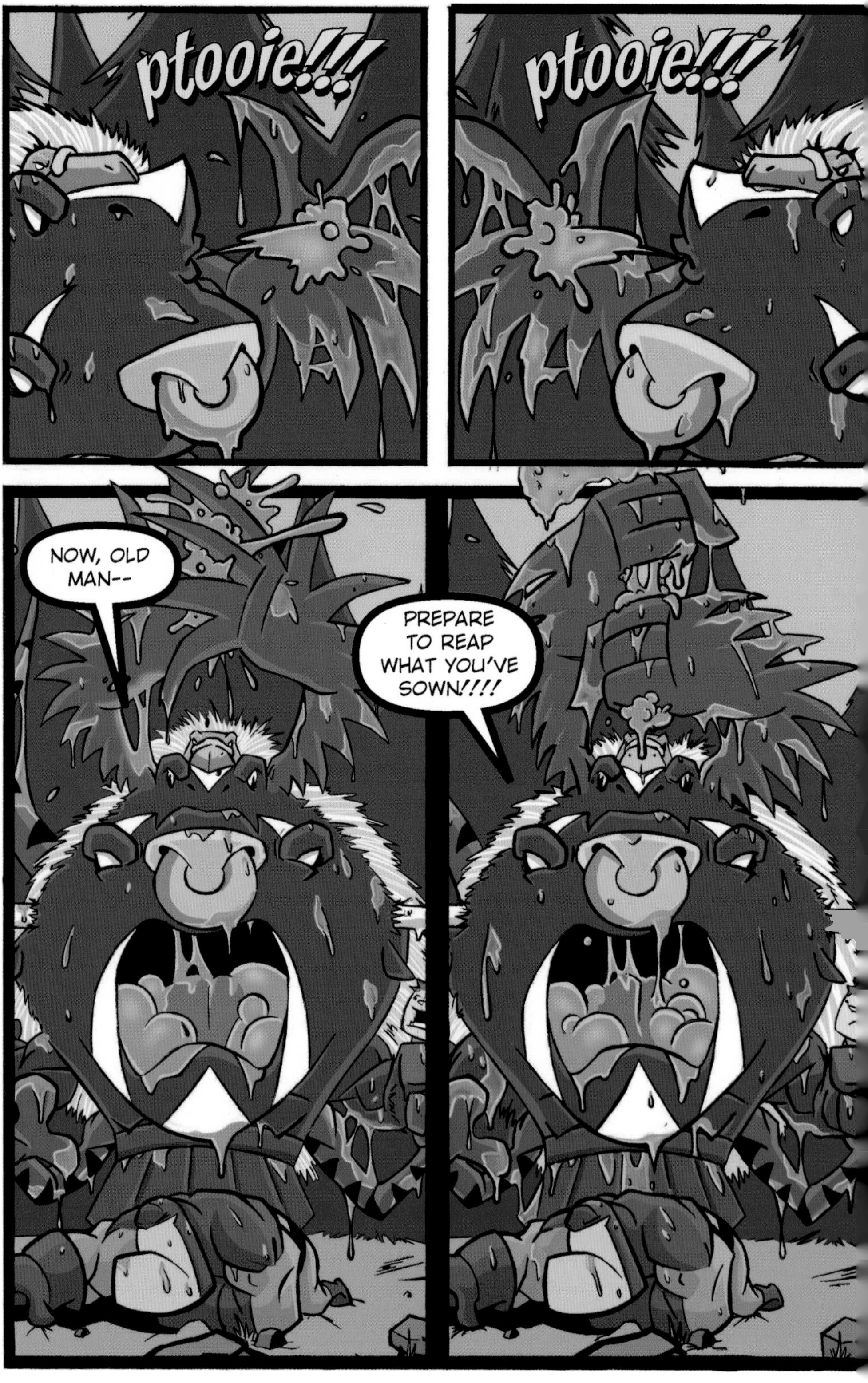
ptooie!!!
ptooie!!!
NOW, OLD MAN--
PREPARE TO REAP WHAT YOU'VE SOWN!!!!

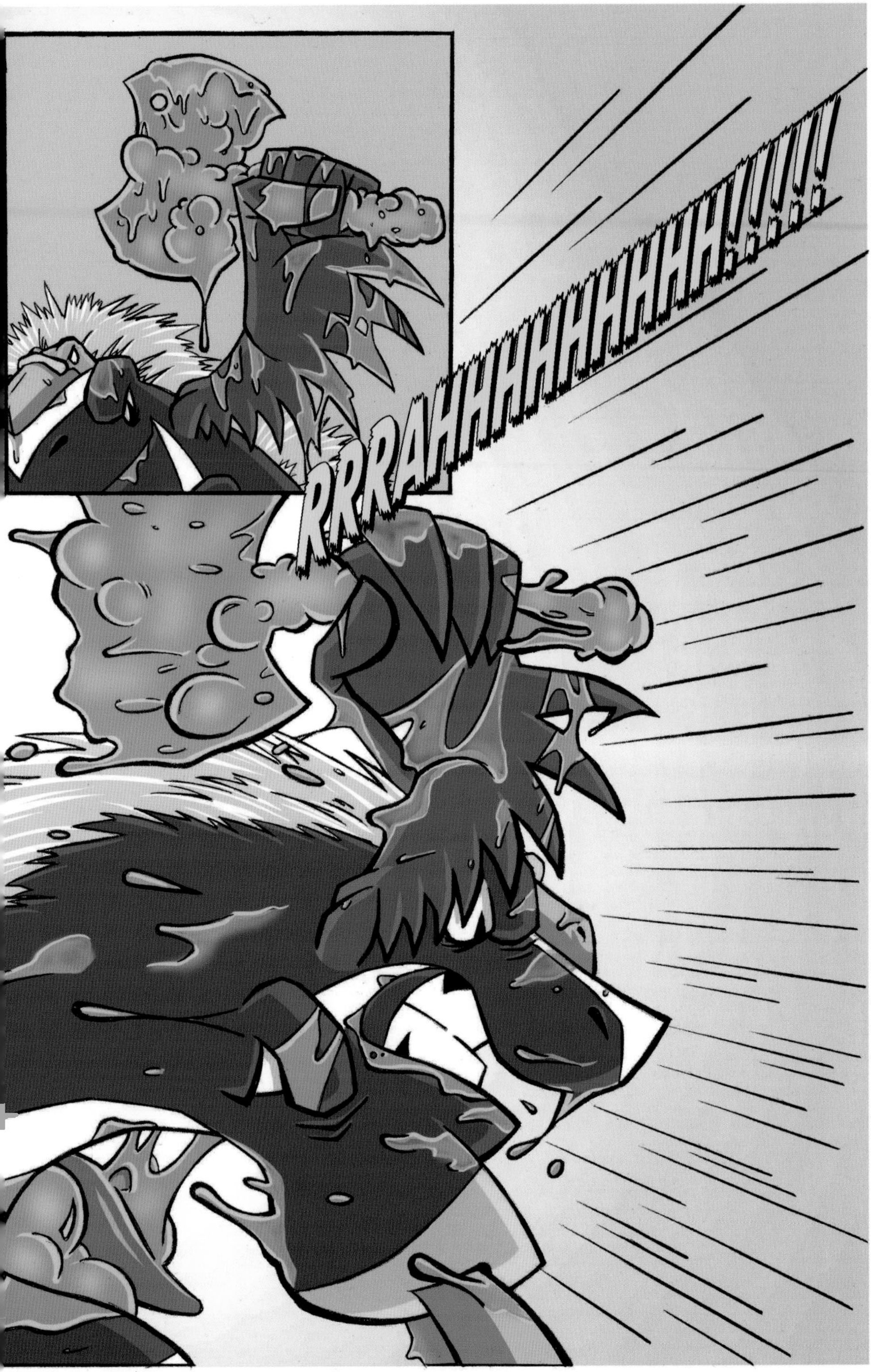
RRRAHHHHHHHHHHH!!!!!

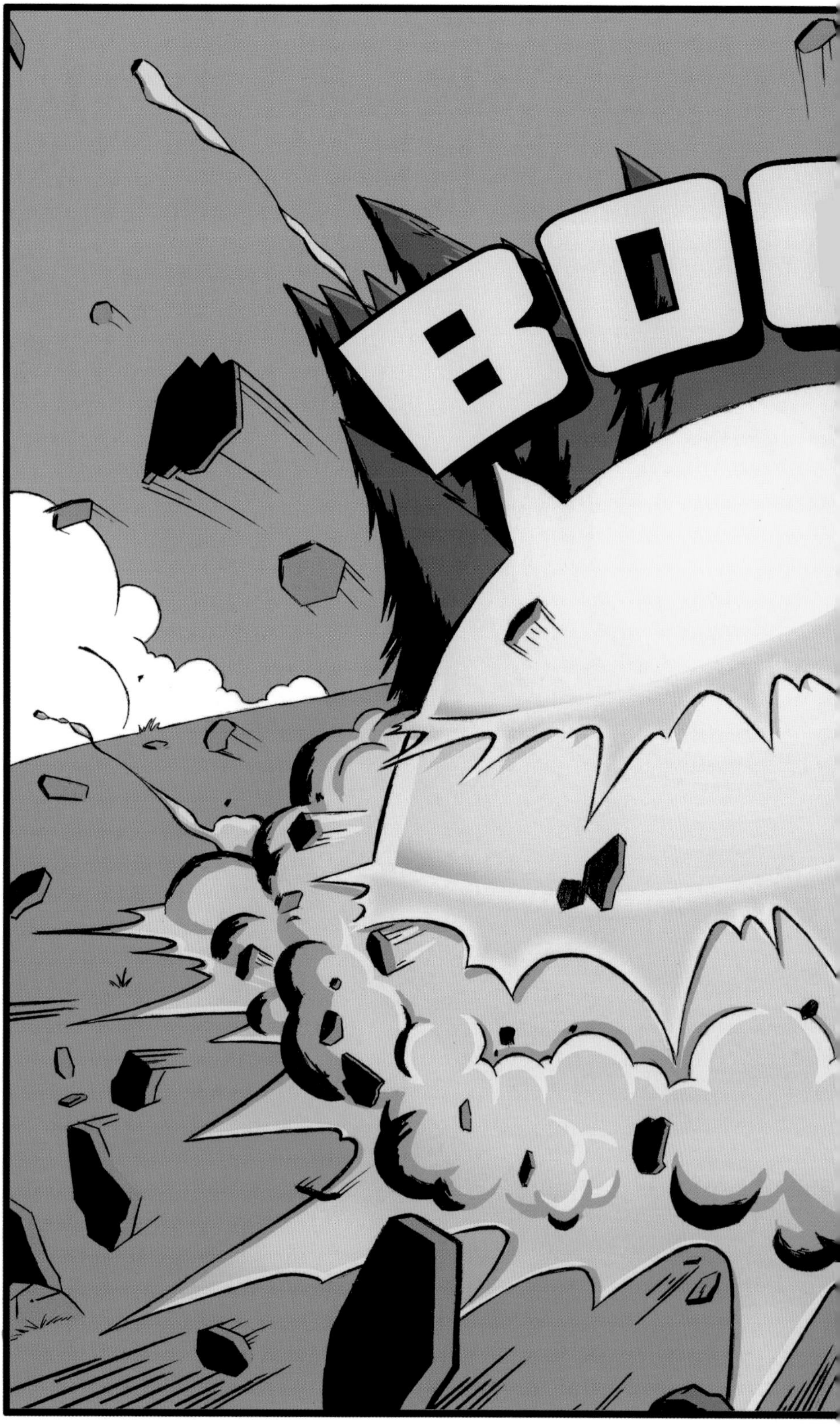
BO

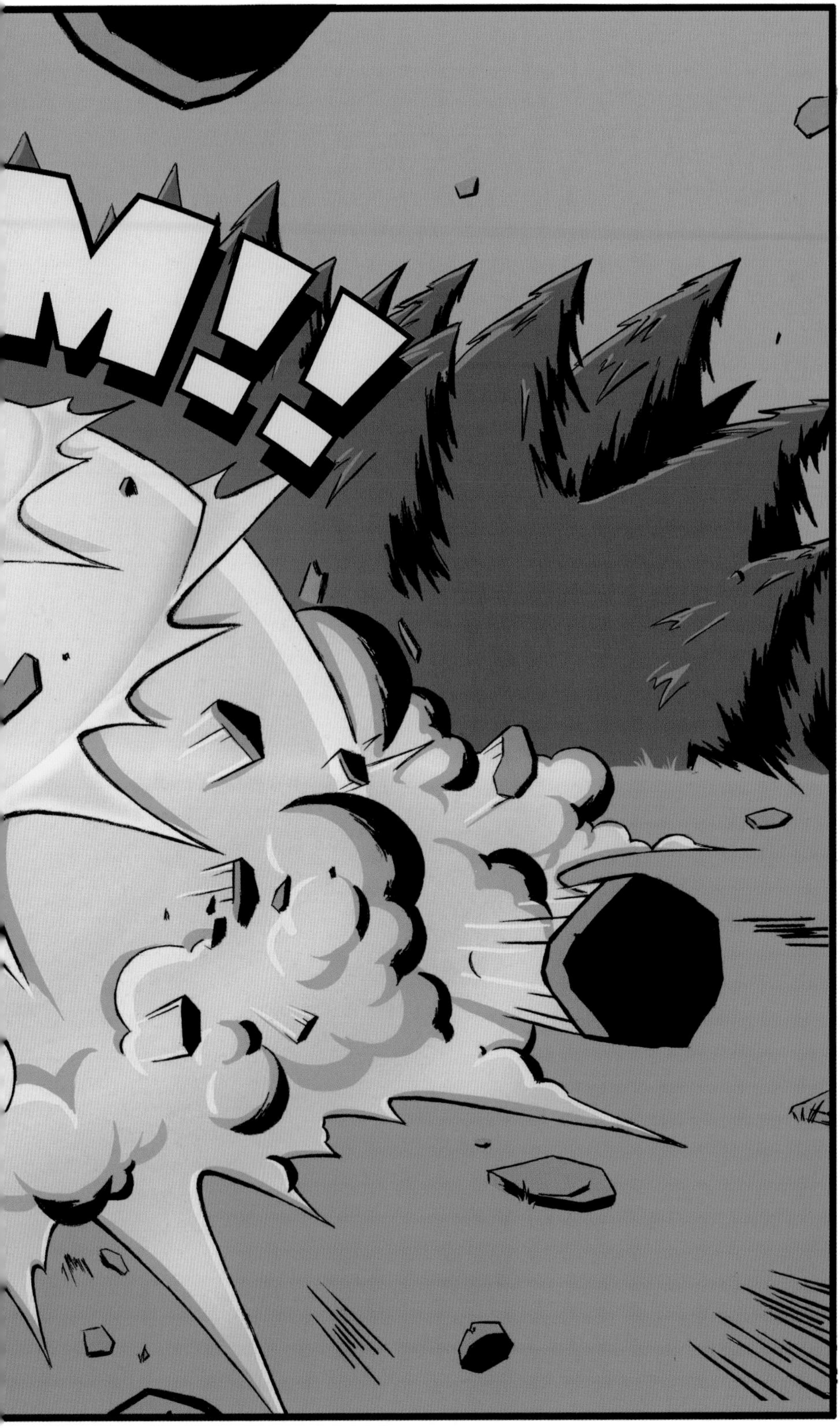
M!!

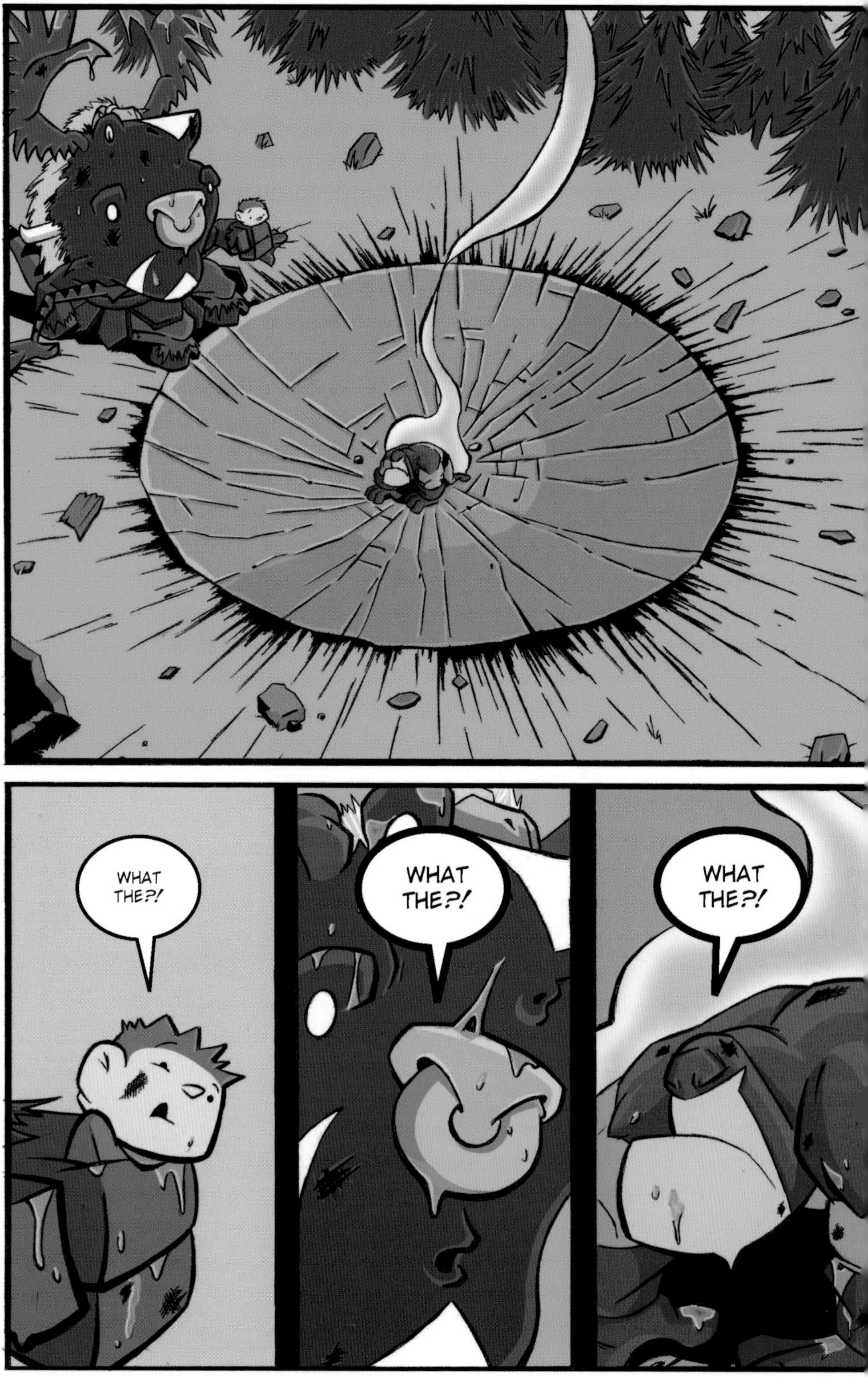
WHAT THE?!
WHAT THE?!
WHAT THE?!

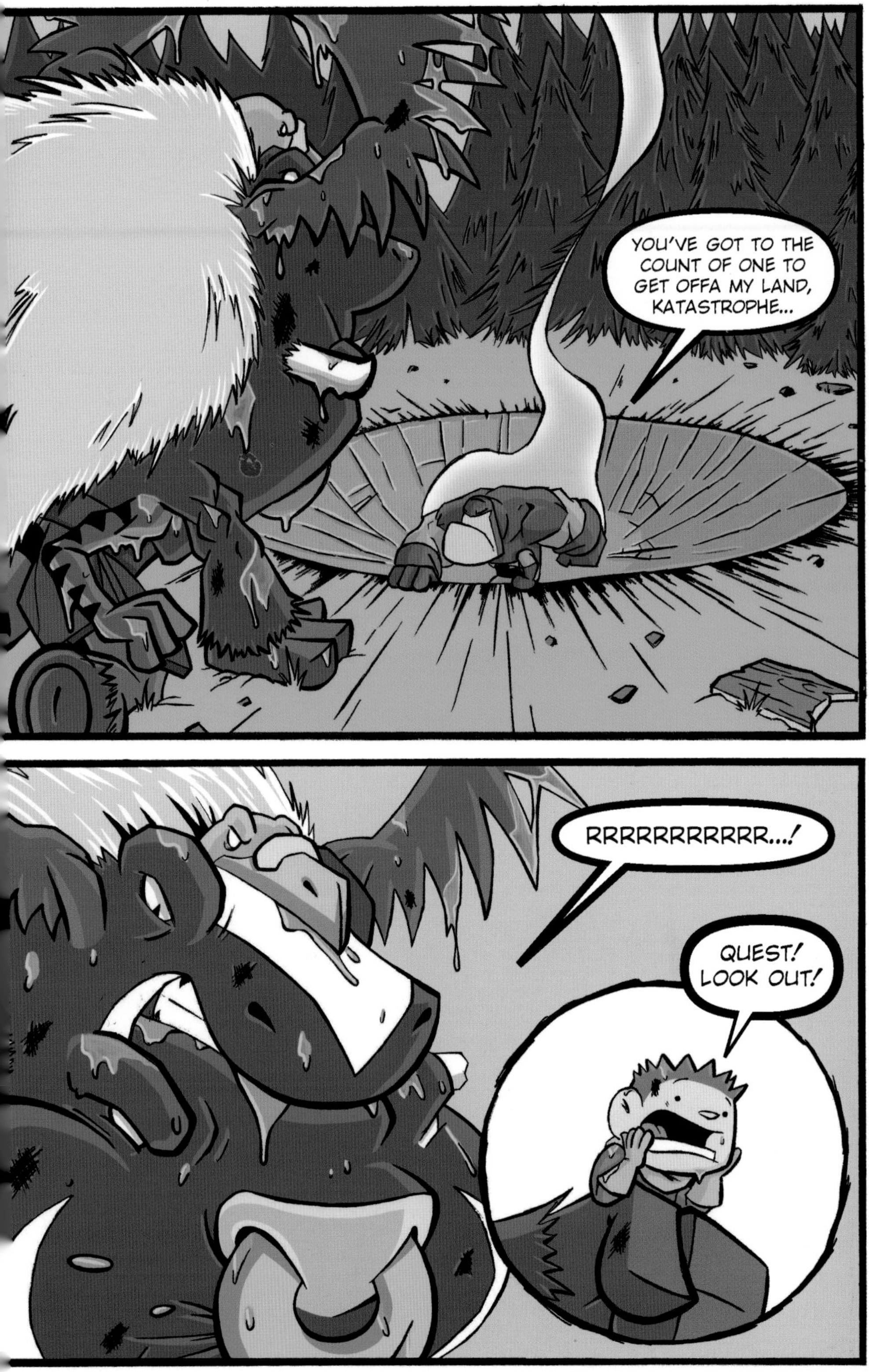
YOU'VE GOT TO THE COUNT OF ONE TO GET OFFA MY LAND, KATASTROPHE...
RRRRRRRRRRR...!
QUEST! LOOK OUT!

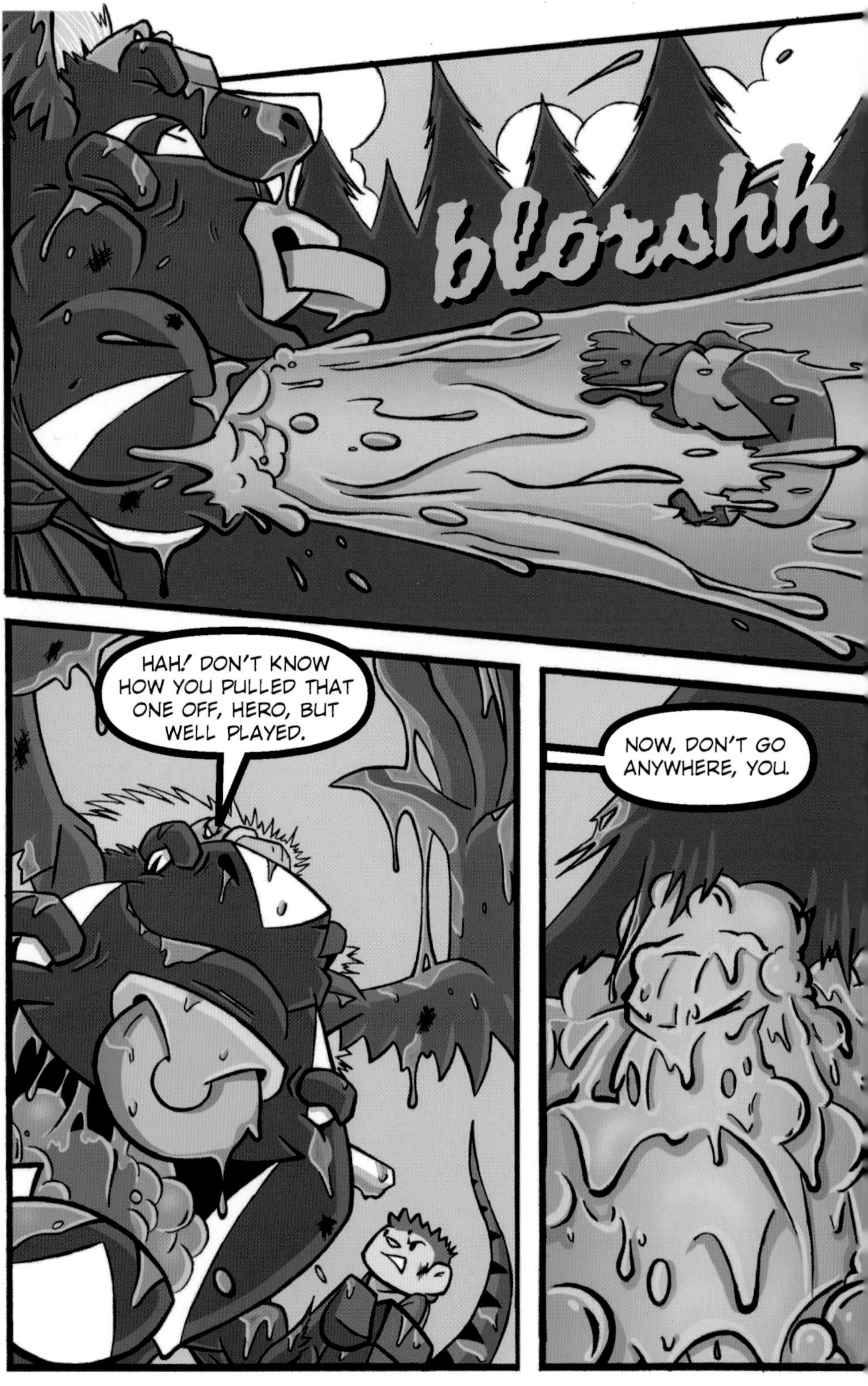
blorshh
HAH! DON'T KNOW HOW YOU PULLED THAT ONE OFF, HERO, BUT WELL PLAYED.
NOW, DON'T GO ANYWHERE, YOU.

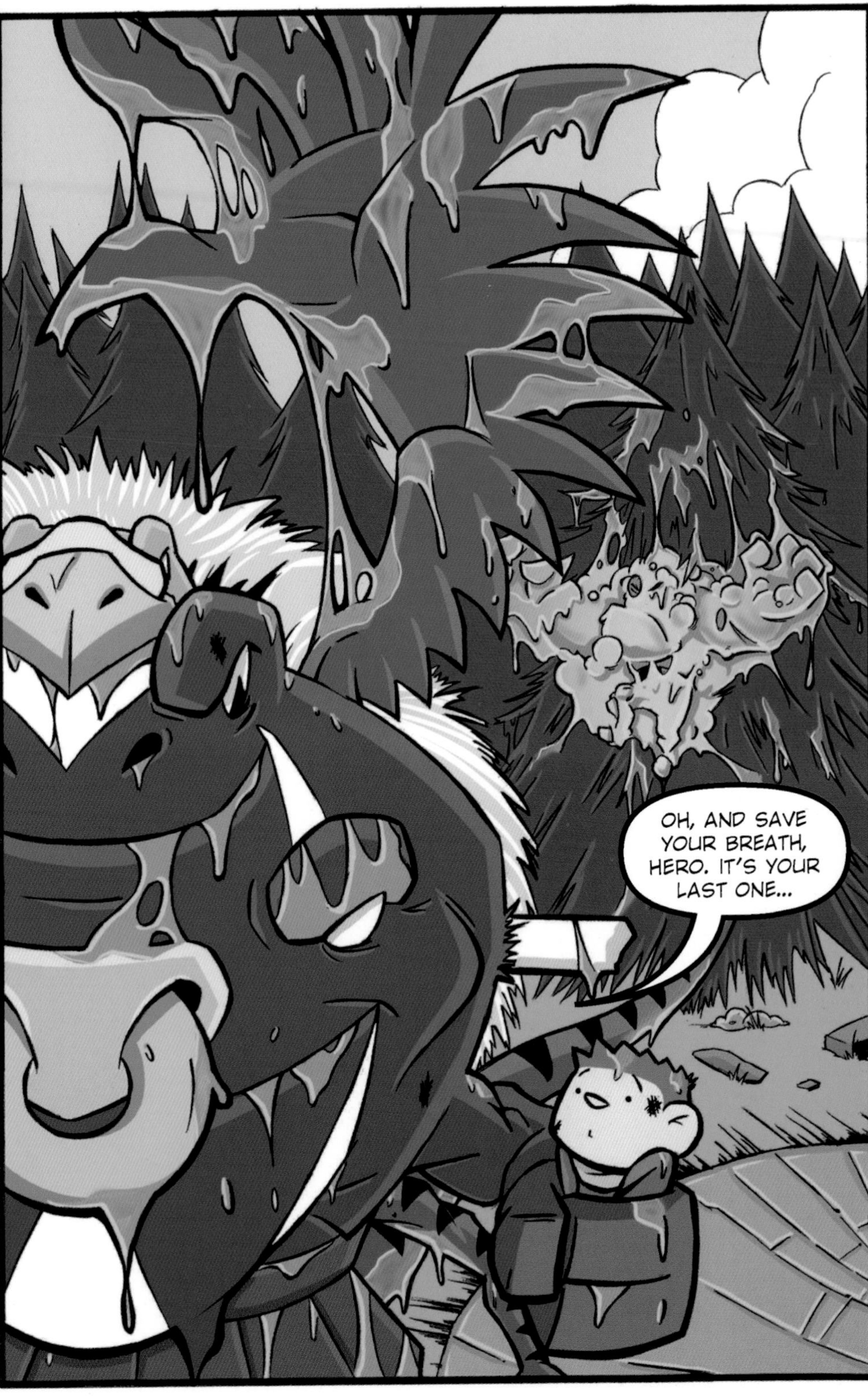
OH, AND SAVE YOUR BREATH, HERO. IT'S YOUR LAST ONE...

INTERLUDE
AN EVIL INTERLUDE...

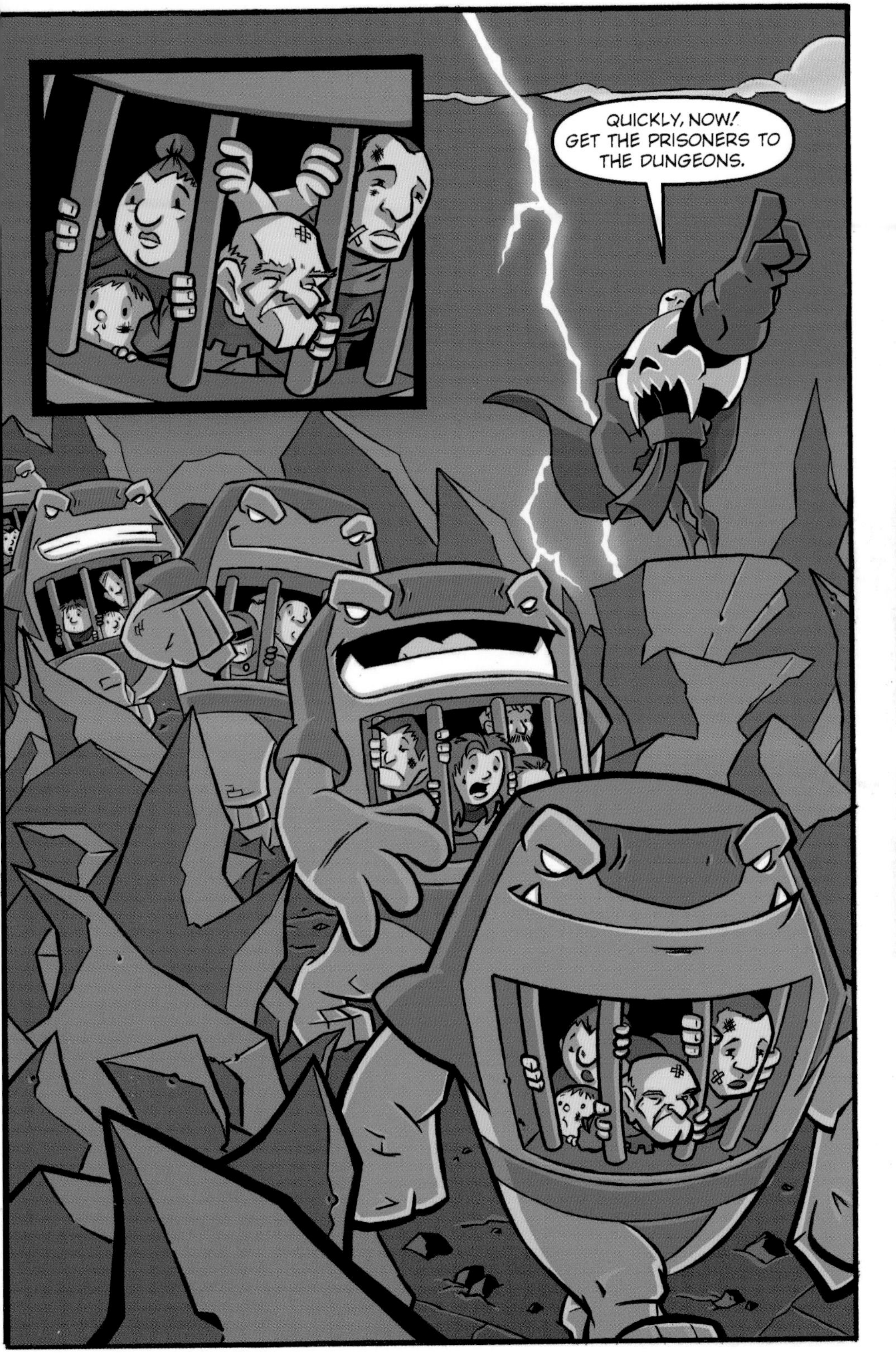
QUICKLY, NOW! GET THE PRISONERS TO THE DUNGEONS.

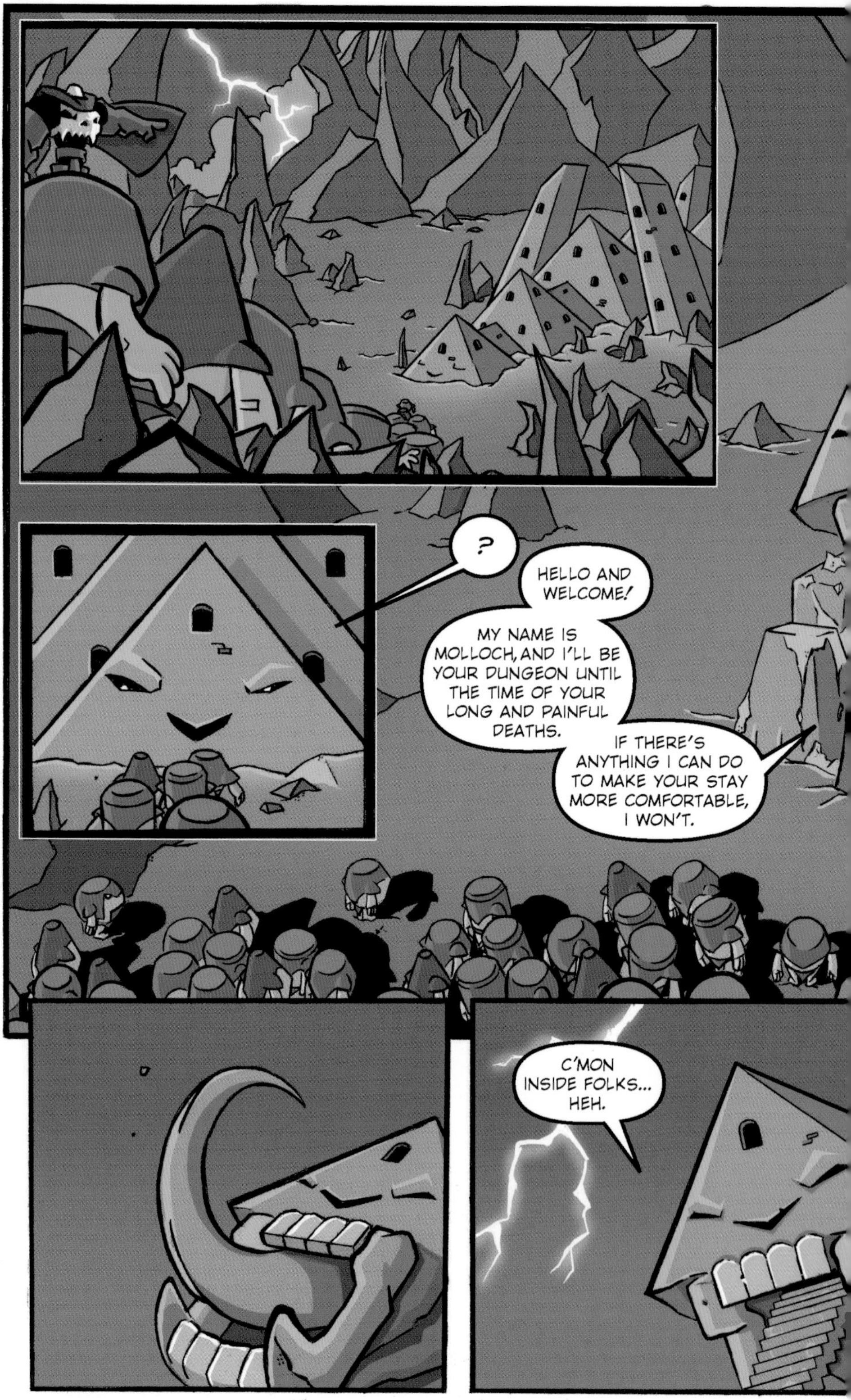
?
HELLO AND WELCOME!
MY NAME IS MOLLOCH, AND I'LL BE YOUR DUNGEON UNTIL THE TIME OF YOUR LONG AND PAINFUL DEATHS.
IF THERE'S ANYTHING I CAN DO TO MAKE YOUR STAY MORE COMFORTABLE, I WON'T.
C'MON INSIDE FOLKS... HEH.

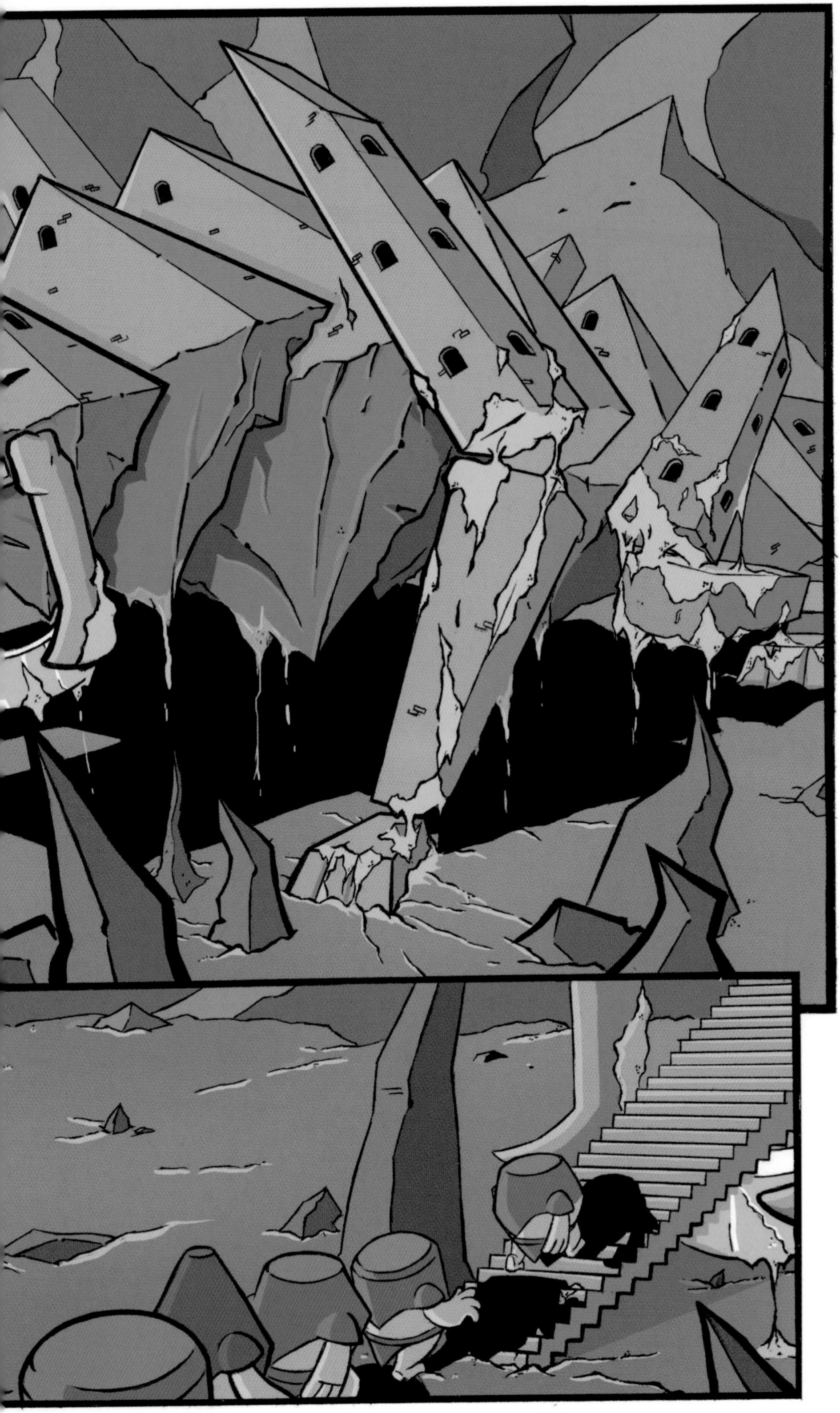

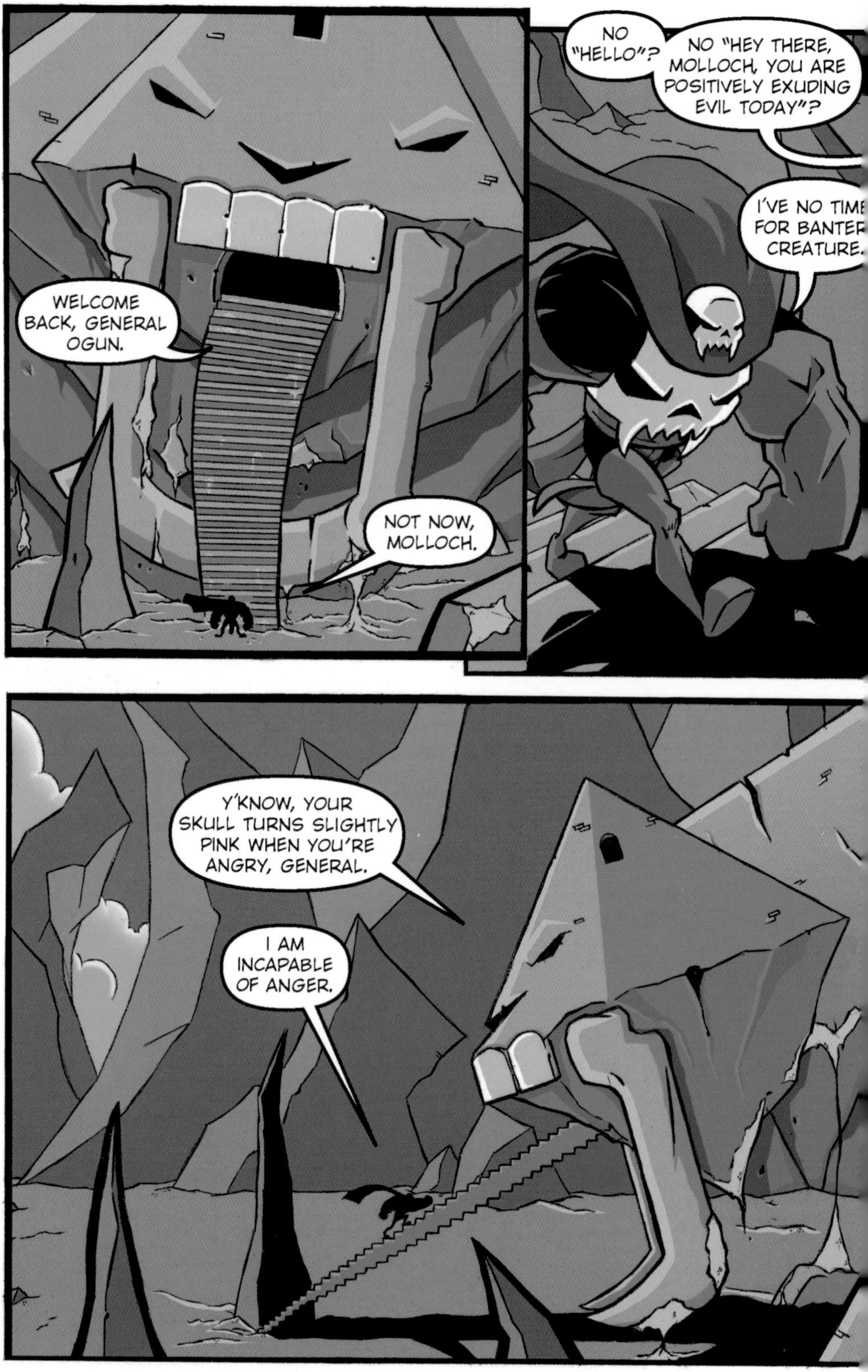
WELCOME BACK, GENERAL OGUN.
NOT NOW, MOLLOCH.
NO "HELLO"?
NO "HEY THERE, MOLLOCH, YOU ARE POSITIVELY EXUDING EVIL TODAY"?
I'VE NO TIME FOR BANTER, CREATURE.
Y'KNOW, YOUR SKULL TURNS SLIGHTLY PINK WHEN YOU'RE ANGRY, GENERAL.
I AM INCAPABLE OF ANGER.

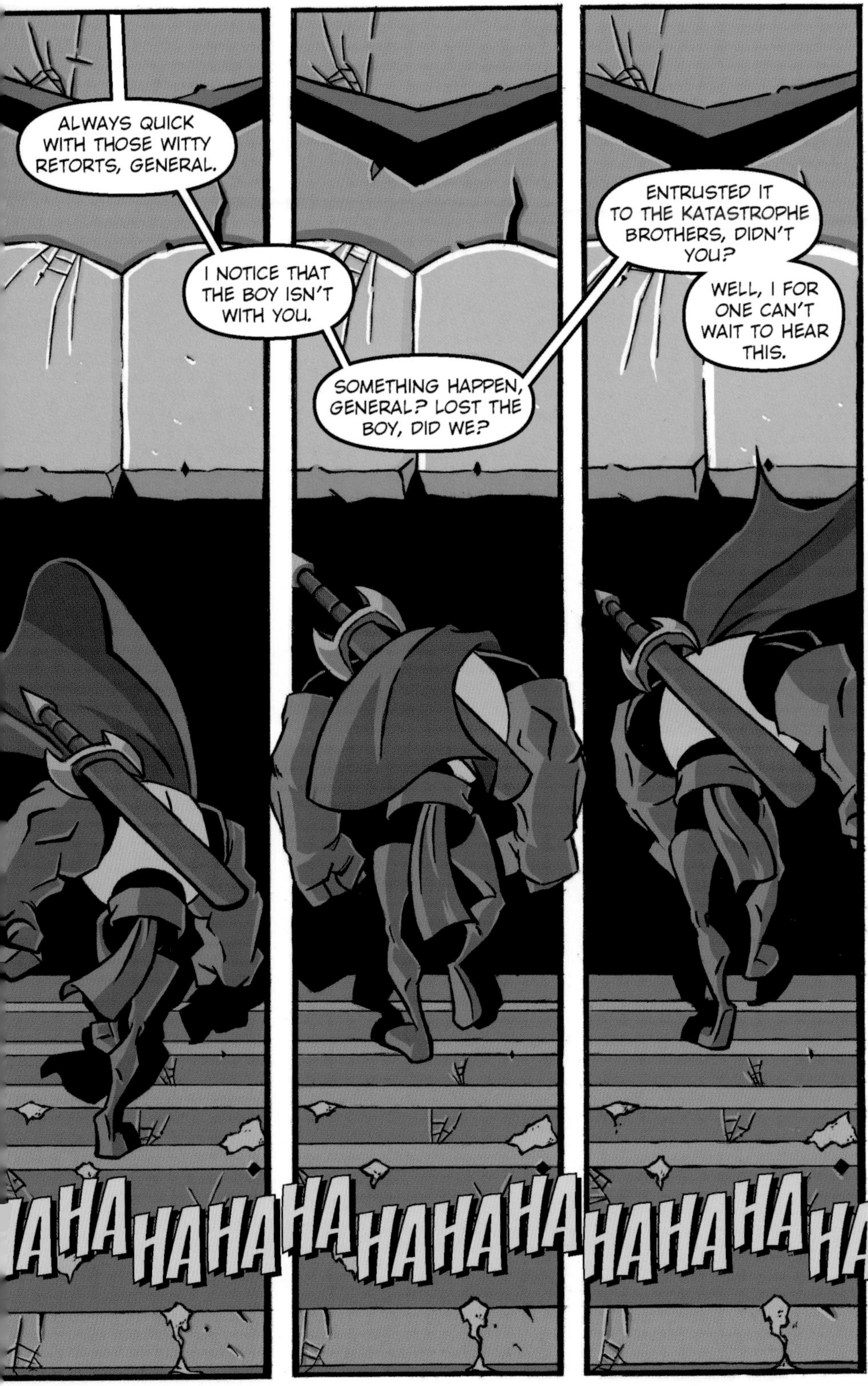
ALWAYS QUICK WITH THOSE WITTY RETORTS, GENERAL.
I NOTICE THAT THE BOY ISN'T WITH YOU.
SOMETHING HAPPEN, GENERAL? LOST THE BOY, DID WE?
ENTRUSTED IT TO THE KATASTROPHE BROTHERS, DIDN'T YOU?
WELL, I FOR ONE CAN'T WAIT TO HEAR THIS.
HAHAHAHAHAHAHAHAHAHAHAHAHAHAHA

CHAPTER THREE
FRIENDS, FRIENDS, FIENDS...

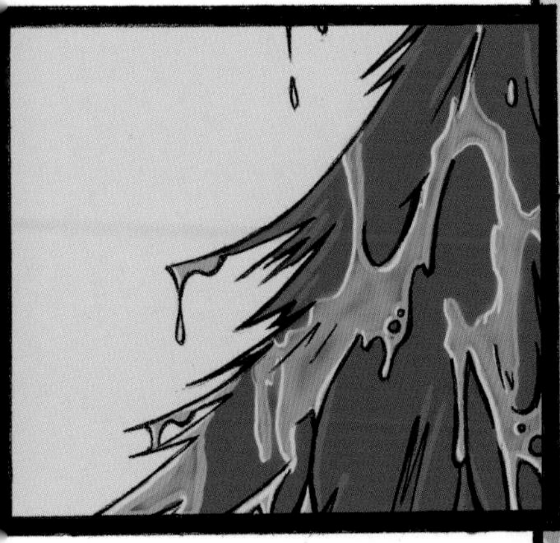

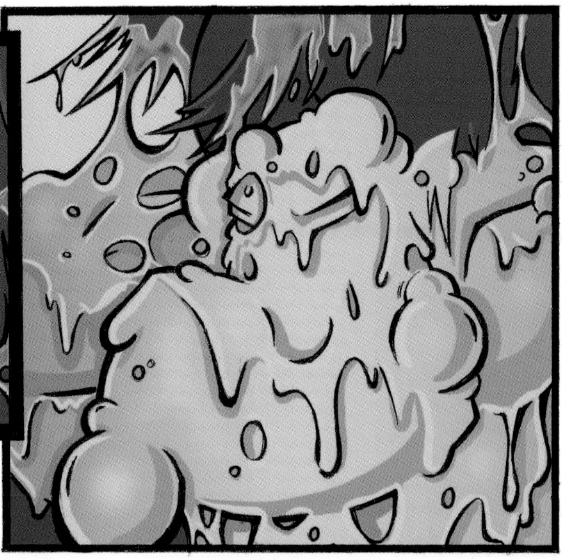

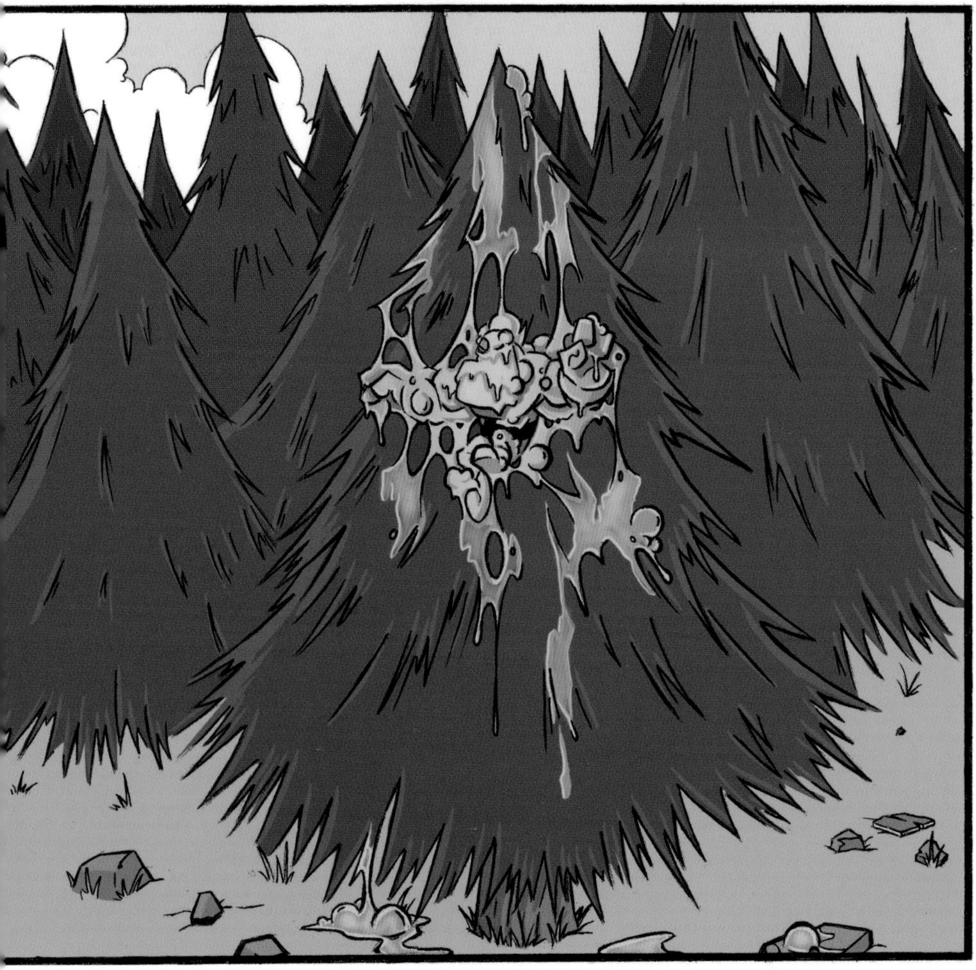

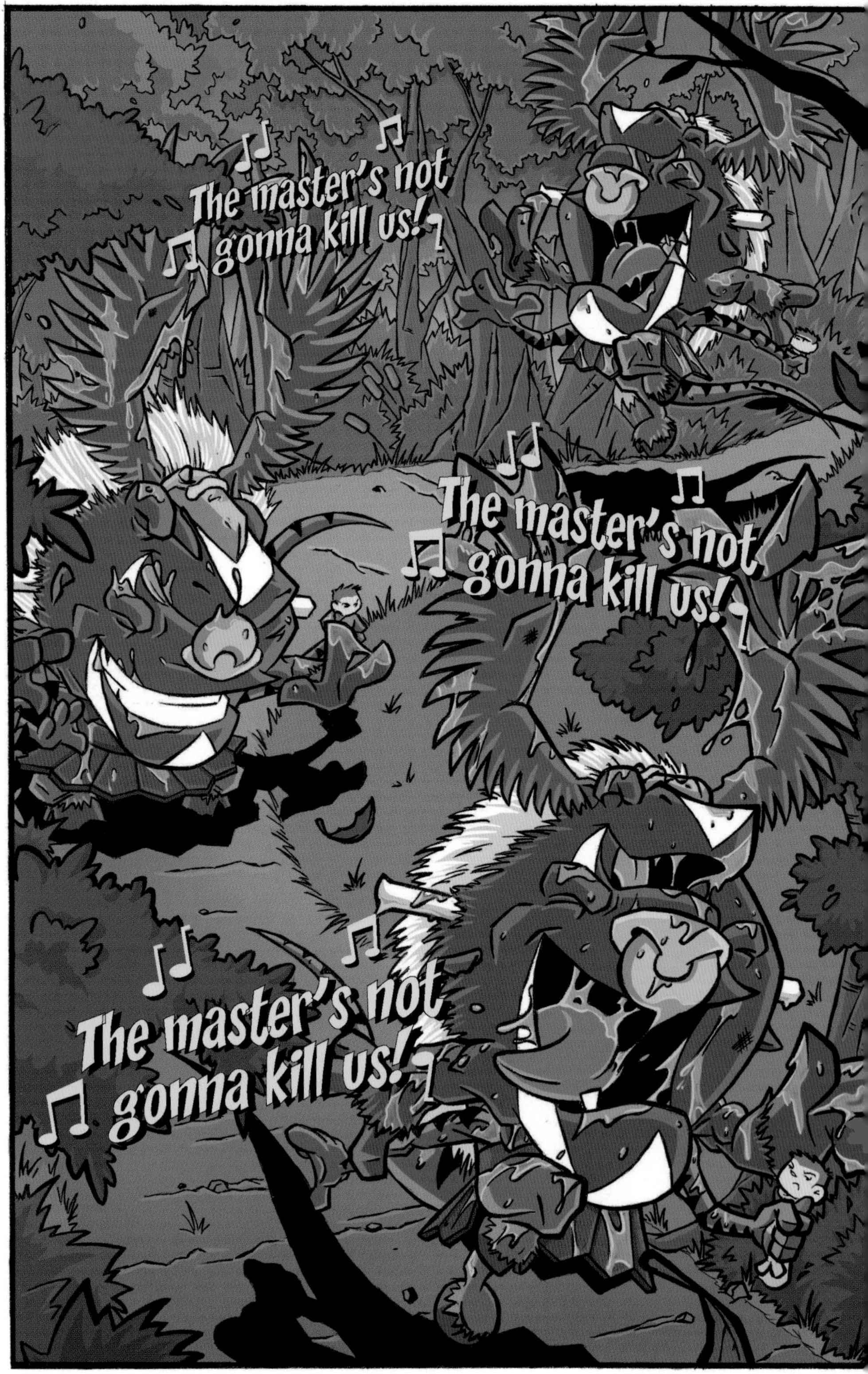
♫ The master's not gonna kill us! ♫
♫ The master's not gonna kill us! ♫
♫ The master's not gonna kill us! ♫

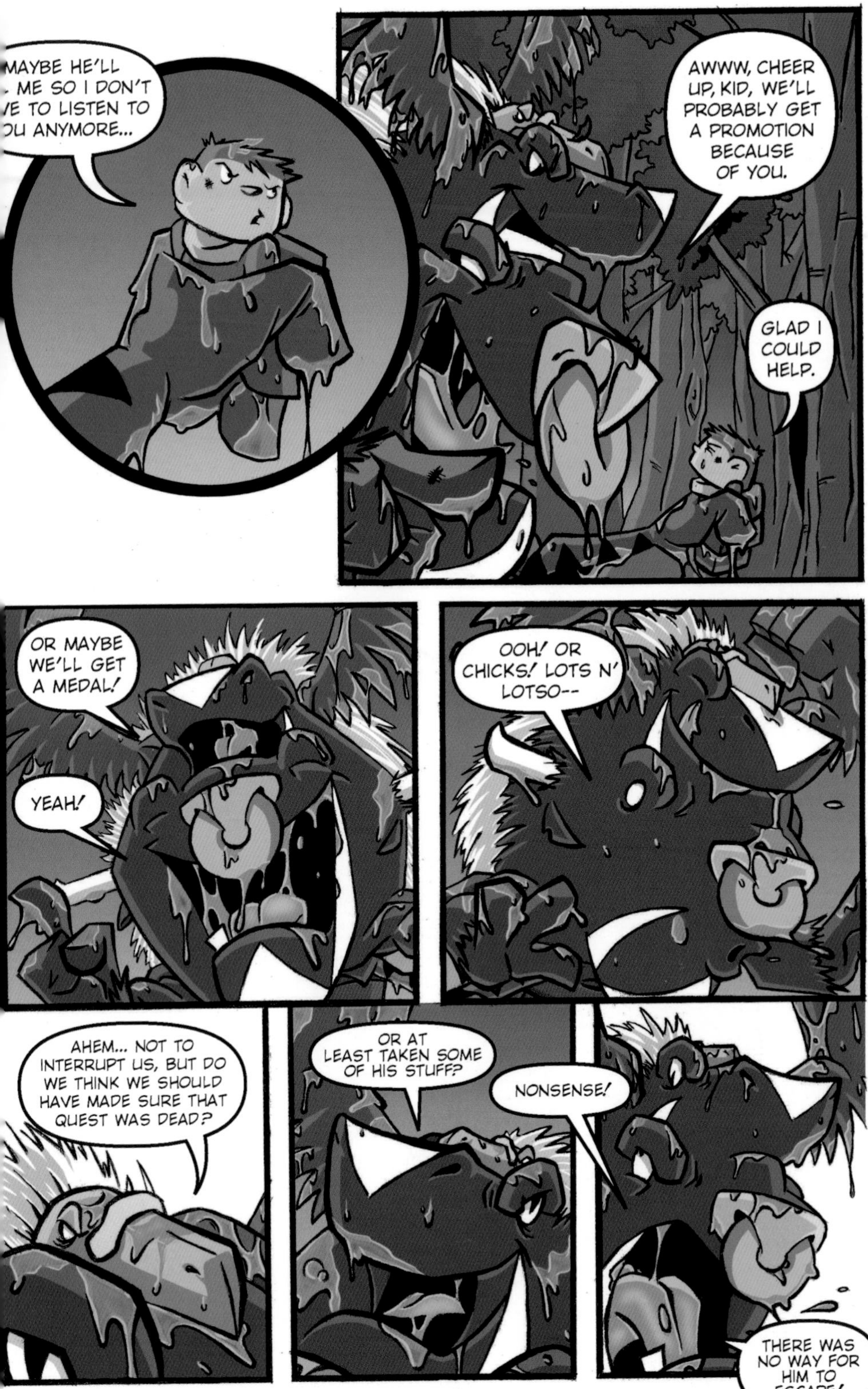
MAYBE HE'LL
ME SO I DON'T
VE TO LISTEN TO
OU ANYMORE...
AWWW, CHEER UP, KID, WE'LL PROBABLY GET A PROMOTION BECAUSE OF YOU.
GLAD I COULD HELP.
OR MAYBE WE'LL GET A MEDAL!
YEAH!
OOH! OR CHICKS! LOTS N' LOTSO--
AHEM... NOT TO INTERRUPT US, BUT DO WE THINK WE SHOULD HAVE MADE SURE THAT QUEST WAS DEAD?
OR AT LEAST TAKEN SOME OF HIS STUFF?
NONSENSE!
THERE WAS NO WAY FOR HIM TO ESCAPE!

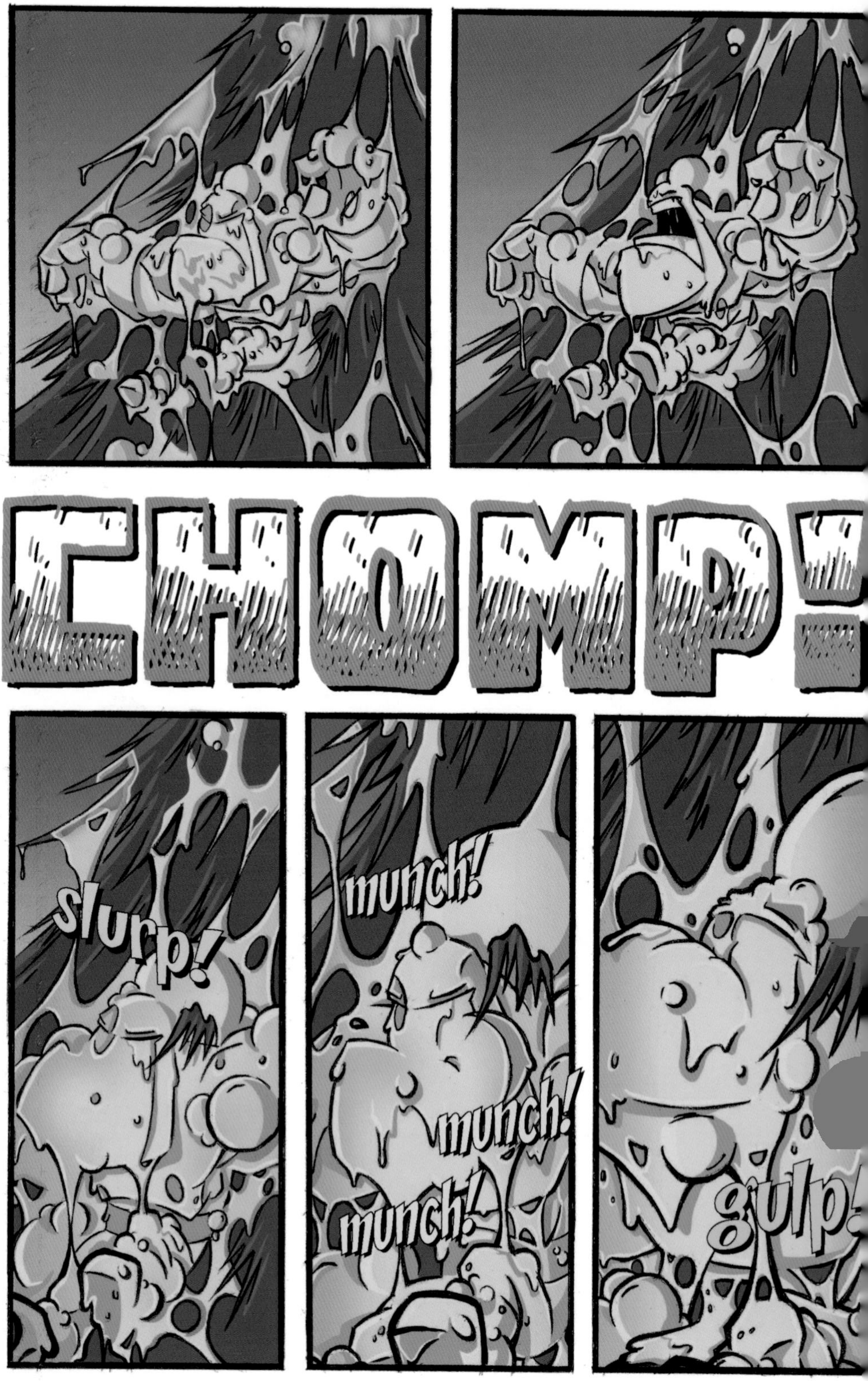
CHOMP!
slurp!
munch!
munch!
munch!
gulp!

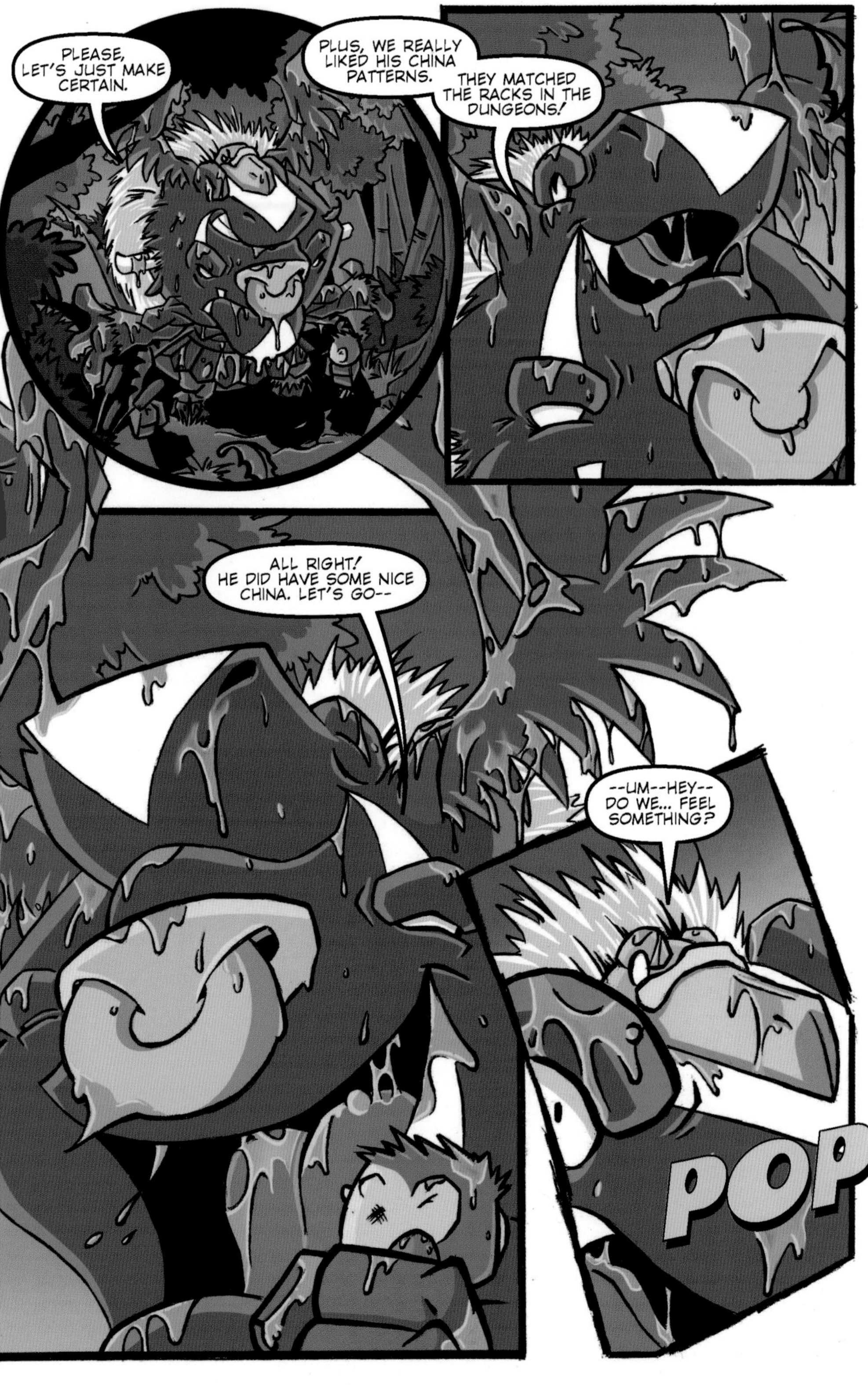
PLEASE, LET'S JUST MAKE CERTAIN.
PLUS, WE REALLY LIKED HIS CHINA PATTERNS.
THEY MATCHED THE RACKS IN THE DUNGEONS!
ALL RIGHT! HE DID HAVE SOME NICE CHINA. LET'S GO--
--UM--HEY-- DO WE... FEEL SOMETHING?
POP

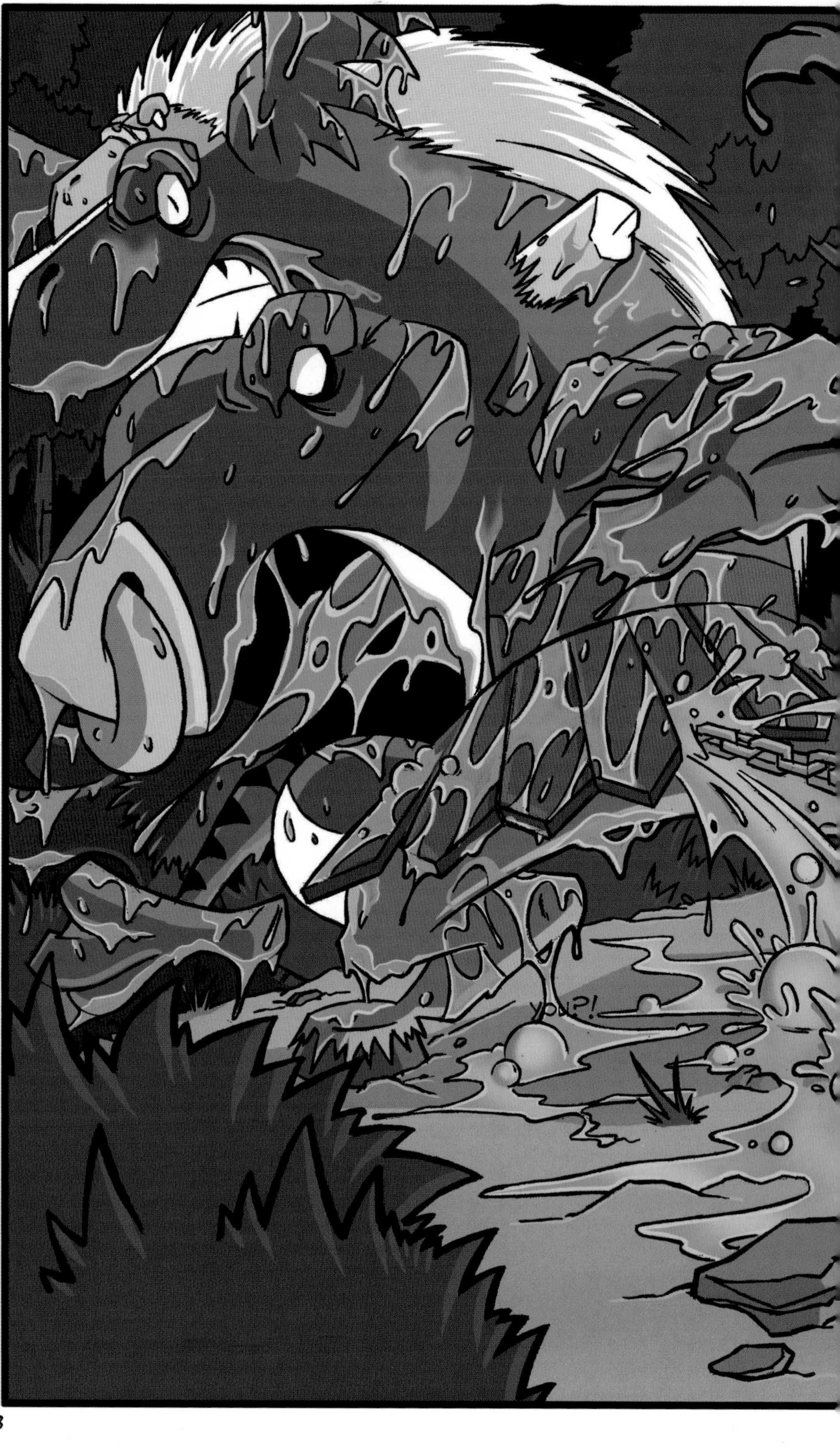
YOU?!

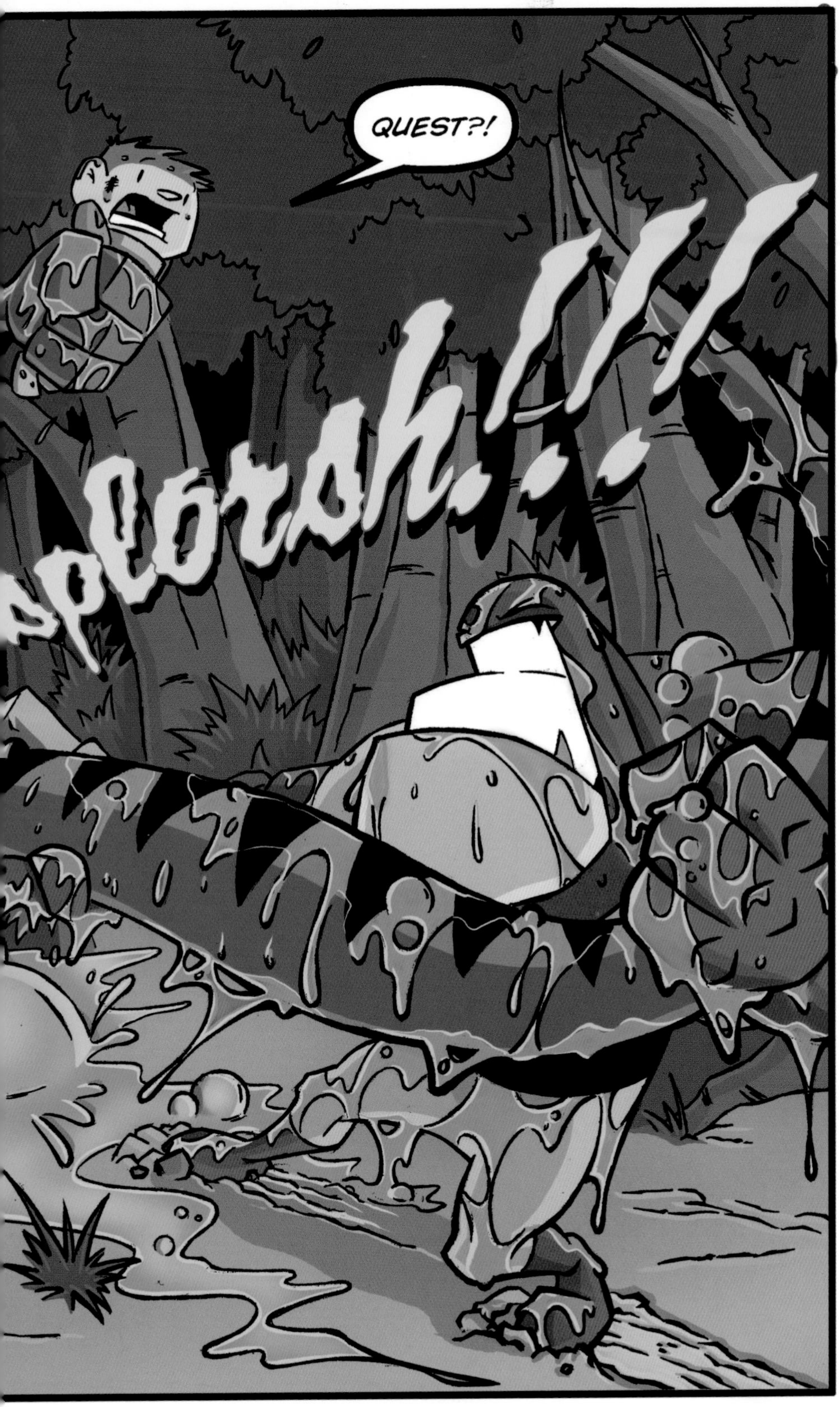
QUEST?!
plorsh!!!!

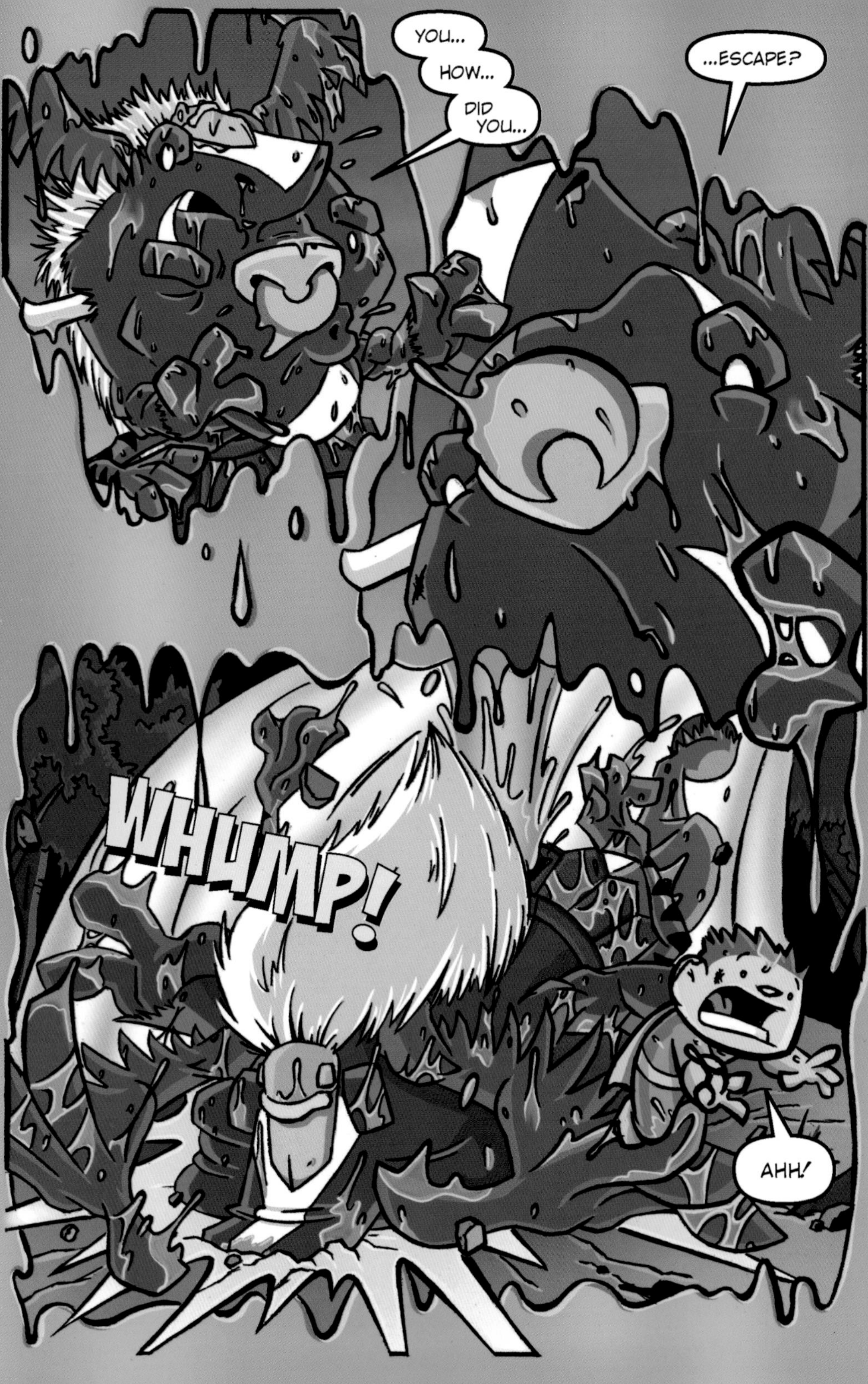
YOU...
HOW...
DID YOU...
...ESCAPE?
WHUMP!
AHH!

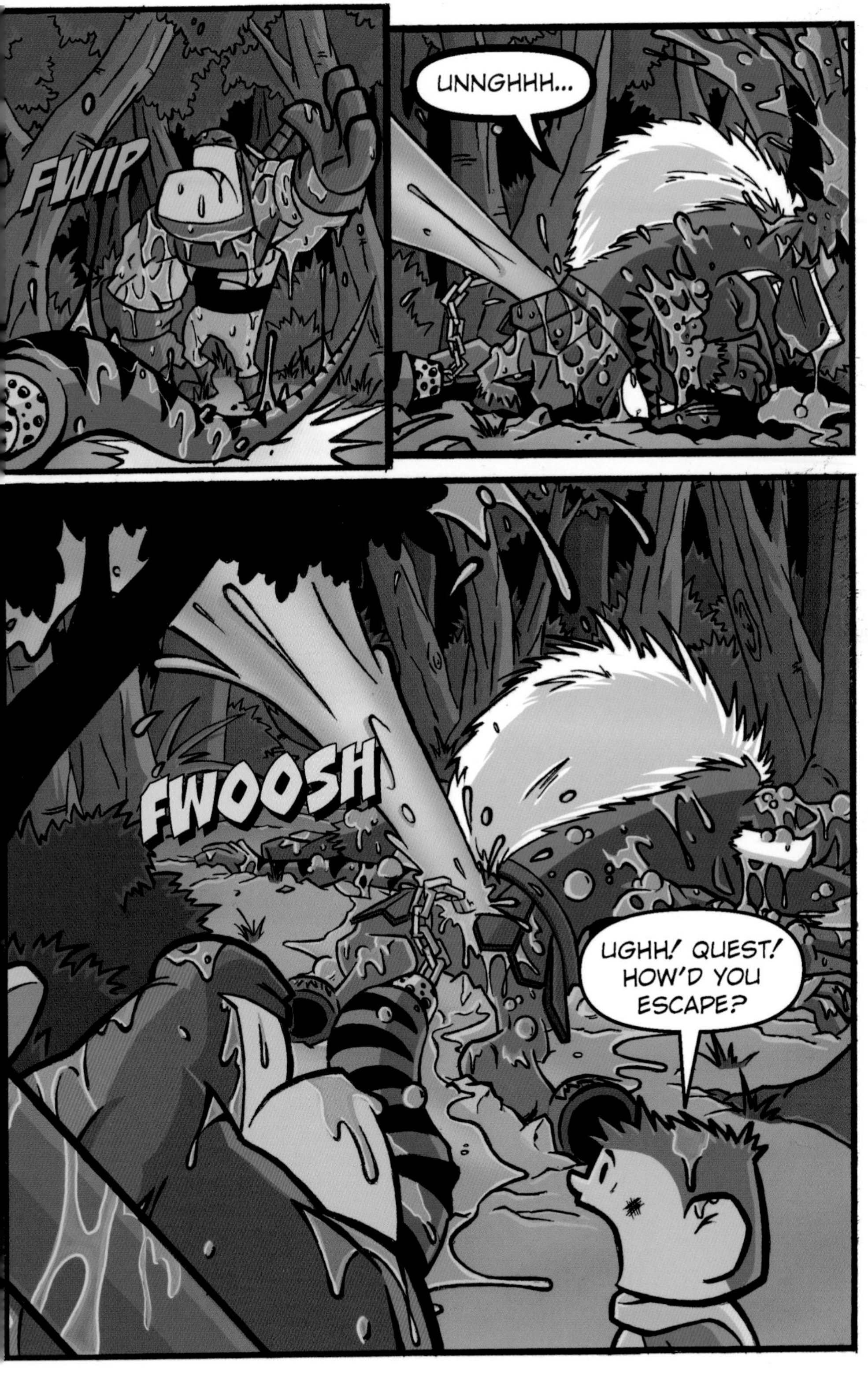
FWIP
UNNGHHH...
FWOOSH
UGHH! QUEST! HOW'D YOU ESCAPE?

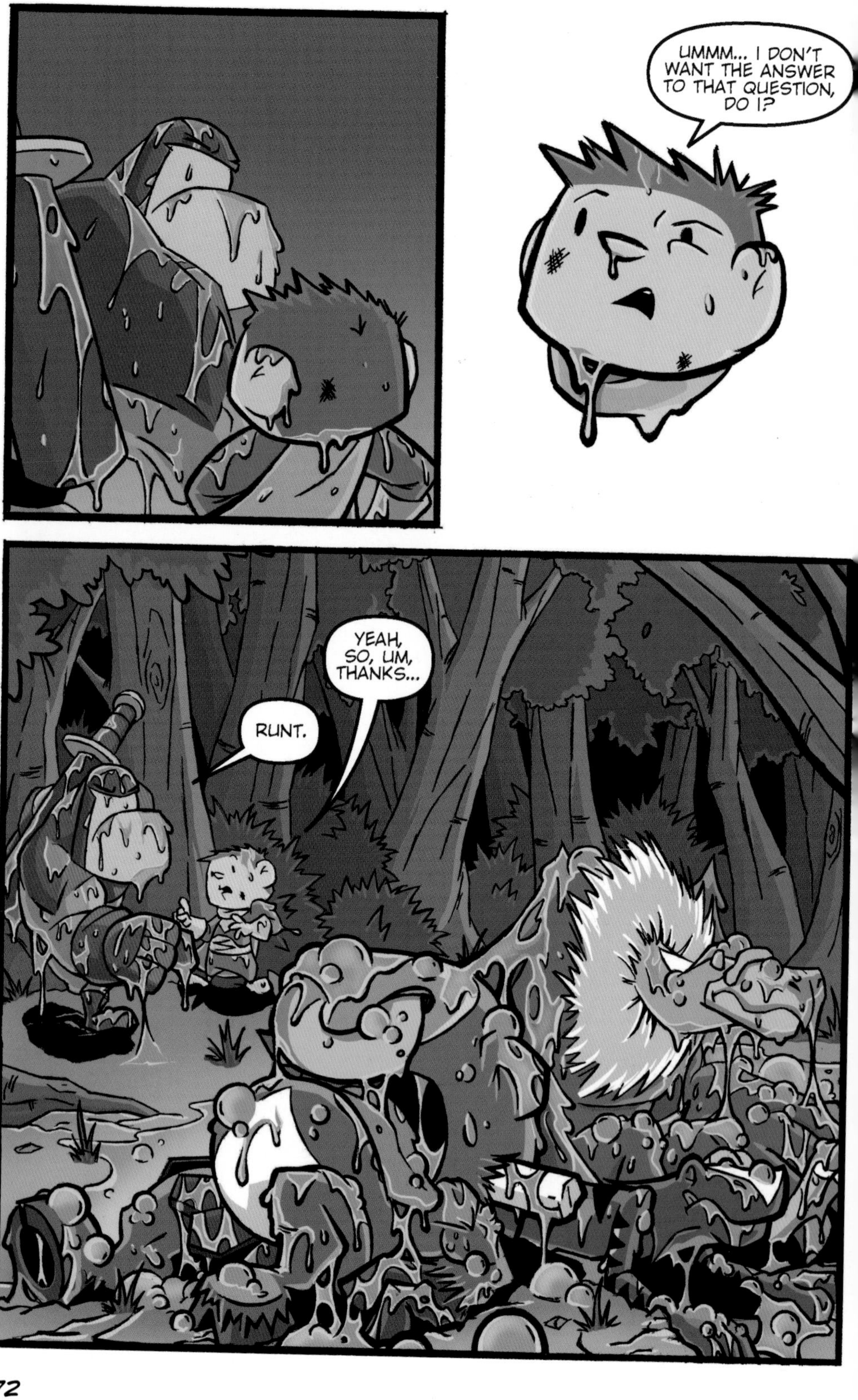
UMMM... I DON'T WANT THE ANSWER TO THAT QUESTION, DO I?
YEAH, SO, UM, THANKS...
RUNT.

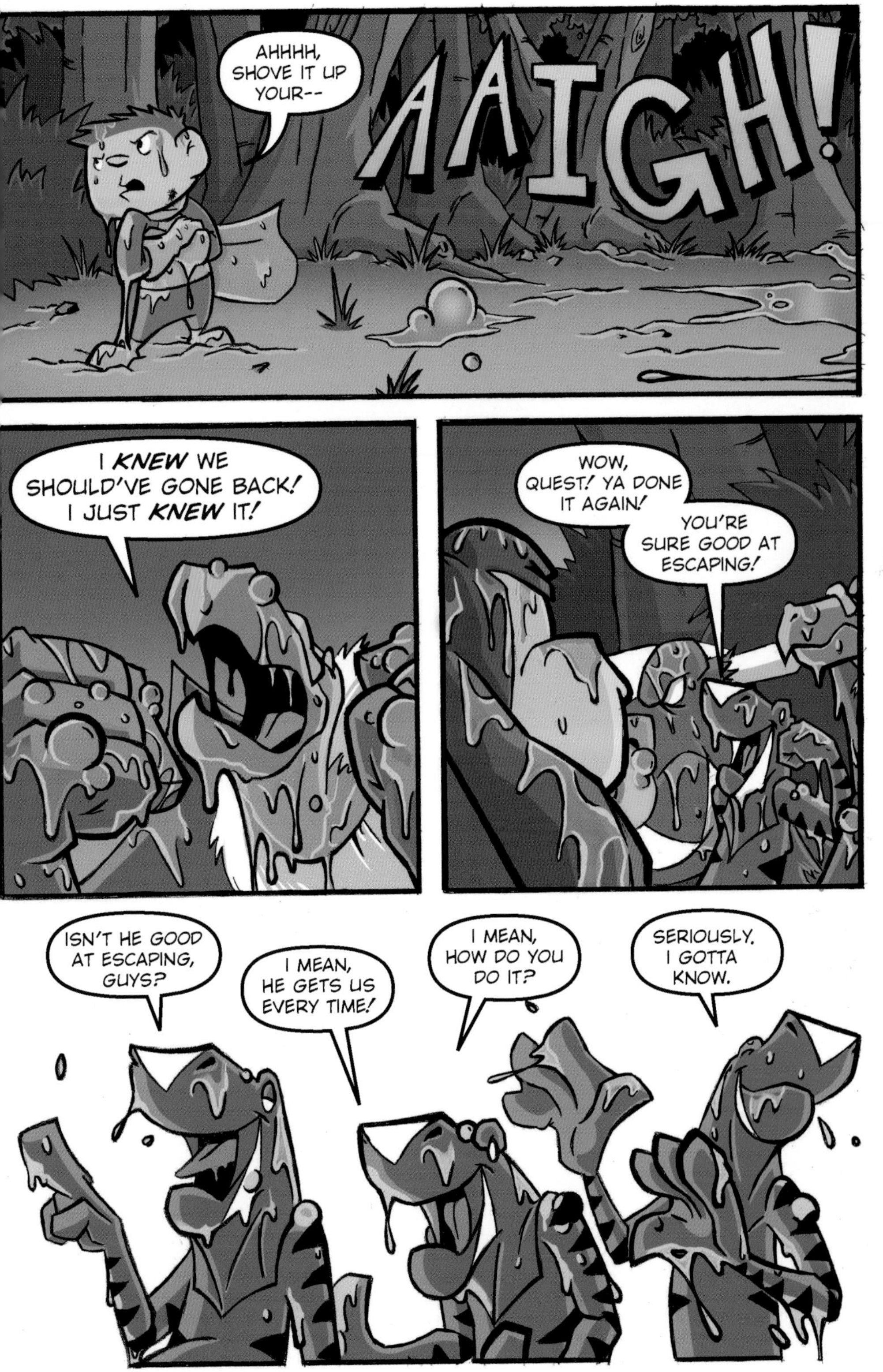
AHHHH, SHOVE IT UP YOUR--
AAIGH!
I *KNEW* WE SHOULD'VE GONE BACK! I JUST *KNEW* IT!
WOW, QUEST! YA DONE IT AGAIN!
YOU'RE SURE GOOD AT ESCAPING!
ISN'T HE GOOD AT ESCAPING, GUYS?
I MEAN, HE GETS US EVERY TIME!
I MEAN, HOW DO YOU DO IT?
SERIOUSLY. I GOTTA KNOW.

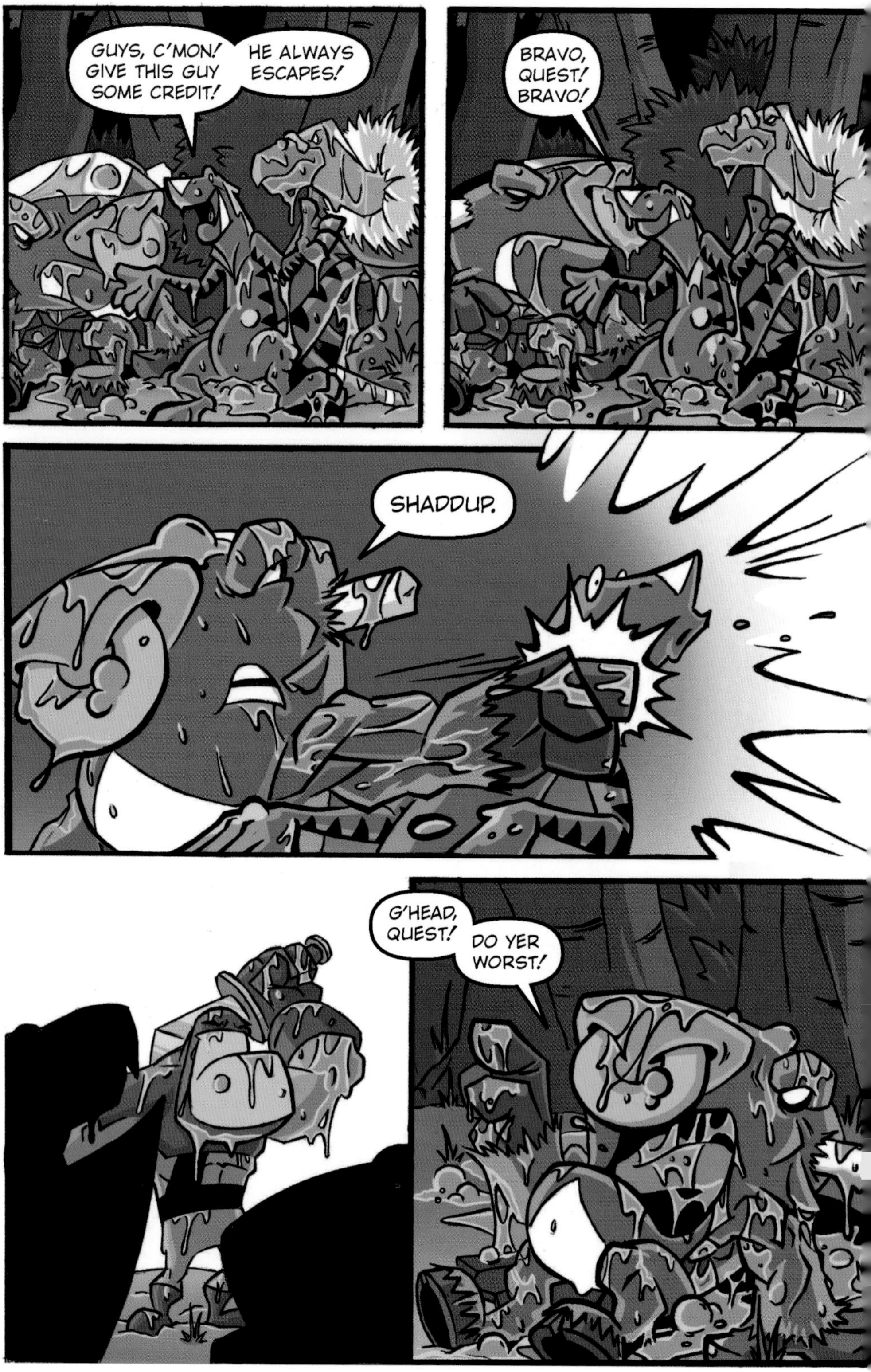
GUYS, C'MON! GIVE THIS GUY SOME CREDIT!
HE ALWAYS ESCAPES!
BRAVO, QUEST! BRAVO!
SHADDUP.
G'HEAD, QUEST!
DO YER WORST!

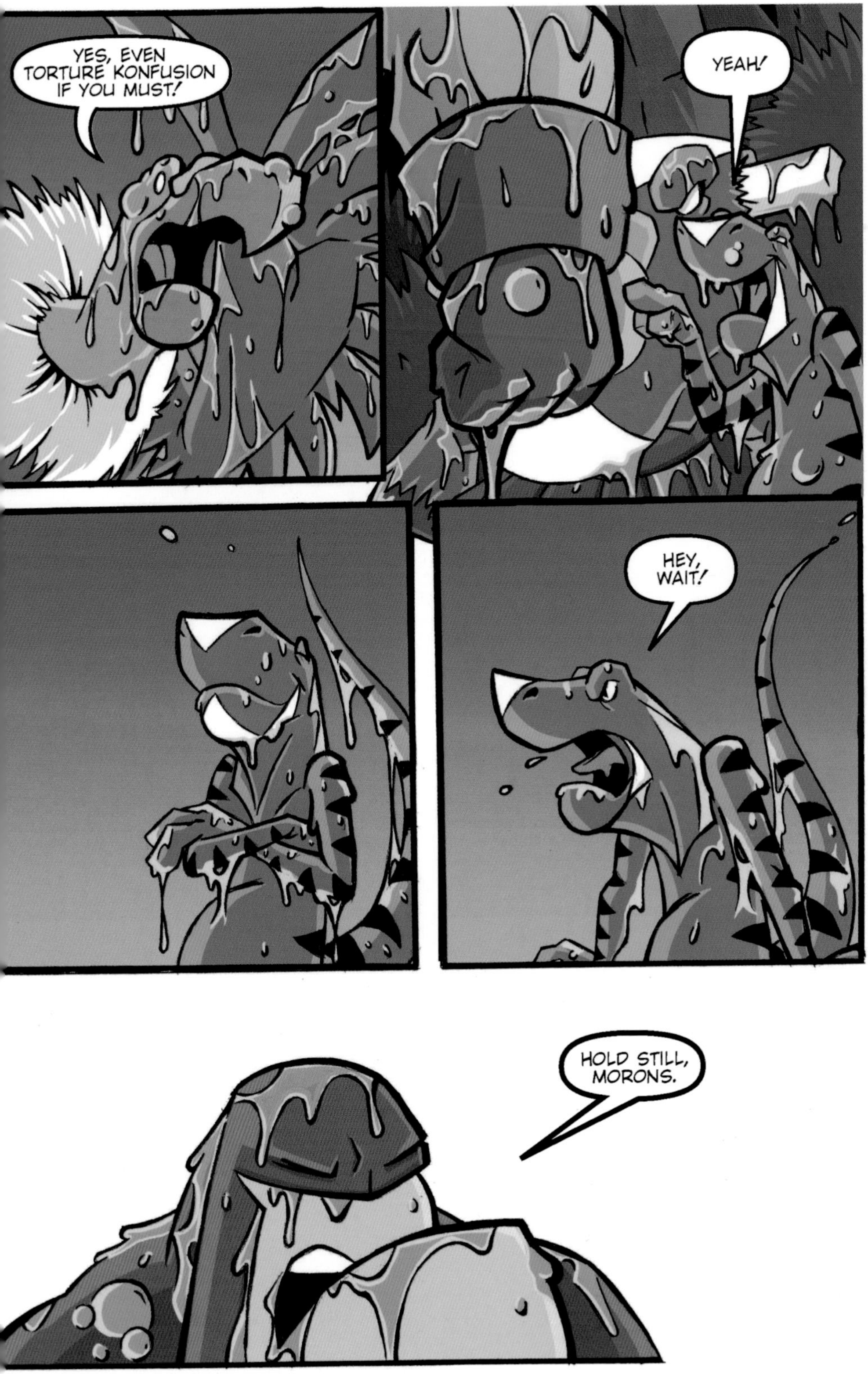
YES, EVEN TORTURE KONFUSION IF YOU MUST!
YEAH!
HEY, WAIT!
HOLD STILL, MORONS.

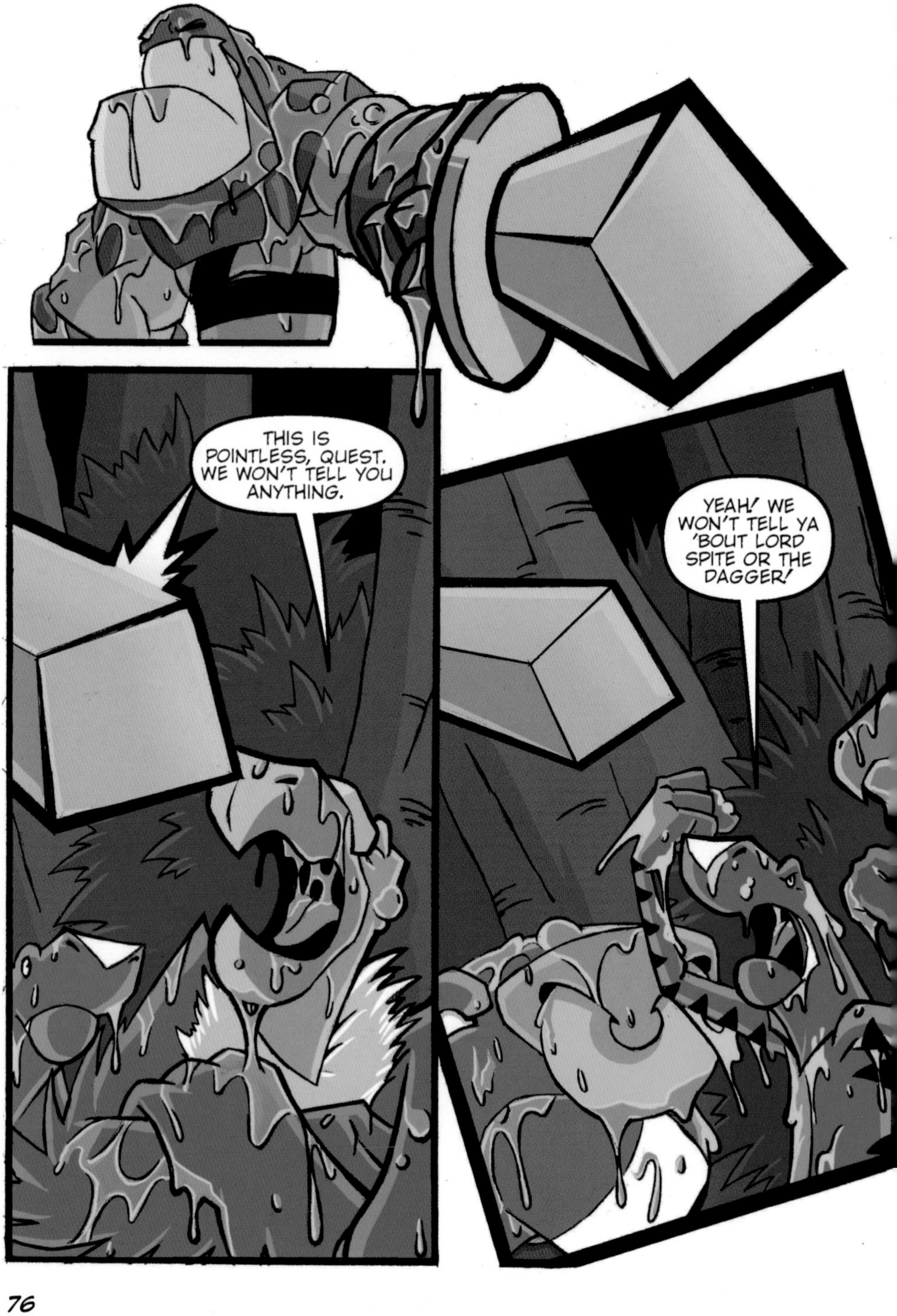
THIS IS POINTLESS, QUEST. WE WON'T TELL YOU ANYTHING.
YEAH! WE WON'T TELL YA 'BOUT LORD SPITE OR THE DAGGER!

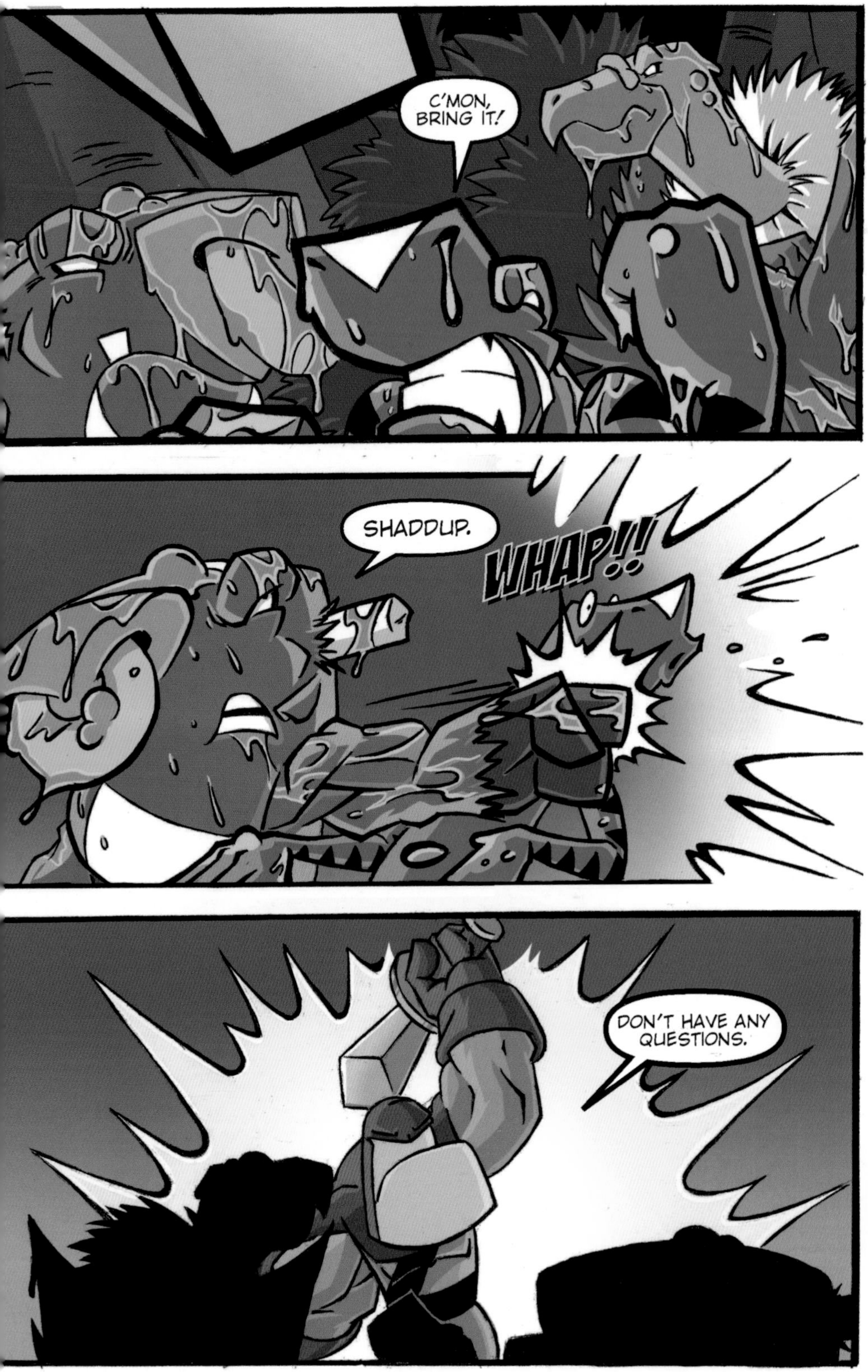

C'MON, BRING IT!
SHADDUP.
WHAP!!
DON'T HAVE ANY QUESTIONS.

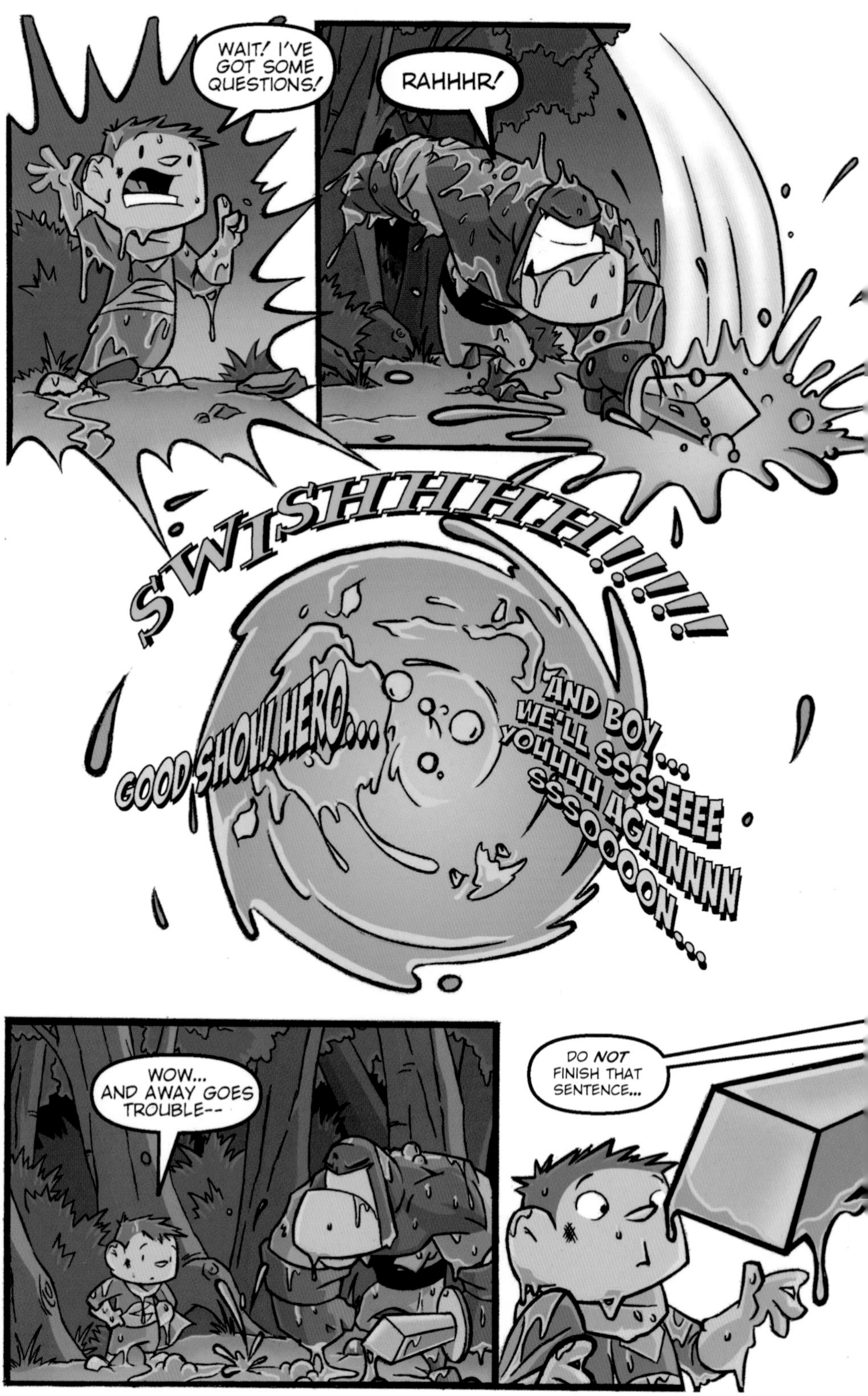
WAIT! I'VE GOT SOME QUESTIONS!
RAHHHR!
SWISHHHHH!!!!!!
GOOD SHOW, HERO...
AND BOY... WE'LL SSSSEEEE YOUUUU AGAINNNN SSSOOOOON...
WOW... AND AWAY GOES TROUBLE--
DO NOT FINISH THAT SENTENCE...

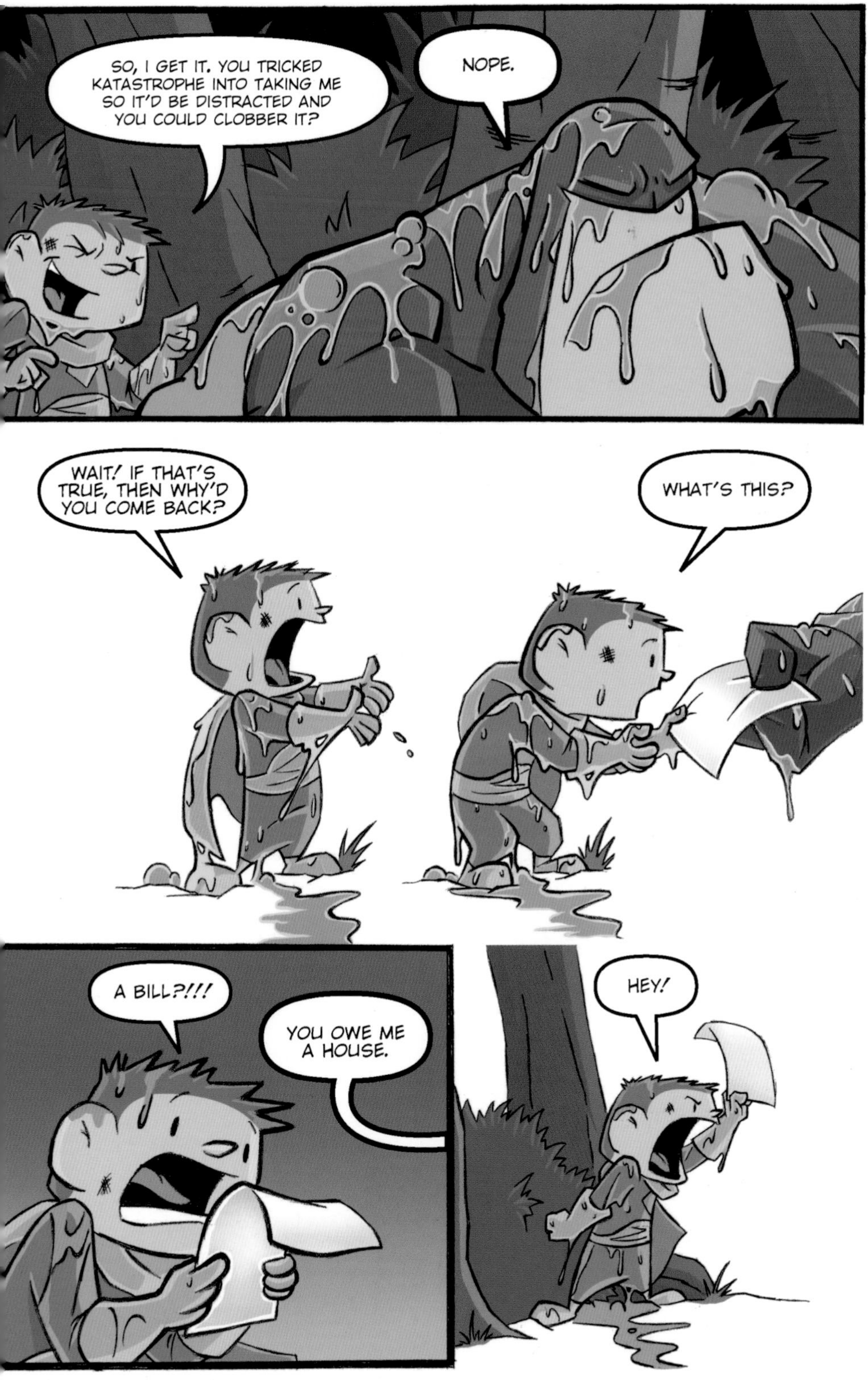
SO, I GET IT. YOU TRICKED KATASTROPHE INTO TAKING ME SO IT'D BE DISTRACTED AND YOU COULD CLOBBER IT?
NOPE.
WAIT! IF THAT'S TRUE, THEN WHY'D YOU COME BACK?
WHAT'S THIS?
A BILL?!!!
YOU OWE ME A HOUSE.
HEY!

CHAPTER FOUR
HEEEEEEEEEEEEERE'S SPITE!

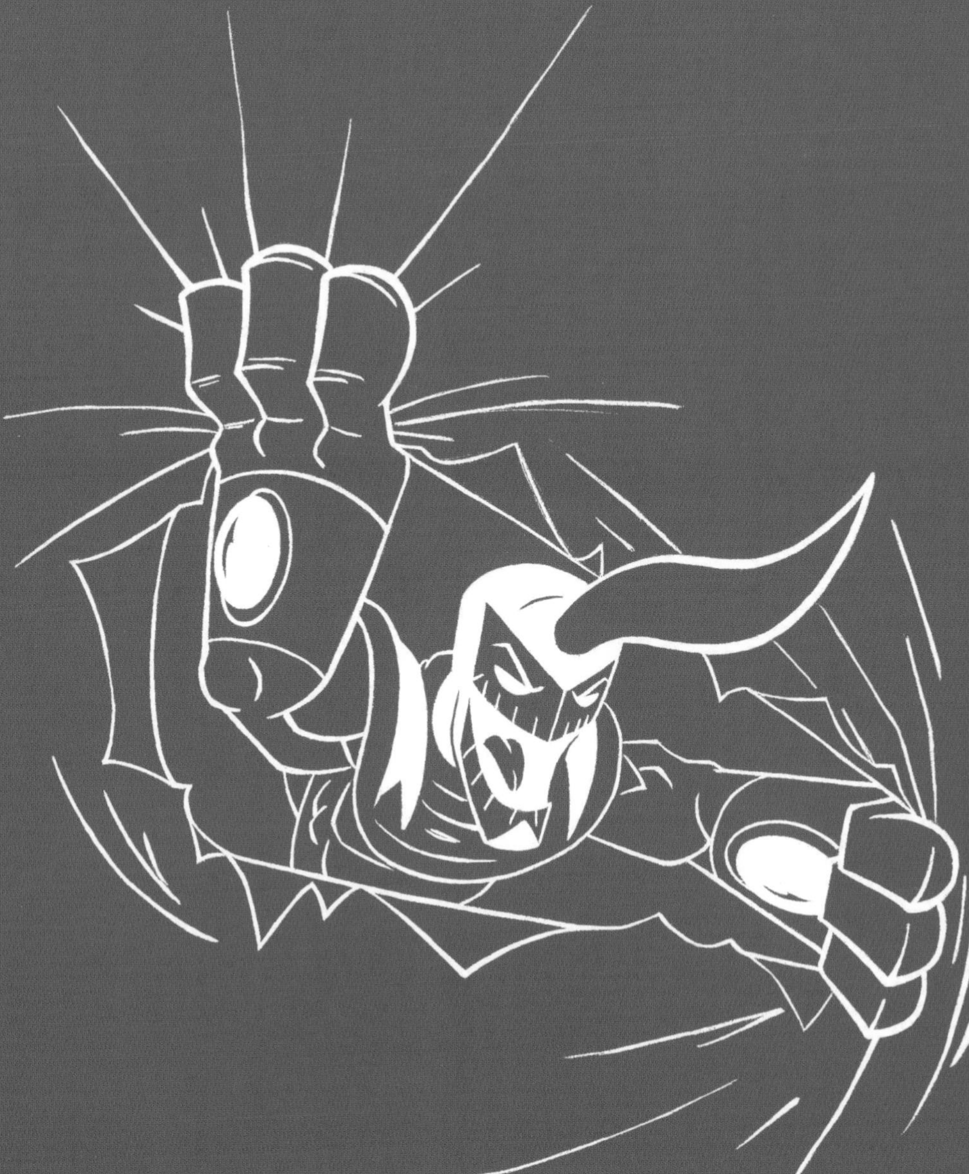

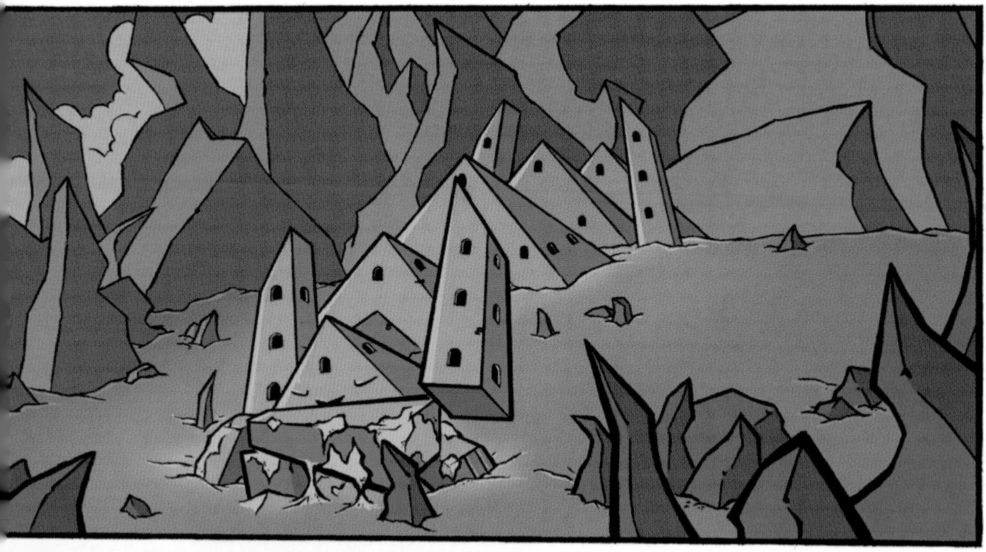

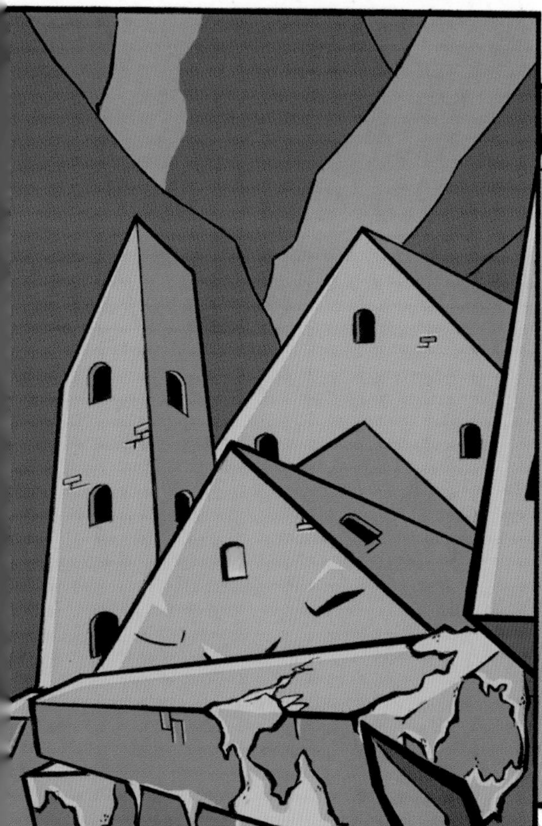

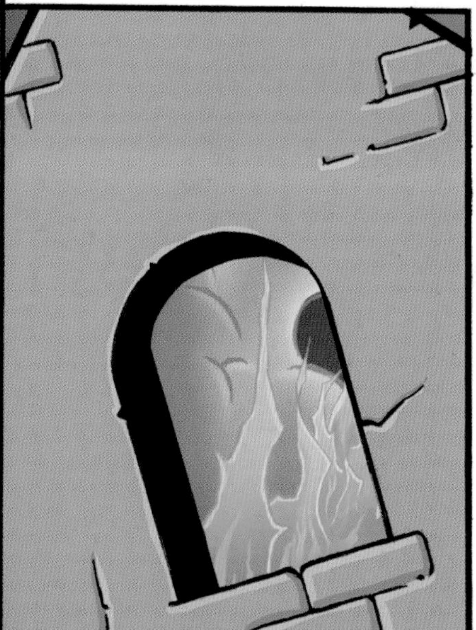

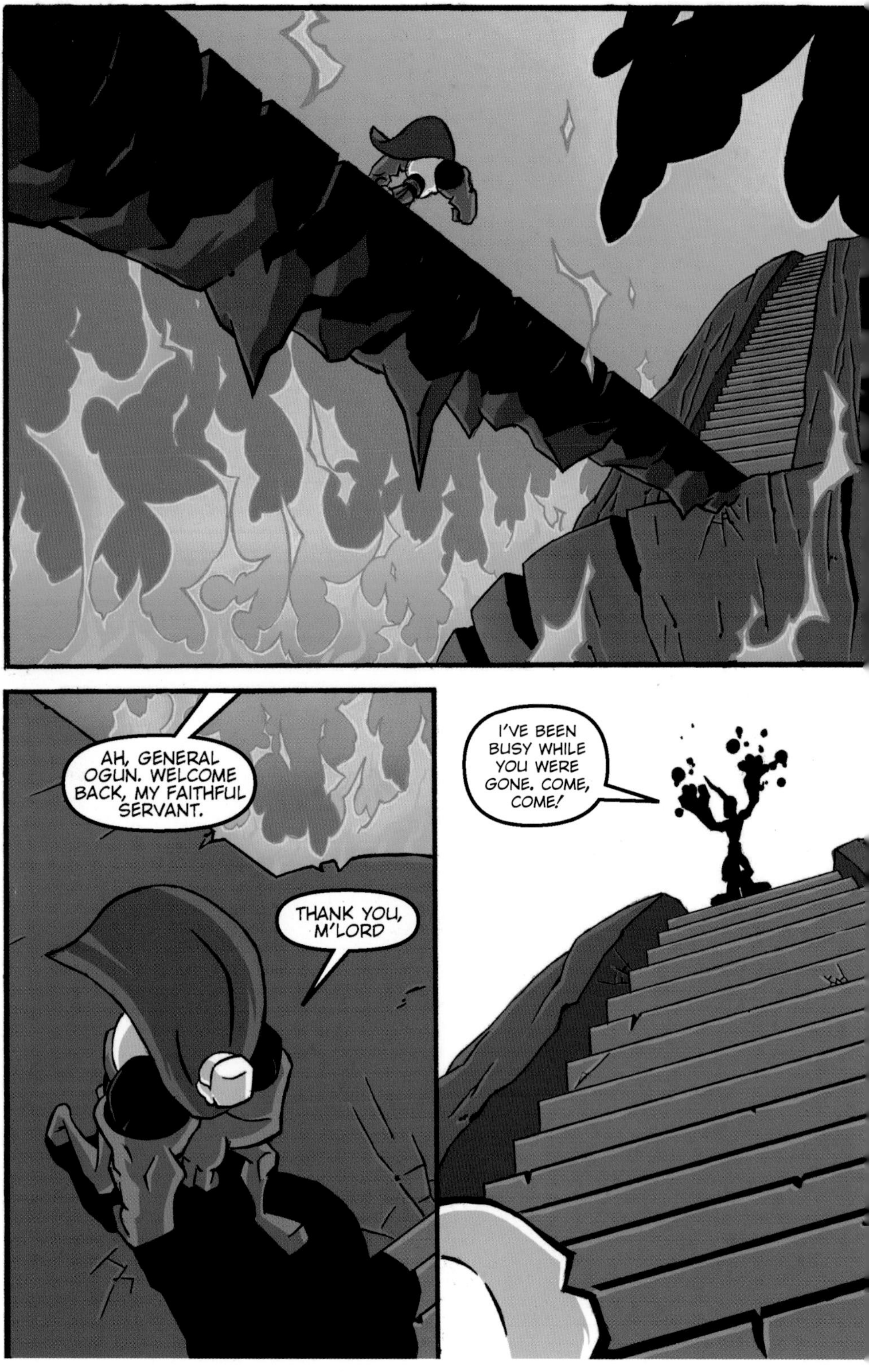
AH, GENERAL OGUN. WELCOME BACK, MY FAITHFUL SERVANT.
THANK YOU, M'LORD
I'VE BEEN BUSY WHILE YOU WERE GONE. COME, COME!

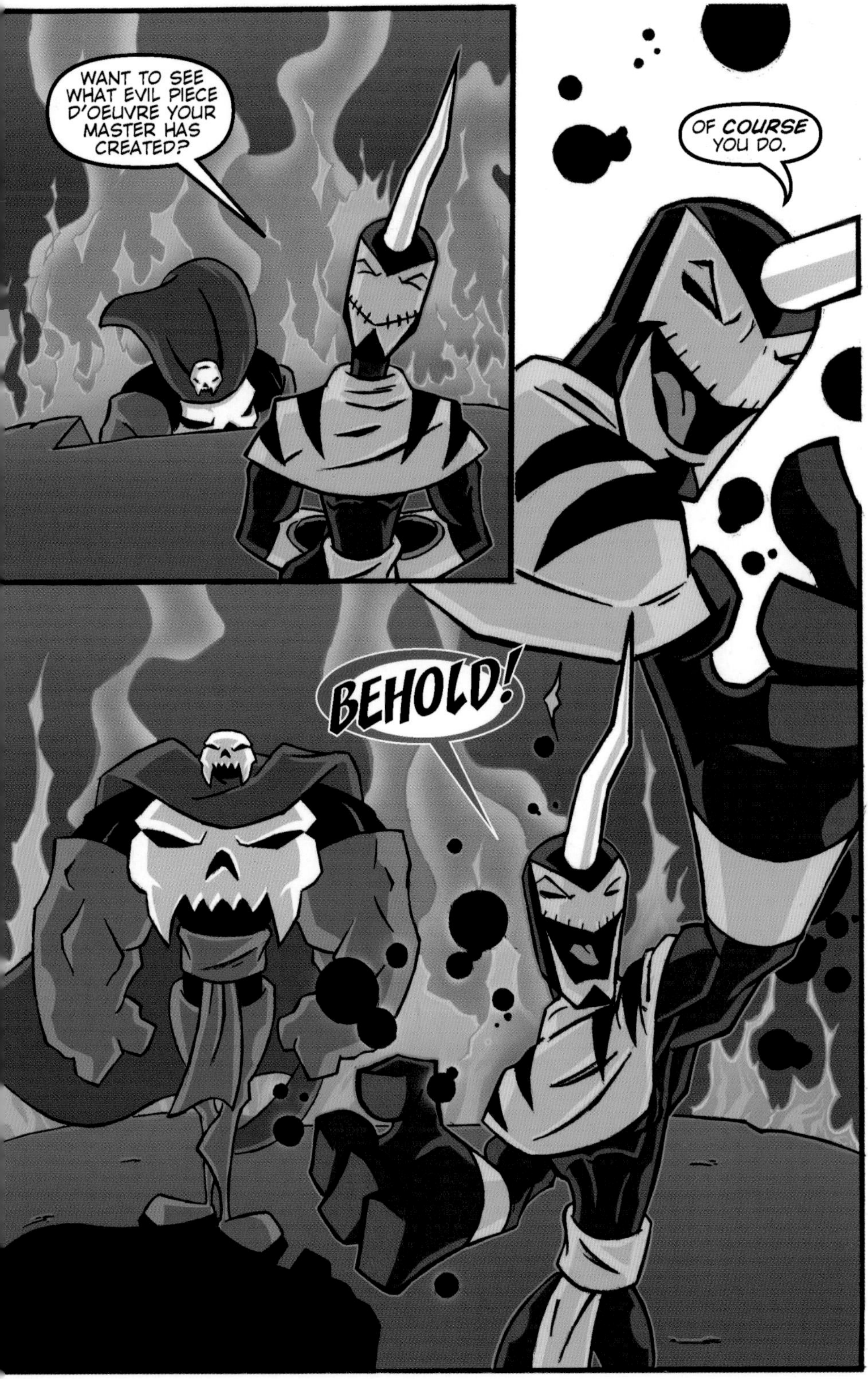
WANT TO SEE WHAT EVIL PIECE D'OEUVRE YOUR MASTER HAS CREATED?
OF COURSE YOU DO.
BEHOLD!

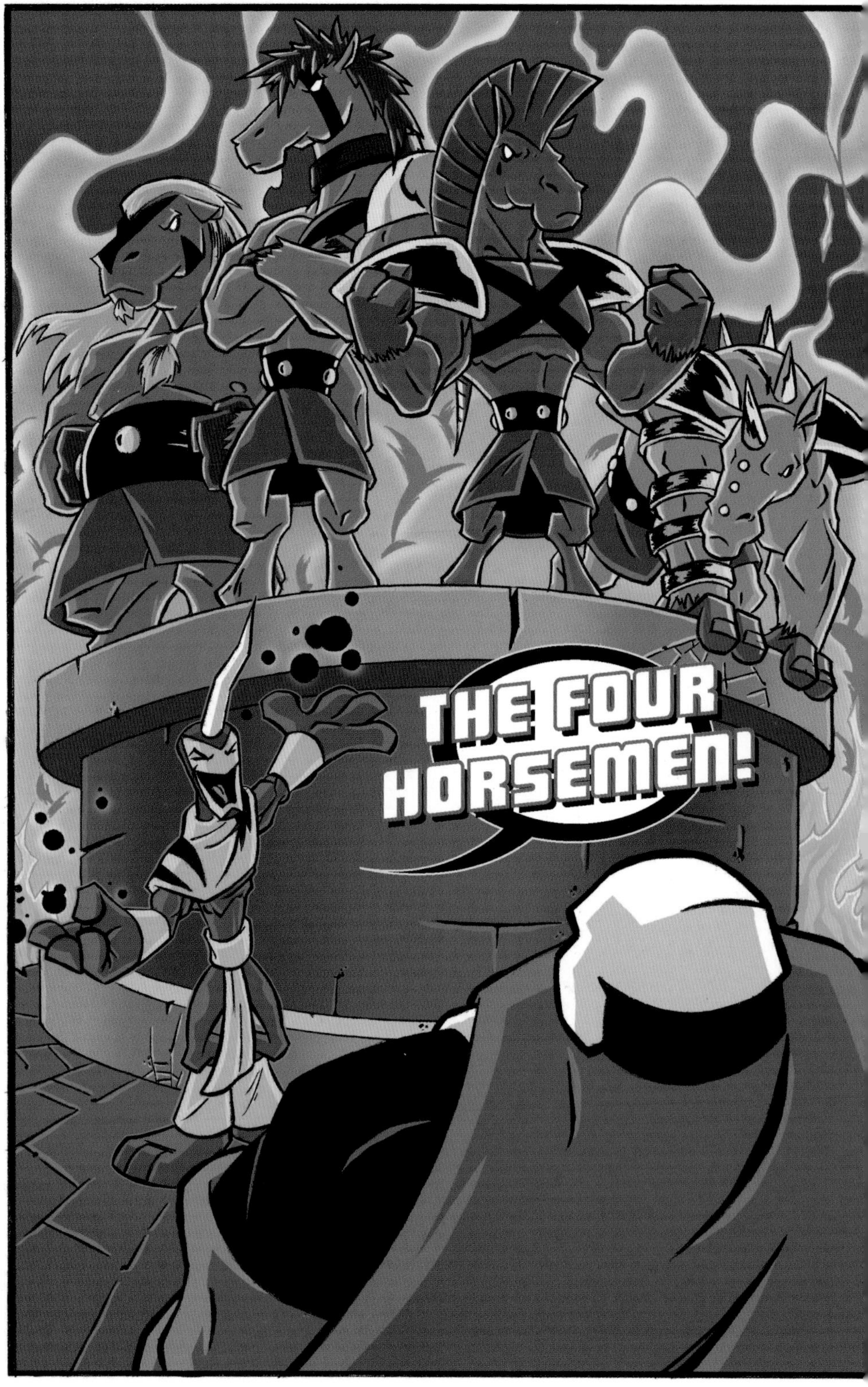
THE FOUR HORSEMEN!

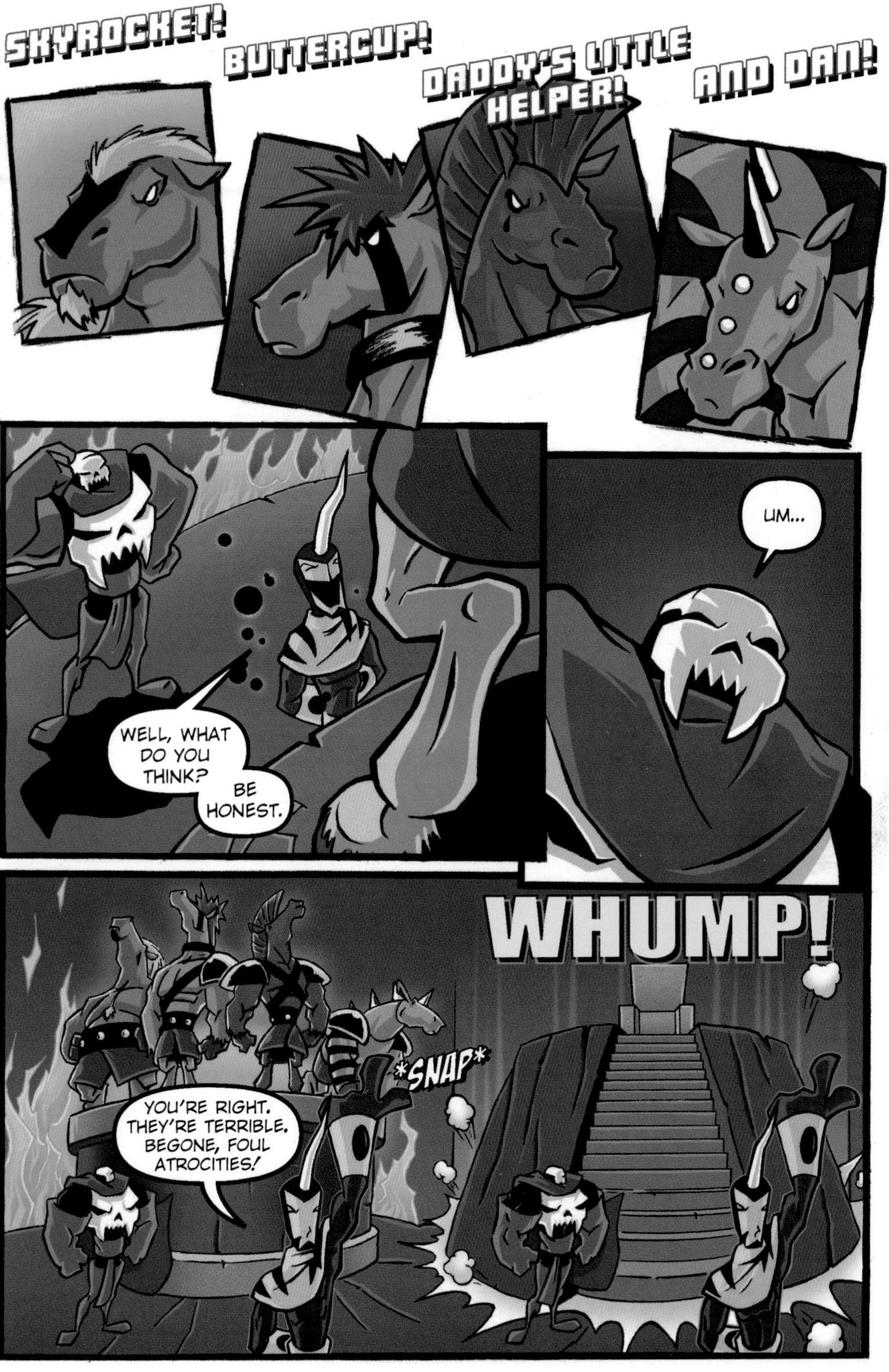
SKYROCKET!
BUTTERCUP!
DADDY'S LITTLE HELPER!
AND DAN!
WELL, WHAT DO YOU THINK?
BE HONEST.
UM...
WHUMP!
YOU'RE RIGHT. THEY'RE TERRIBLE. BEGONE, FOUL ATROCITIES!
SNAP

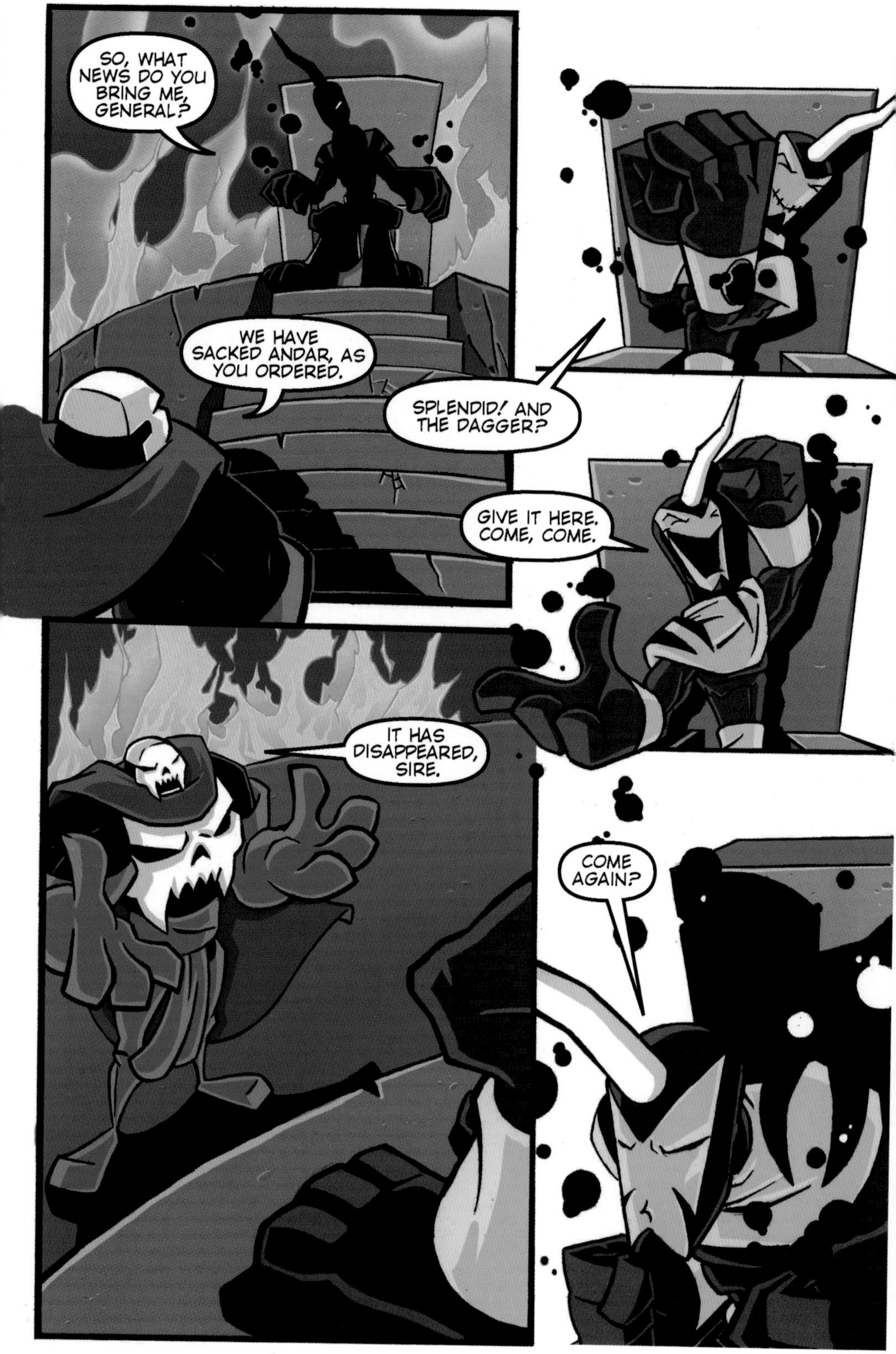
SO, WHAT NEWS DO YOU BRING ME, GENERAL?
WE HAVE SACKED ANDAR, AS YOU ORDERED.
SPLENDID! AND THE DAGGER?
GIVE IT HERE. COME, COME.
IT HAS DISAPPEARED, SIRE.
COME AGAIN?

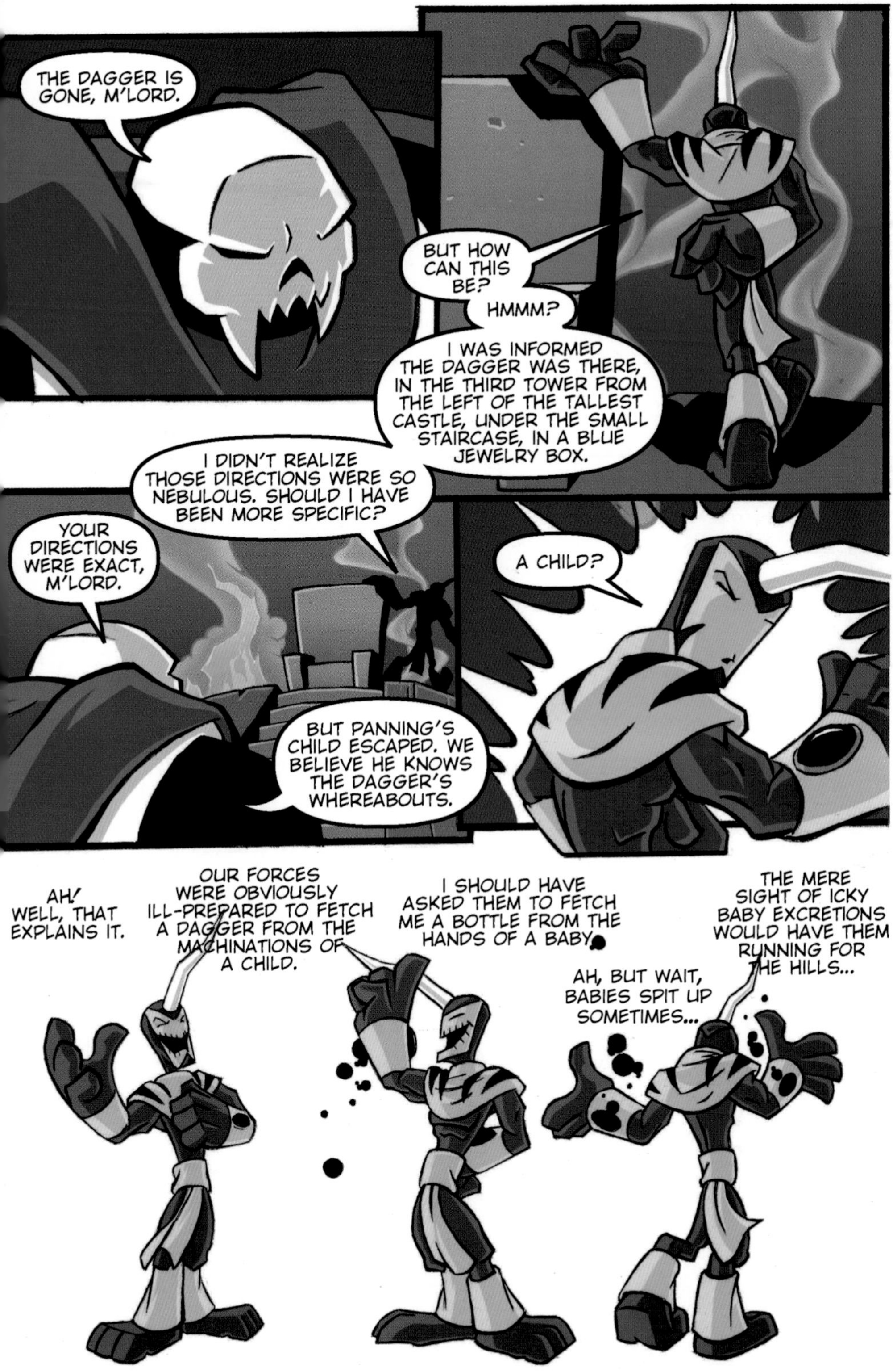

THE DAGGER IS GONE, M'LORD.
BUT HOW CAN THIS BE?
HMMM?
I WAS INFORMED THE DAGGER WAS THERE, IN THE THIRD TOWER FROM THE LEFT OF THE TALLEST CASTLE, UNDER THE SMALL STAIRCASE, IN A BLUE JEWELRY BOX.
I DIDN'T REALIZE THOSE DIRECTIONS WERE SO NEBULOUS. SHOULD I HAVE BEEN MORE SPECIFIC?
YOUR DIRECTIONS WERE EXACT, M'LORD.
BUT PANNING'S CHILD ESCAPED. WE BELIEVE HE KNOWS THE DAGGER'S WHEREABOUTS.
A CHILD?
AH! WELL, THAT EXPLAINS IT.
OUR FORCES WERE OBVIOUSLY ILL-PREPARED TO FETCH A DAGGER FROM THE MACHINATIONS OF A CHILD.
I SHOULD HAVE ASKED THEM TO FETCH ME A BOTTLE FROM THE HANDS OF A BABY.
THE MERE SIGHT OF ICKY BABY EXCRETIONS WOULD HAVE THEM RUNNING FOR THE HILLS...
AH, BUT WAIT, BABIES SPIT UP SOMETIMES...

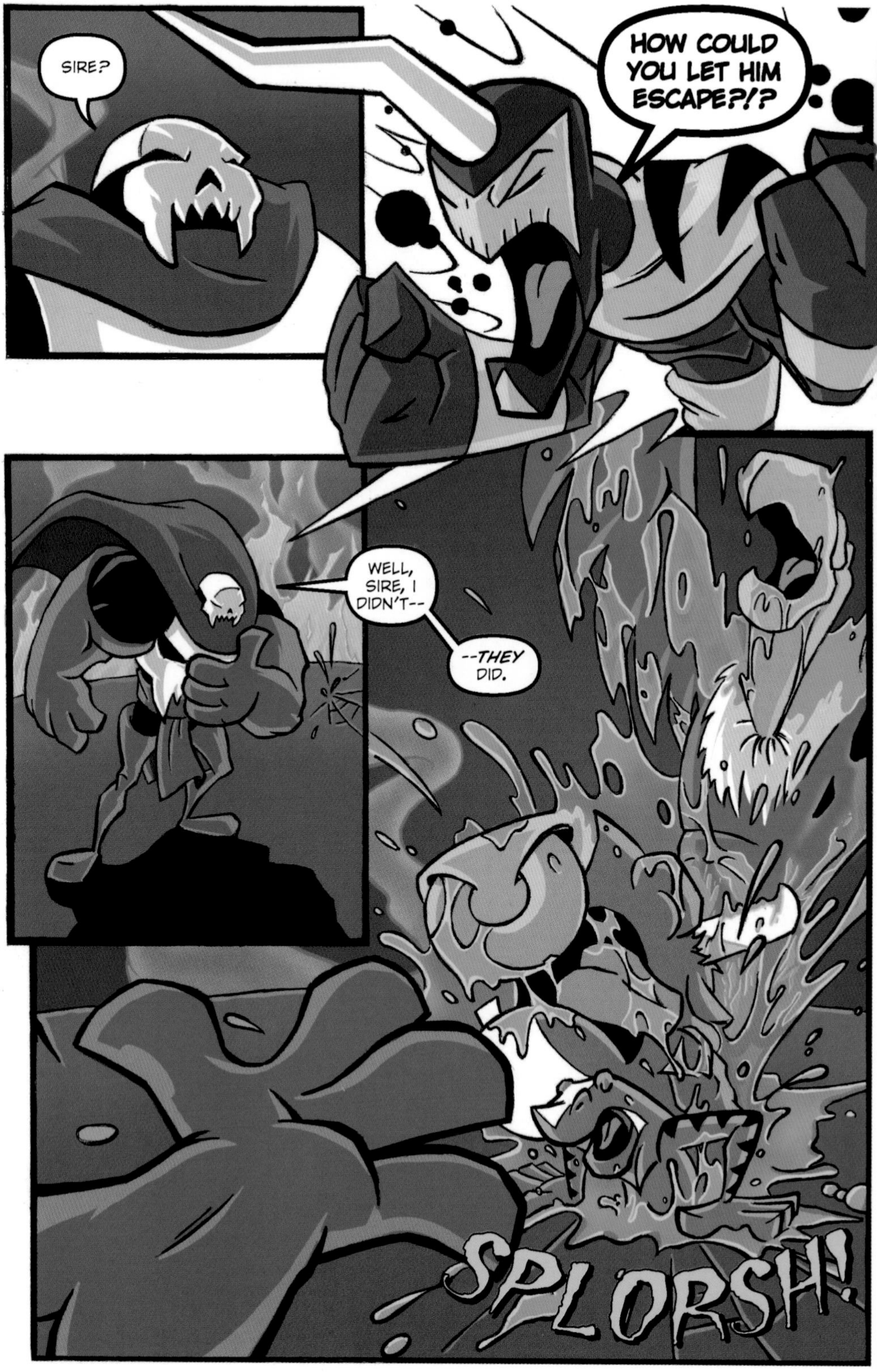
SIRE?
HOW COULD YOU LET HIM ESCAPE?!?
WELL, SIRE, I DIDN'T--
--THEY DID.
SPLORSH!

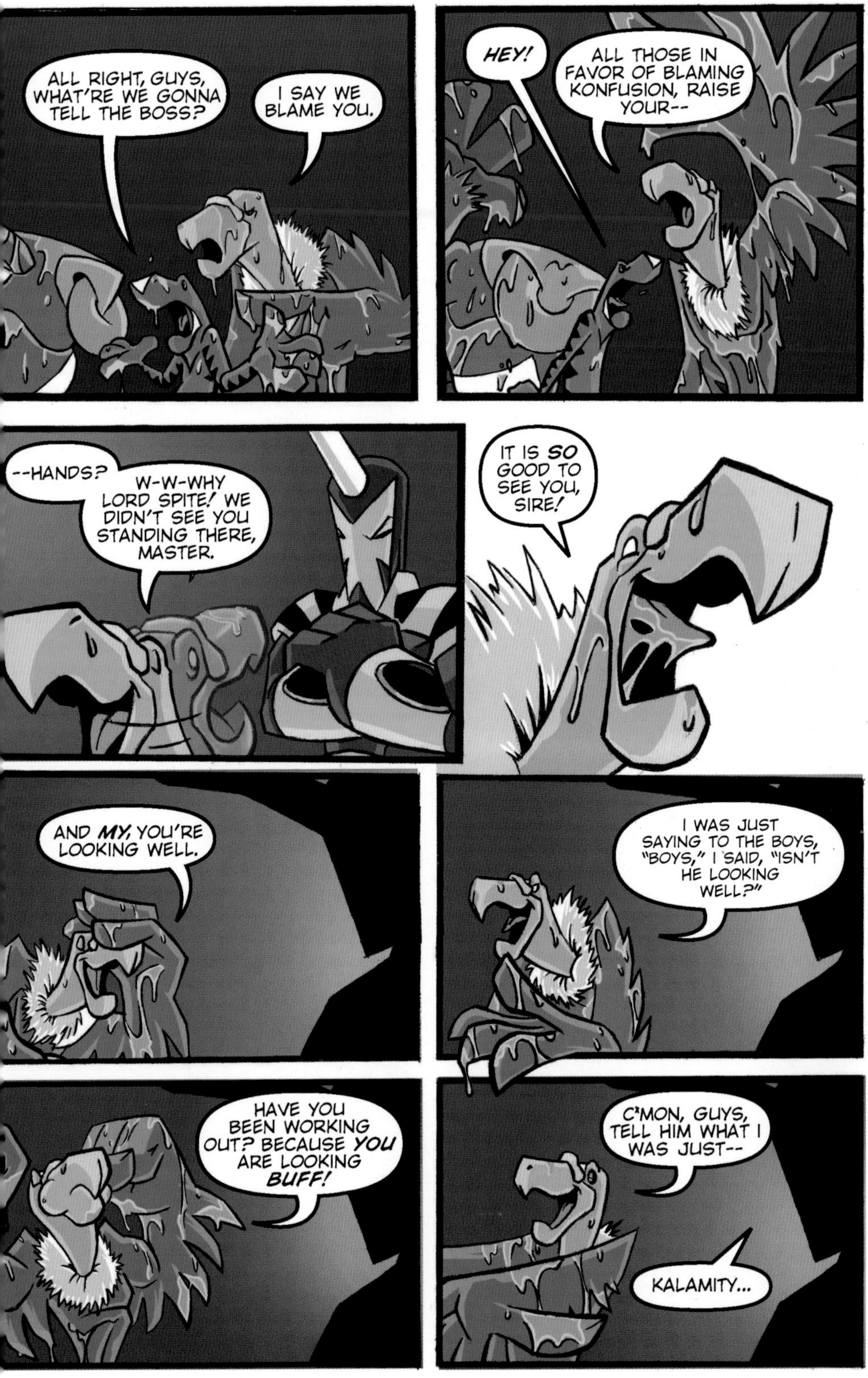
ALL RIGHT, GUYS, WHAT'RE WE GONNA TELL THE BOSS?
I SAY WE BLAME YOU.
HEY!
ALL THOSE IN FAVOR OF BLAMING KONFUSION, RAISE YOUR--
--HANDS?
W-W-WHY LORD SPITE! WE DIDN'T SEE YOU STANDING THERE, MASTER.
IT IS *SO* GOOD TO SEE YOU, SIRE!
AND *MY*, YOU'RE LOOKING WELL.
I WAS JUST SAYING TO THE BOYS, "BOYS," I SAID, "ISN'T HE LOOKING WELL?"
HAVE YOU BEEN WORKING OUT? BECAUSE *YOU* ARE LOOKING *BUFF!*
C'MON, GUYS, TELL HIM WHAT I WAS JUST--
KALAMITY...

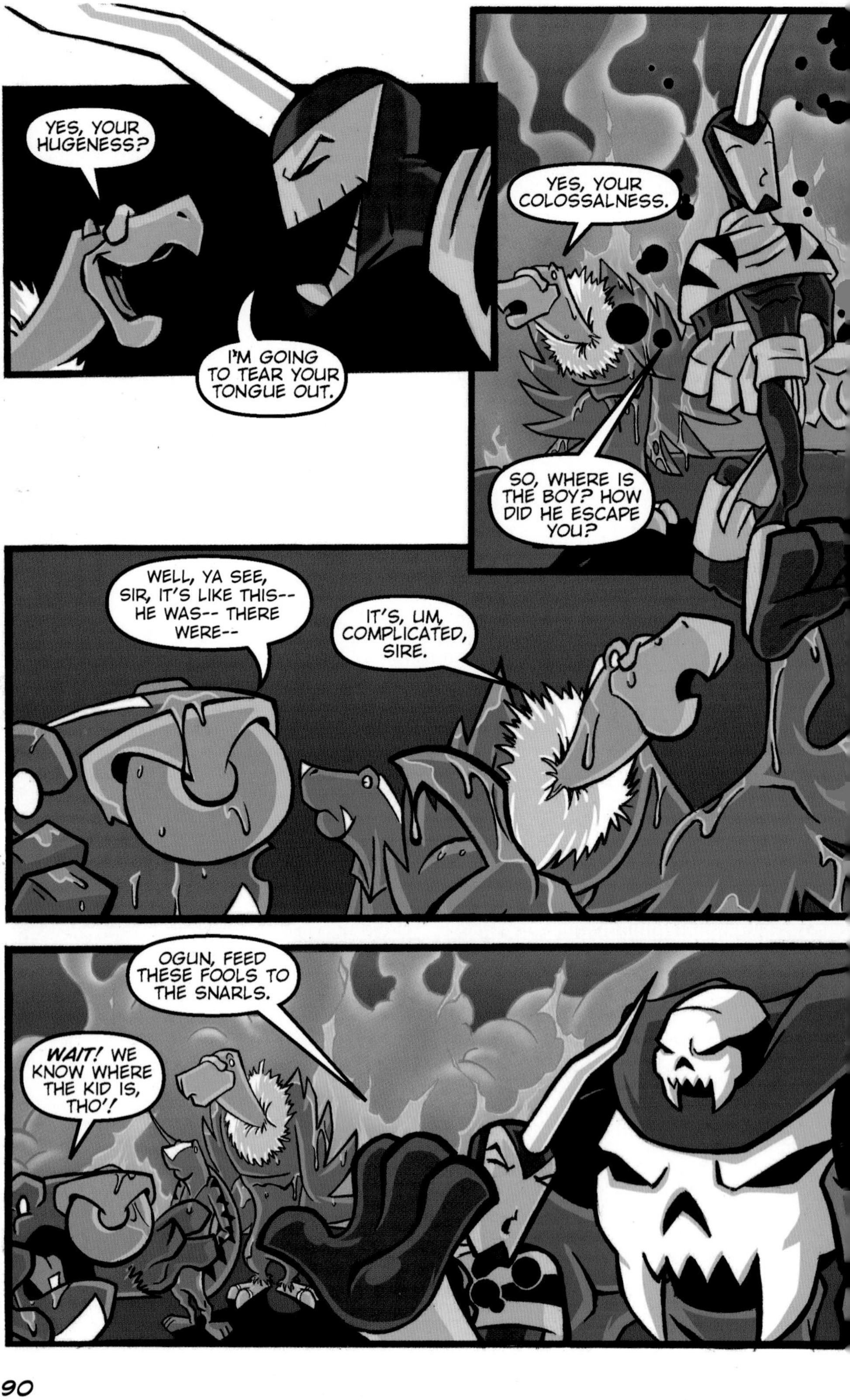
YES, YOUR HUGENESS?
I'M GOING TO TEAR YOUR TONGUE OUT.
YES, YOUR COLOSSALNESS.
SO, WHERE IS THE BOY? HOW DID HE ESCAPE YOU?
WELL, YA SEE, SIR, IT'S LIKE THIS-- HE WAS-- THERE WERE--
IT'S, UM, COMPLICATED, SIRE.
OGUN, FEED THESE FOOLS TO THE SNARLS.
WAIT! WE KNOW WHERE THE KID IS, THO'!

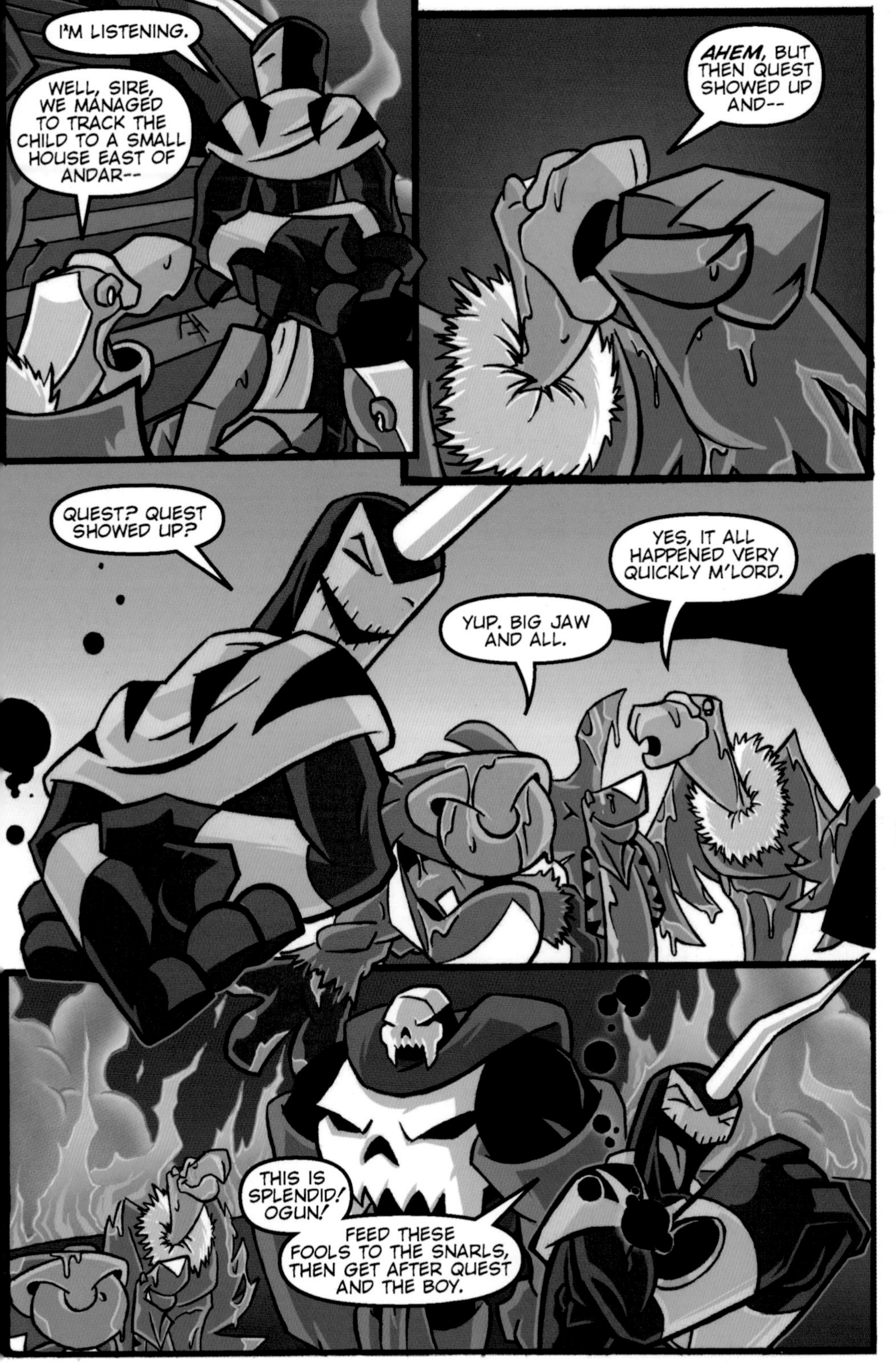
I'M LISTENING.
WELL, SIRE, WE MANAGED TO TRACK THE CHILD TO A SMALL HOUSE EAST OF ANDAR--
AHEM, BUT THEN QUEST SHOWED UP AND--
QUEST? QUEST SHOWED UP?
YUP. BIG JAW AND ALL.
YES, IT ALL HAPPENED VERY QUICKLY M'LORD.
THIS IS SPLENDID! OGUN!
FEED THESE FOOLS TO THE SNARLS, THEN GET AFTER QUEST AND THE BOY.

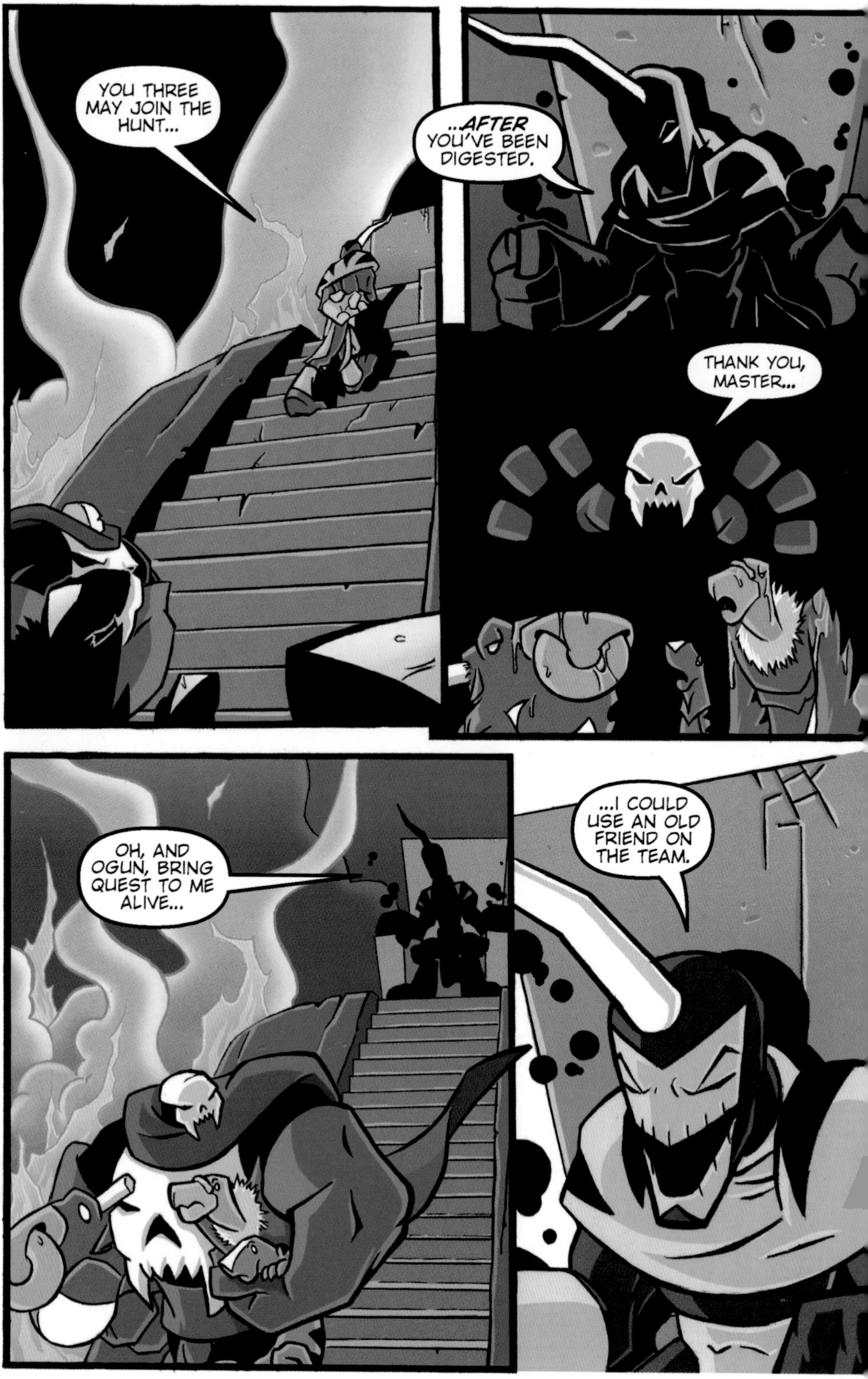
YOU THREE MAY JOIN THE HUNT...
...AFTER YOU'VE BEEN DIGESTED.
THANK YOU, MASTER...
OH, AND OGUN, BRING QUEST TO ME ALIVE...
...I COULD USE AN OLD FRIEND ON THE TEAM.

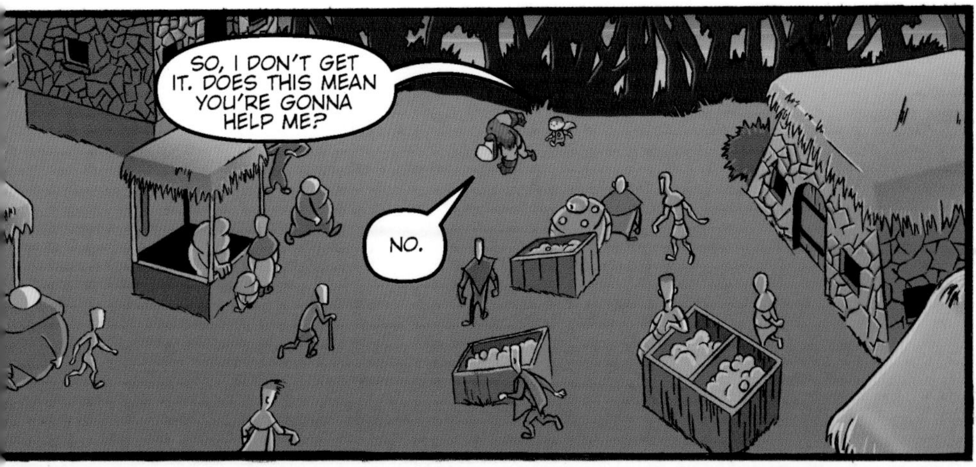
SO, I DON'T GET IT. DOES THIS MEAN YOU'RE GONNA HELP ME?
NO.

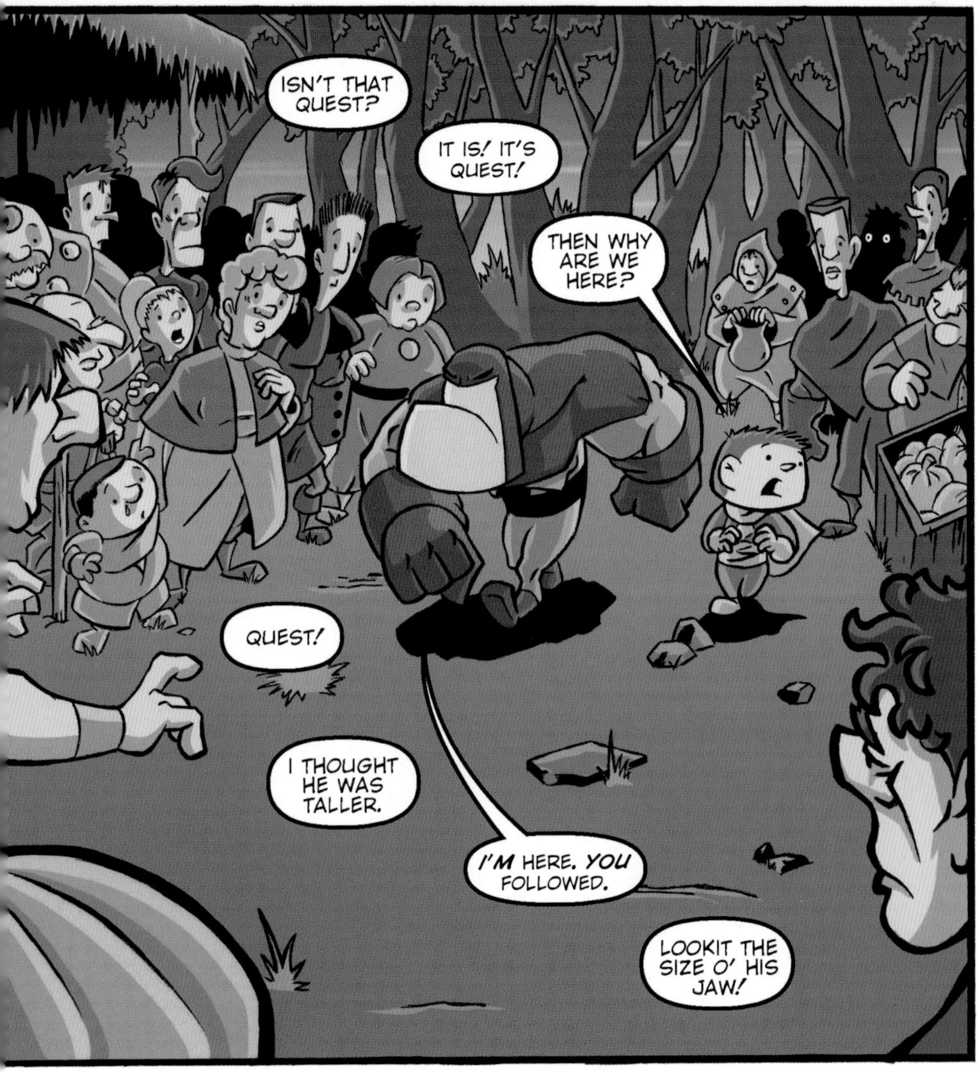
ISN'T THAT QUEST?
IT IS! IT'S QUEST!
THEN WHY ARE WE HERE?
QUEST!
I THOUGHT HE WAS TALLER.
I'M HERE. YOU FOLLOWED.
LOOKIT THE SIZE O' HIS JAW!

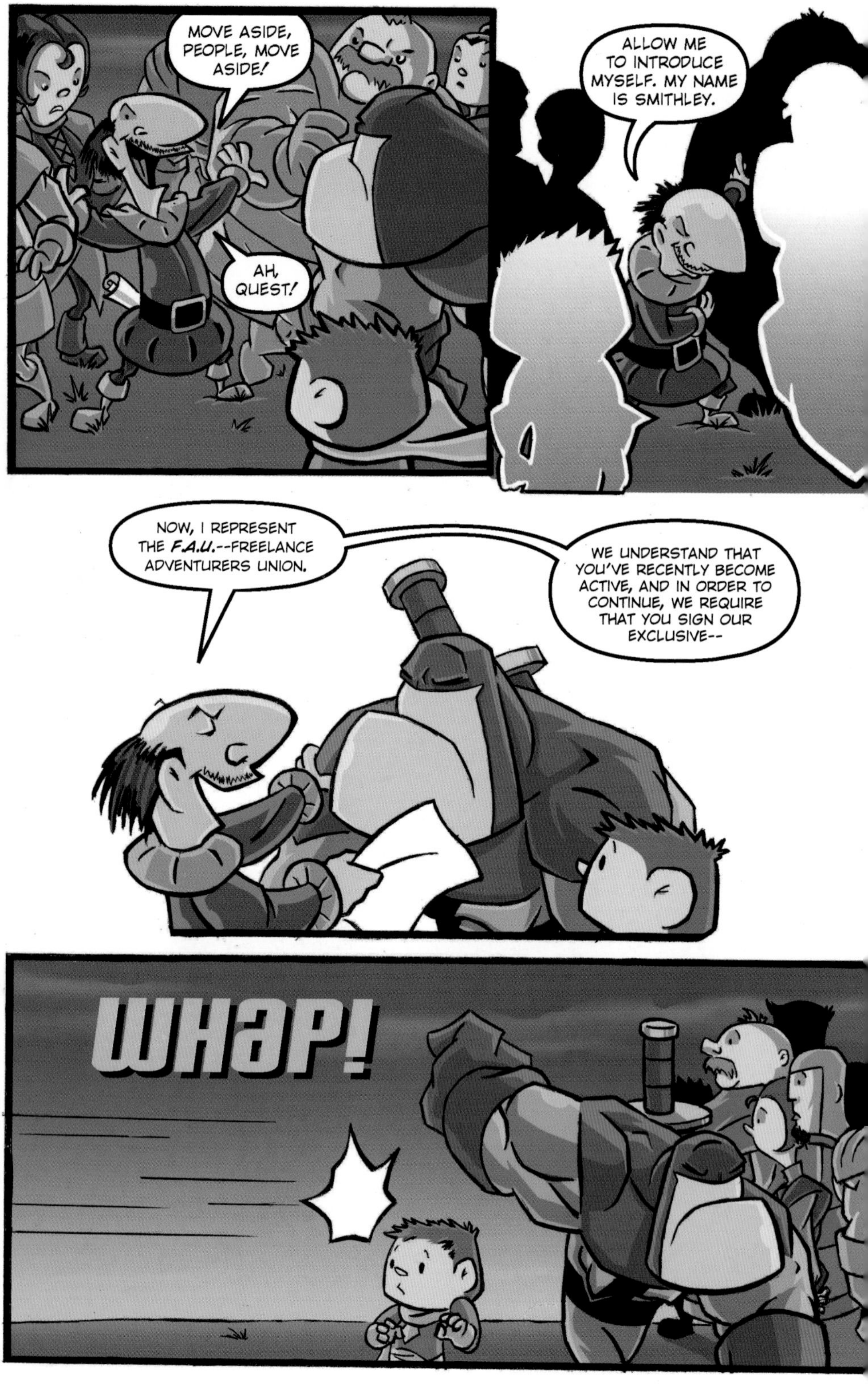
MOVE ASIDE, PEOPLE, MOVE ASIDE!
AH, QUEST!
ALLOW ME TO INTRODUCE MYSELF. MY NAME IS SMITHLEY.
NOW, I REPRESENT THE F.A.U.--FREELANCE ADVENTURERS UNION.
WE UNDERSTAND THAT YOU'VE RECENTLY BECOME ACTIVE, AND IN ORDER TO CONTINUE, WE REQUIRE THAT YOU SIGN OUR EXCLUSIVE--
WHAP!

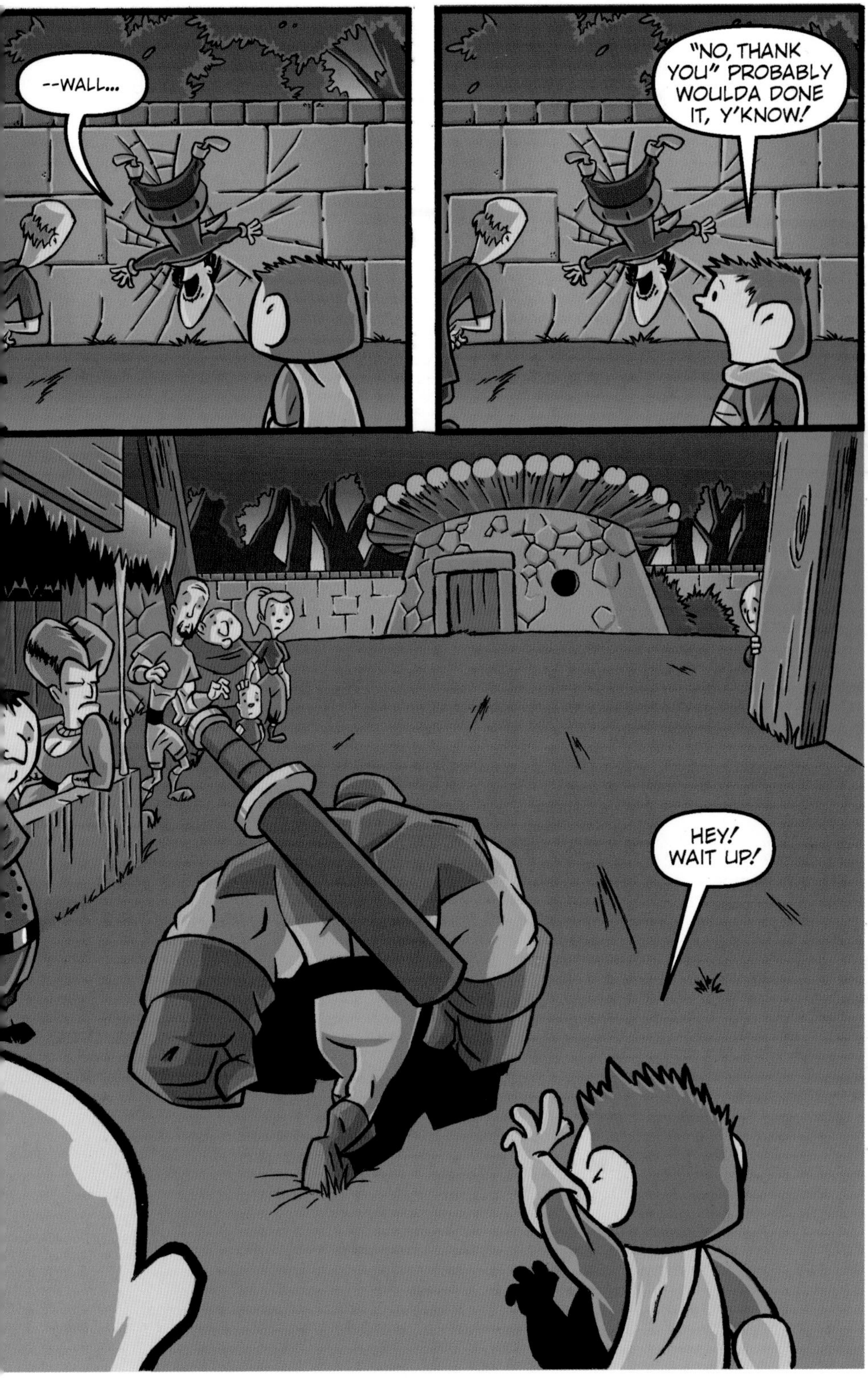
--WALL...
"NO, THANK YOU" PROBABLY WOULDA DONE IT, Y'KNOW!
HEY! WAIT UP!

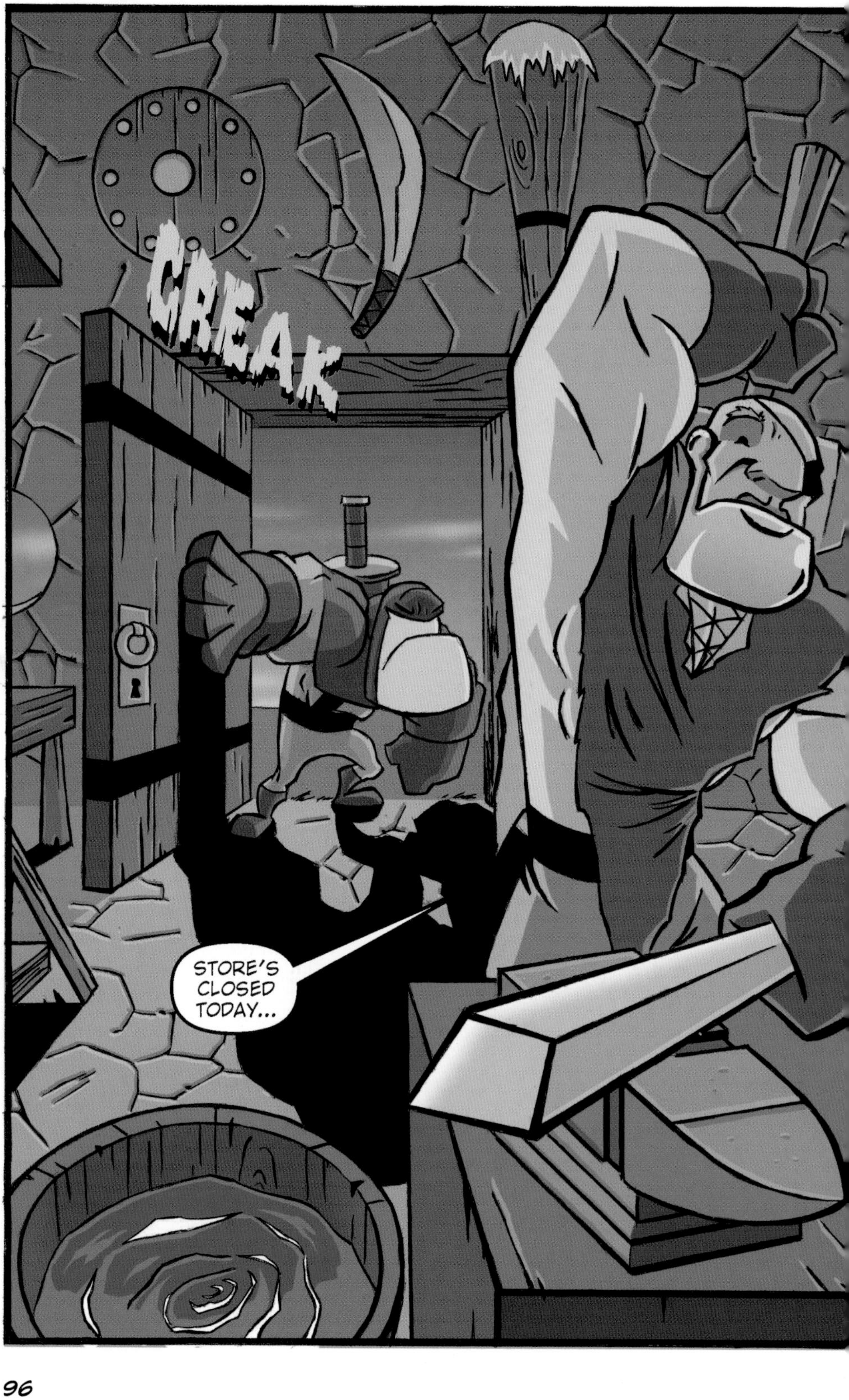
CREAK
STORE'S CLOSED TODAY...

CLANK!
THWANNNGGG!!!
ESPECIALLY TO YOU--
--QUEST.

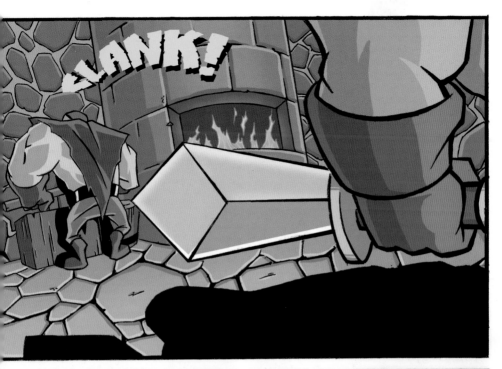

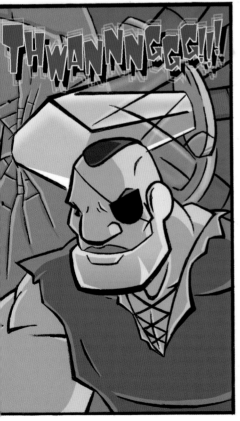

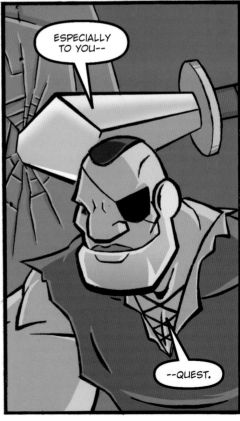

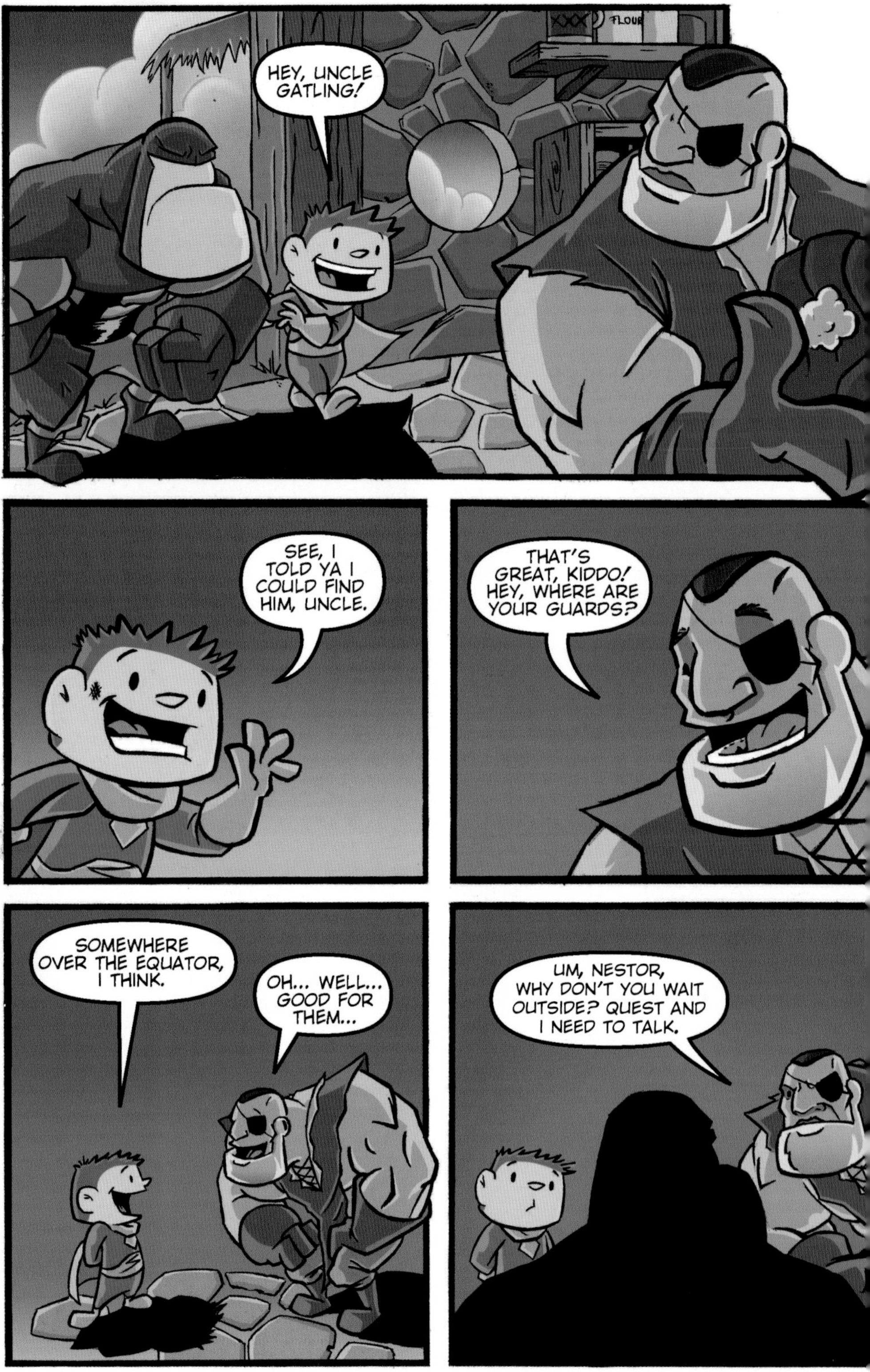
HEY, UNCLE GATLING!
FLOUR
SEE, I TOLD YA I COULD FIND HIM, UNCLE.
THAT'S GREAT, KIDDO! HEY, WHERE ARE YOUR GUARDS?
SOMEWHERE OVER THE EQUATOR, I THINK.
OH... WELL... GOOD FOR THEM...
UM, NESTOR, WHY DON'T YOU WAIT OUTSIDE? QUEST AND I NEED TO TALK.

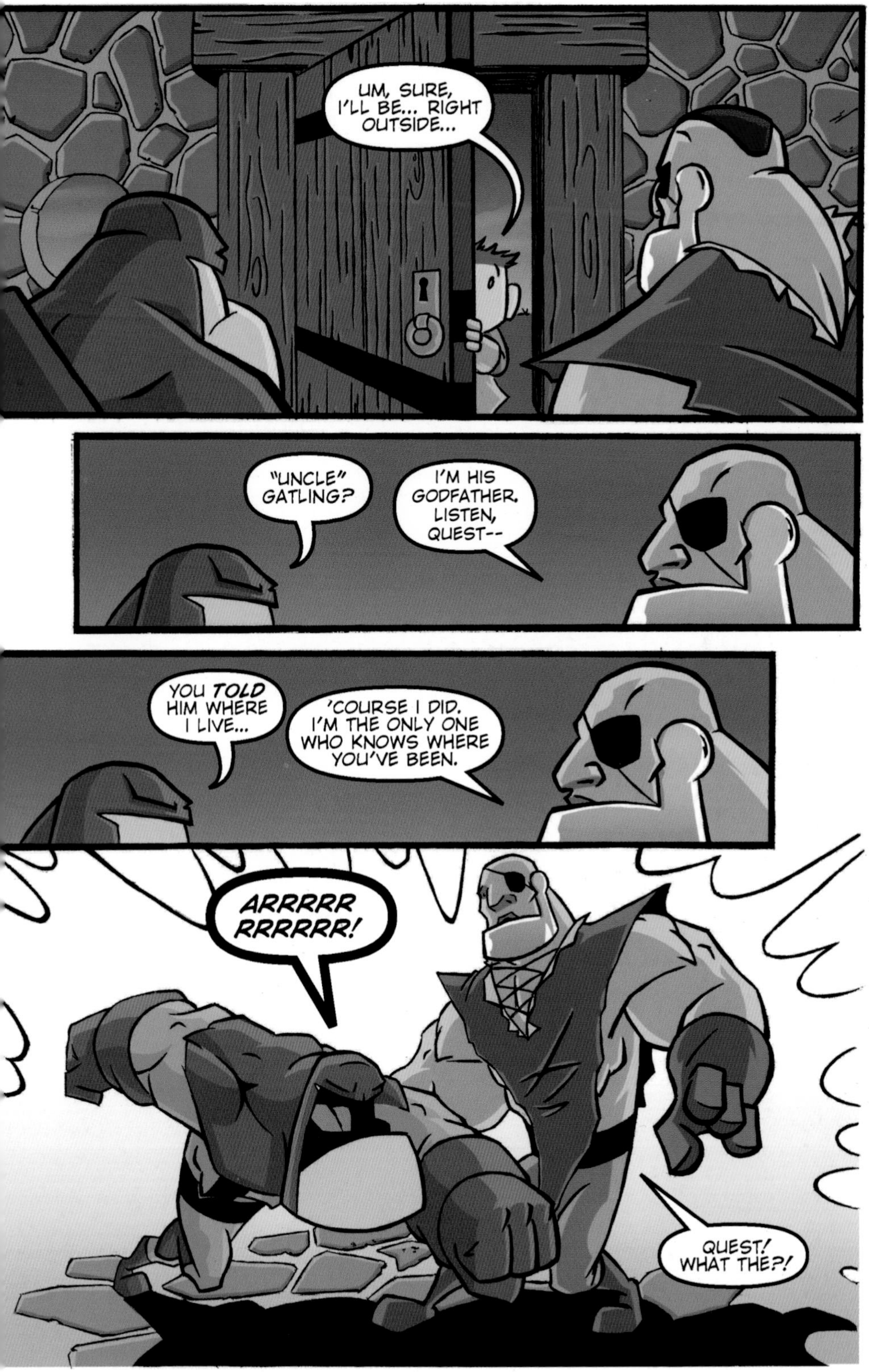
UM, SURE, I'LL BE... RIGHT OUTSIDE...
"UNCLE" GATLING?
I'M HIS GODFATHER. LISTEN, QUEST--
YOU *TOLD* HIM WHERE I LIVE...
'COURSE I DID. I'M THE ONLY ONE WHO KNOWS WHERE YOU'VE BEEN.
ARRRRR RRRRRR!
QUEST! WHAT THE?!

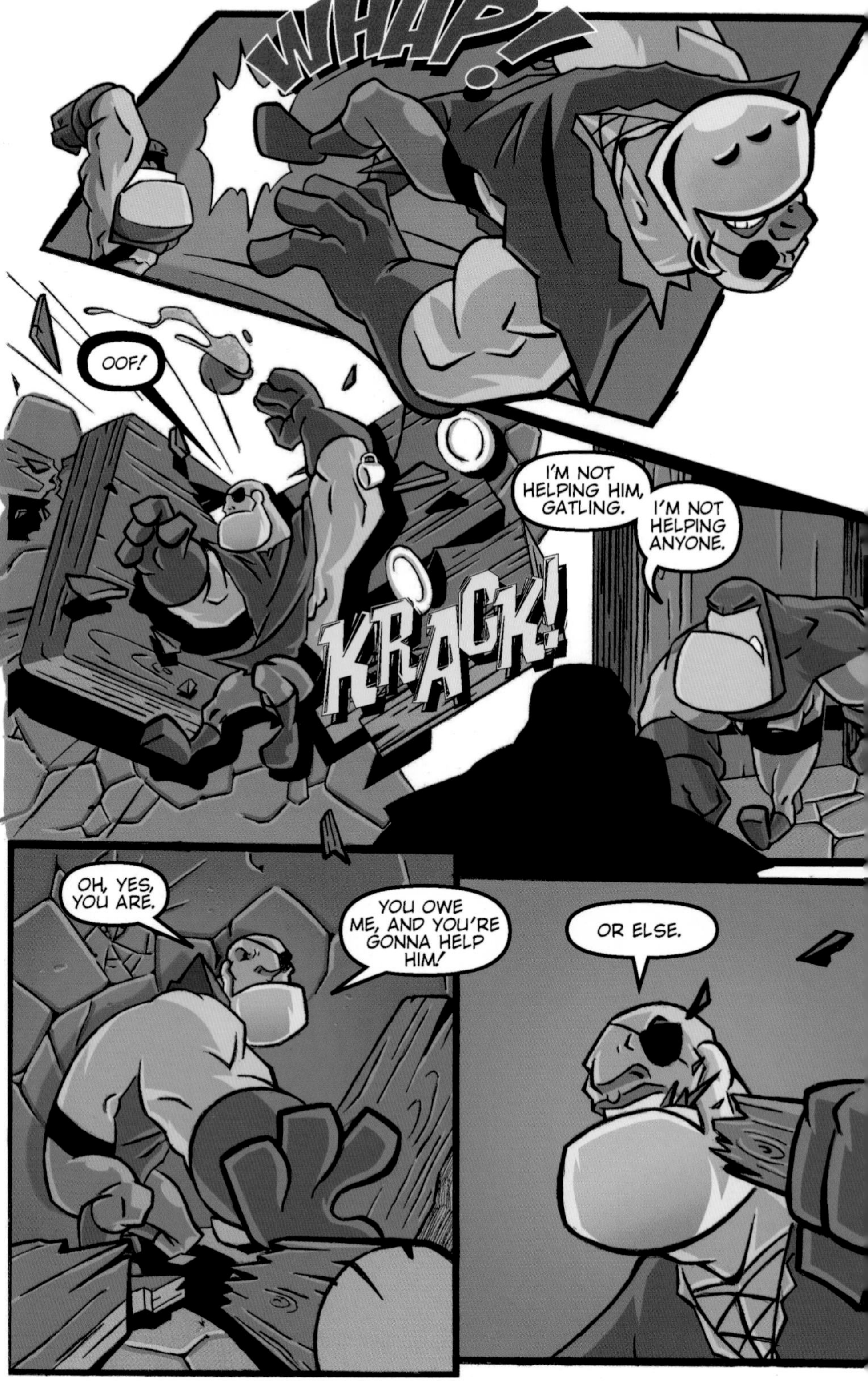
WHAP!
OOF!
KRACK!
I'M NOT HELPING HIM, GATLING.
I'M NOT HELPING ANYONE.
OH, YES, YOU ARE.
YOU OWE ME, AND YOU'RE GONNA HELP HIM!
OR ELSE.

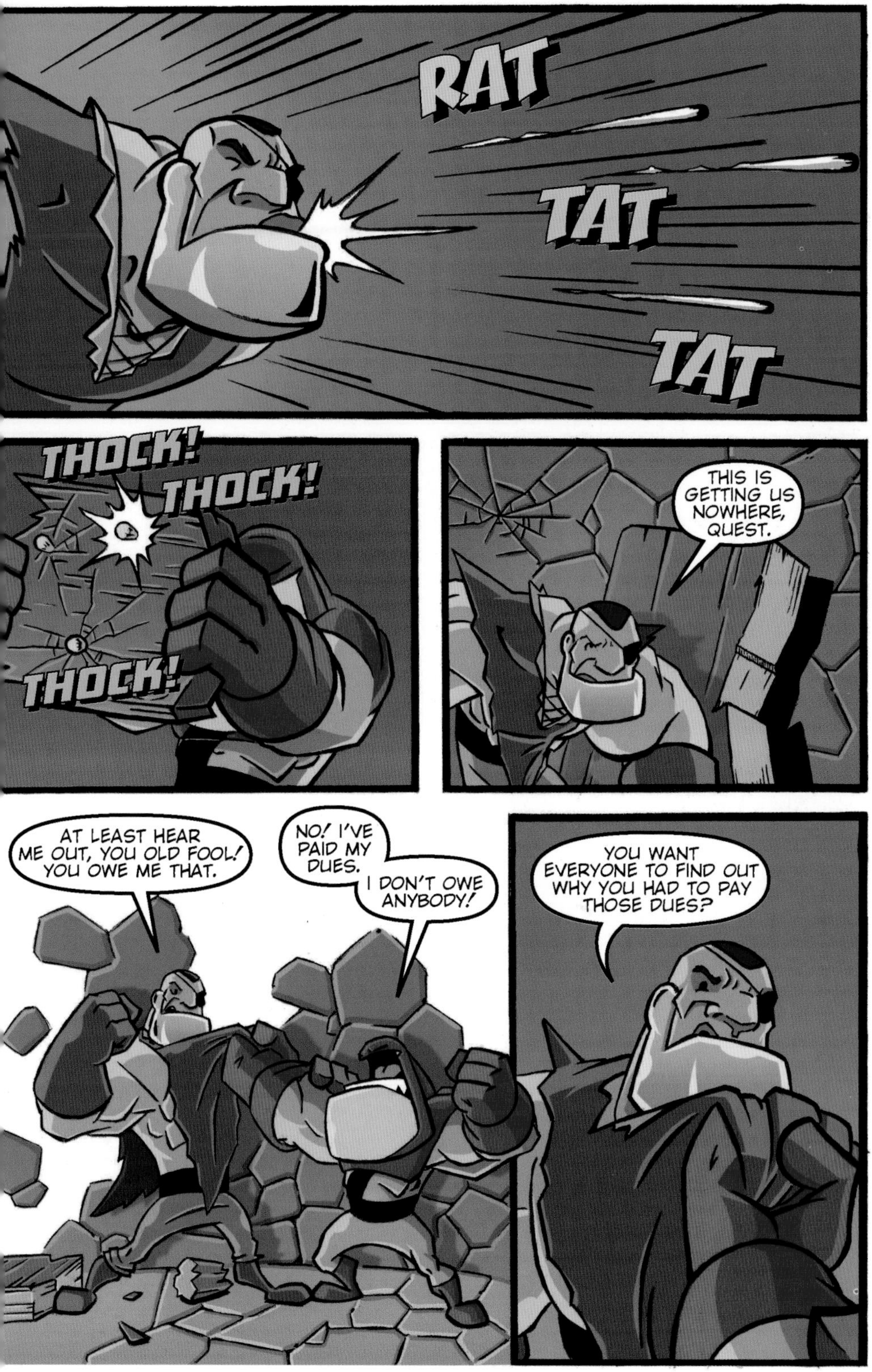
RAT
TAT
TAT
THOCK!
THOCK!
THOCK!
THIS IS GETTING US NOWHERE, QUEST.
AT LEAST HEAR ME OUT, YOU OLD FOOL! YOU OWE ME THAT.
NO! I'VE PAID MY DUES.
I DON'T OWE ANYBODY!
YOU WANT EVERYONE TO FIND OUT WHY YOU HAD TO PAY THOSE DUES?

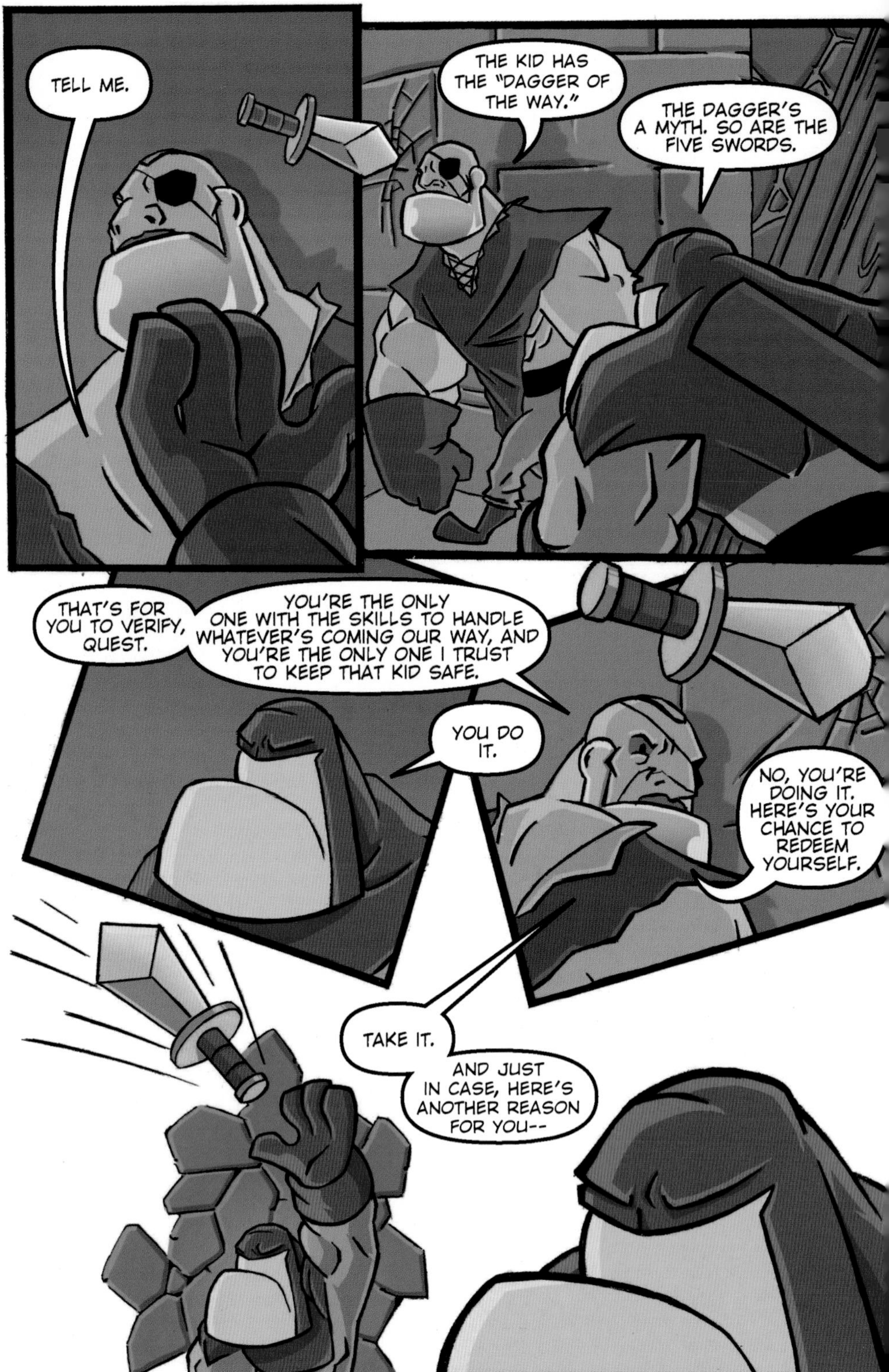
TELL ME.
THE KID HAS THE "DAGGER OF THE WAY."
THE DAGGER'S A MYTH. SO ARE THE FIVE SWORDS.
THAT'S FOR YOU TO VERIFY, QUEST.
YOU'RE THE ONLY ONE WITH THE SKILLS TO HANDLE WHATEVER'S COMING OUR WAY, AND YOU'RE THE ONLY ONE I TRUST TO KEEP THAT KID SAFE.
YOU DO IT.
NO, YOU'RE DOING IT. HERE'S YOUR CHANCE TO REDEEM YOURSELF.
TAKE IT.
AND JUST IN CASE, HERE'S ANOTHER REASON FOR YOU--

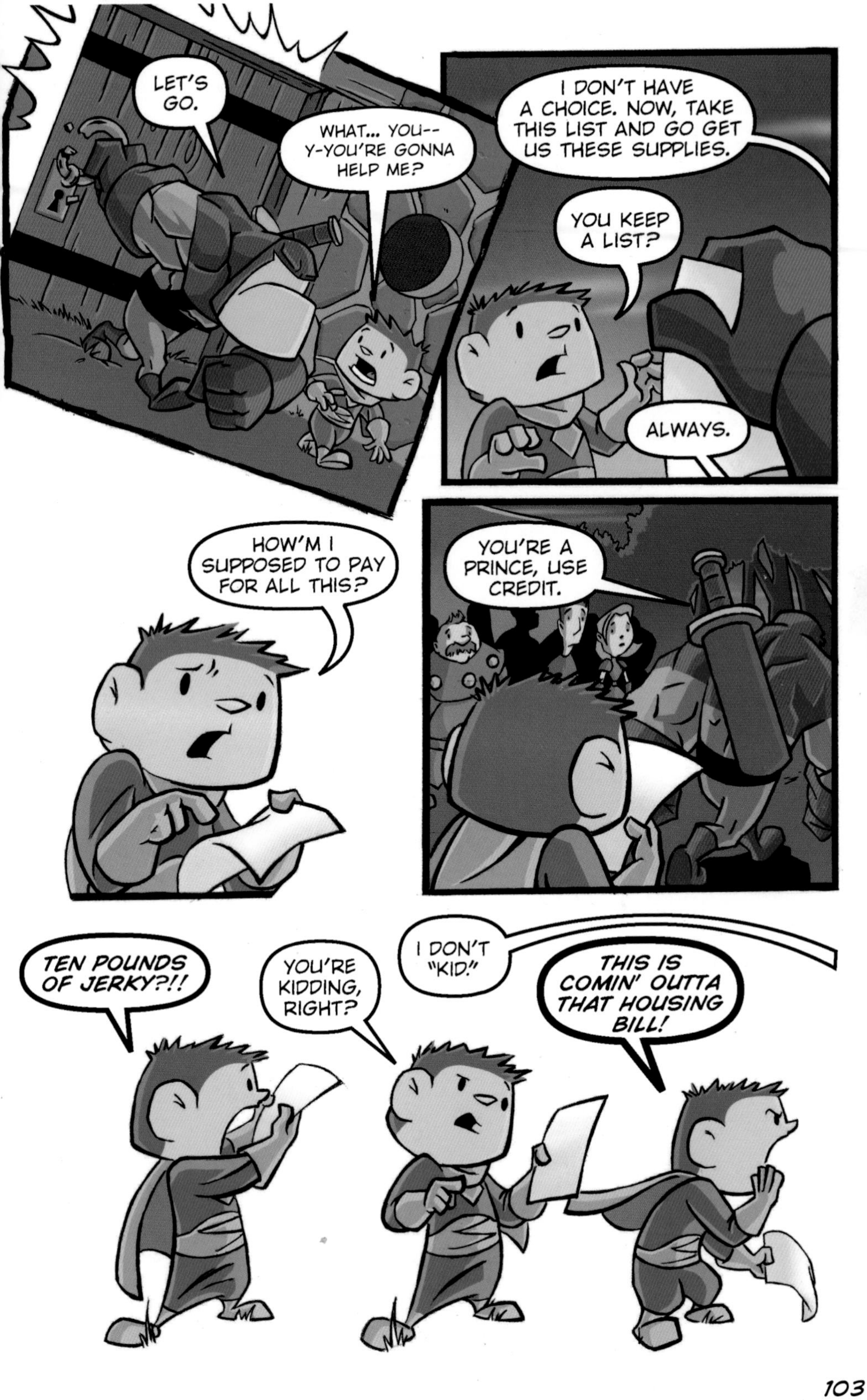
LET'S GO.
WHAT... YOU-- Y-YOU'RE GONNA HELP ME?
I DON'T HAVE A CHOICE. NOW, TAKE THIS LIST AND GO GET US THESE SUPPLIES.
YOU KEEP A LIST?
ALWAYS.
HOW'M I SUPPOSED TO PAY FOR ALL THIS?
YOU'RE A PRINCE, USE CREDIT.
TEN POUNDS OF JERKY?!!
YOU'RE KIDDING, RIGHT?
I DON'T "KID."
THIS IS COMIN' OUTTA THAT HOUSING BILL!

CHAPTER FIVE
PRISON BREAK

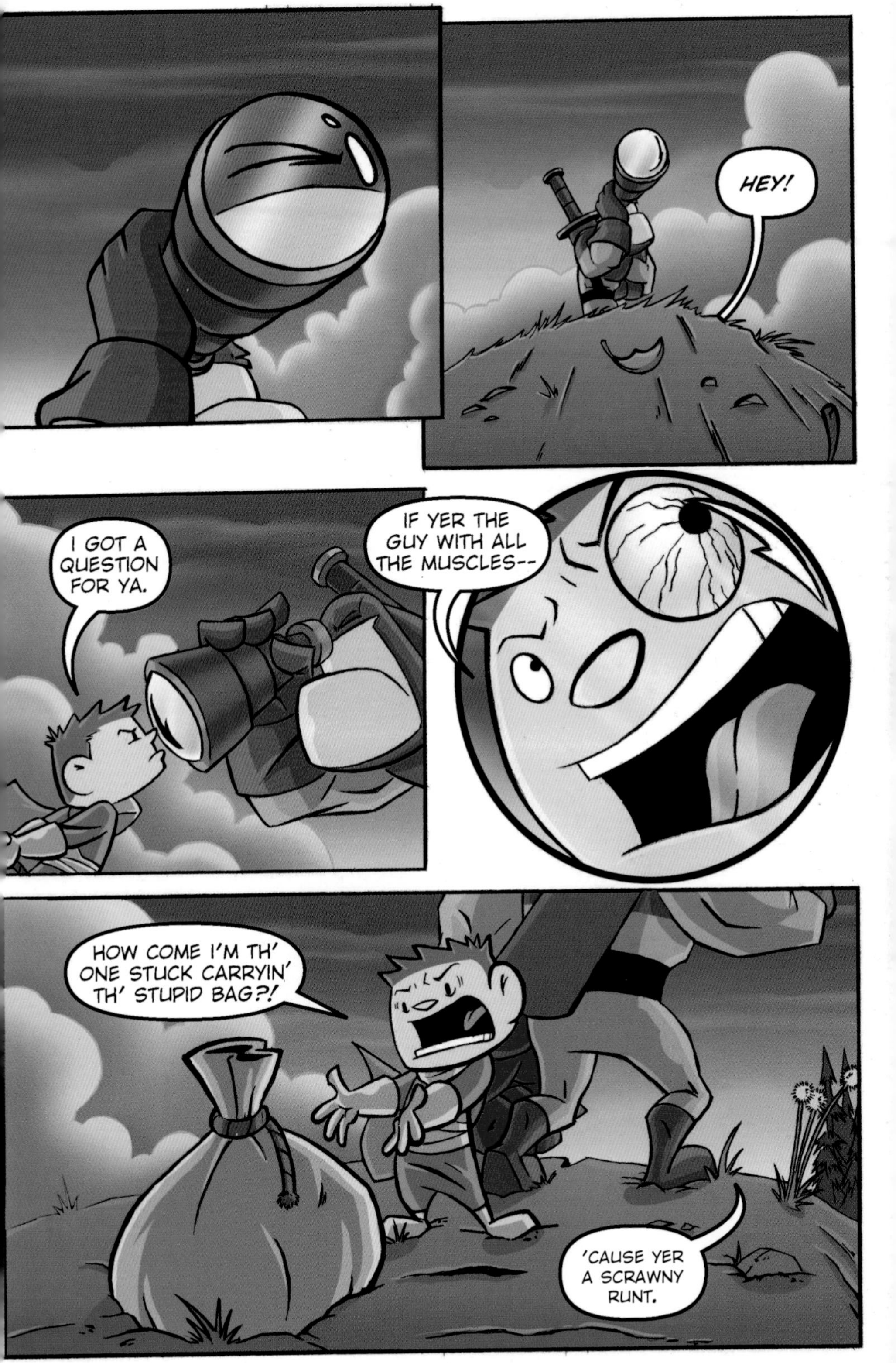
HEY!
I GOT A QUESTION FOR YA.
IF YER THE GUY WITH ALL THE MUSCLES--
HOW COME I'M TH' ONE STUCK CARRYIN' TH' STUPID BAG?!
'CAUSE YER A SCRAWNY RUNT.

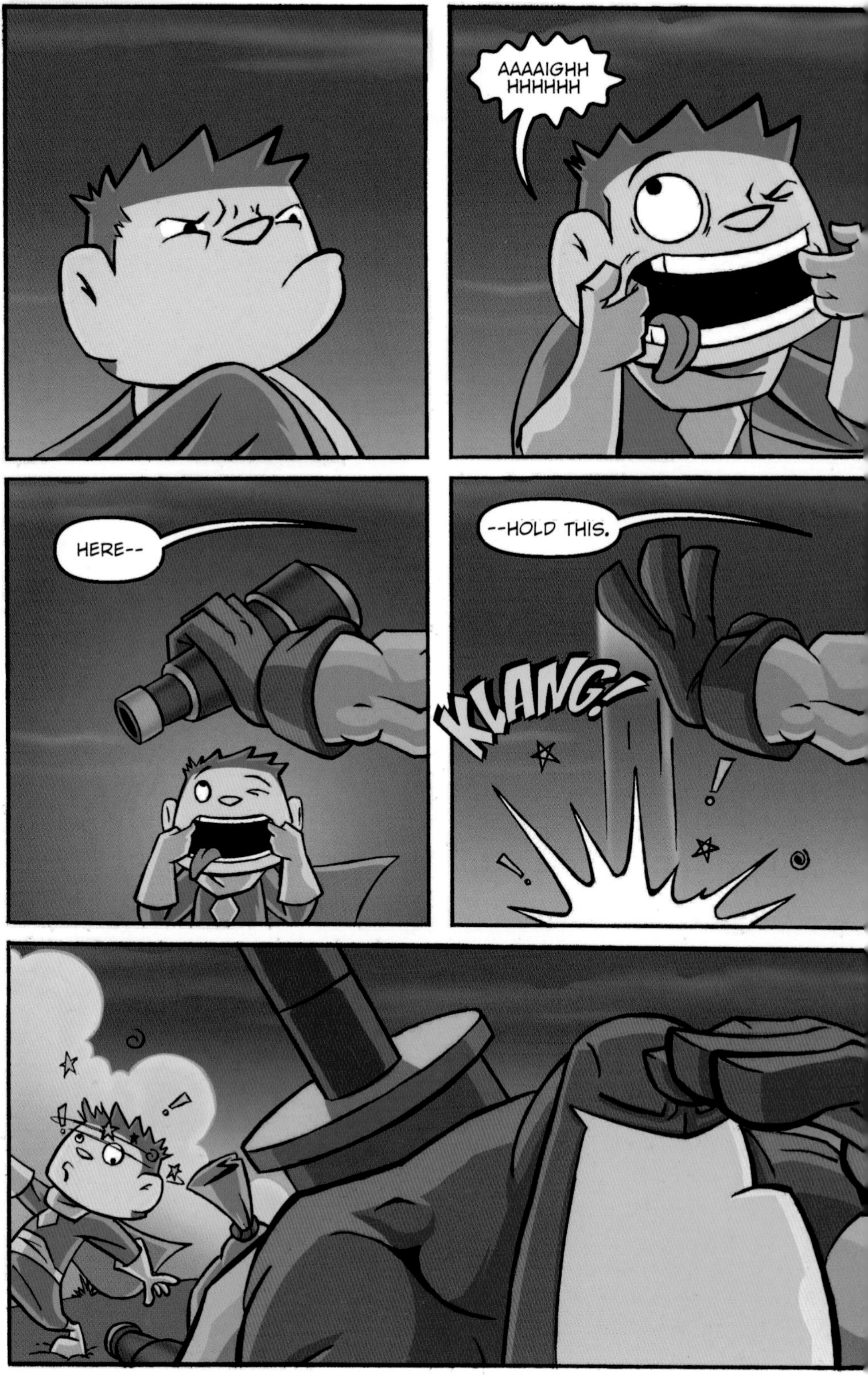
AAAAIGHH HHHHHH
HERE--
--HOLD THIS.
KLANG!

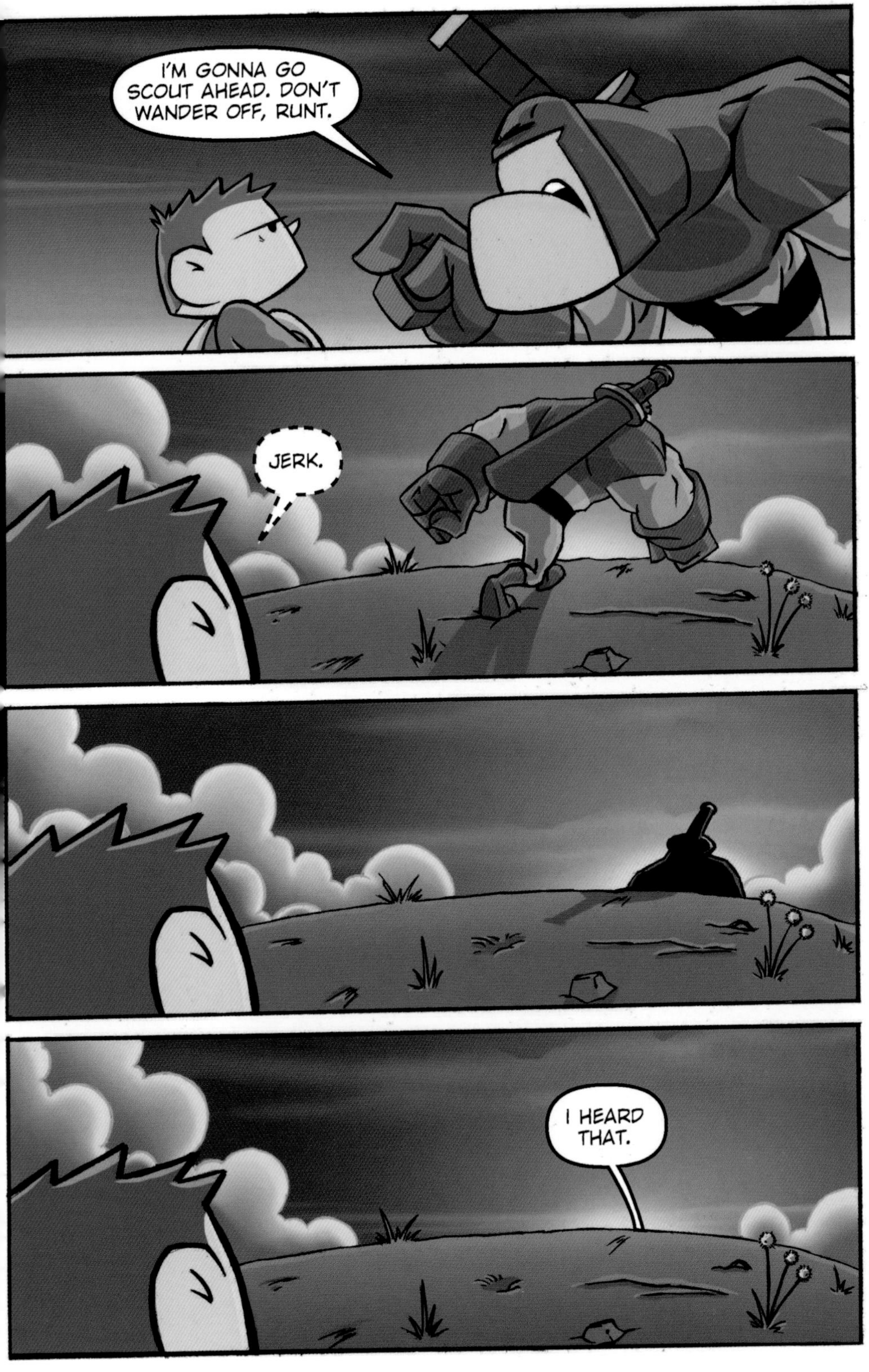
I'M GONNA GO SCOUT AHEAD. DON'T WANDER OFF, RUNT.
JERK.
I HEARD THAT.

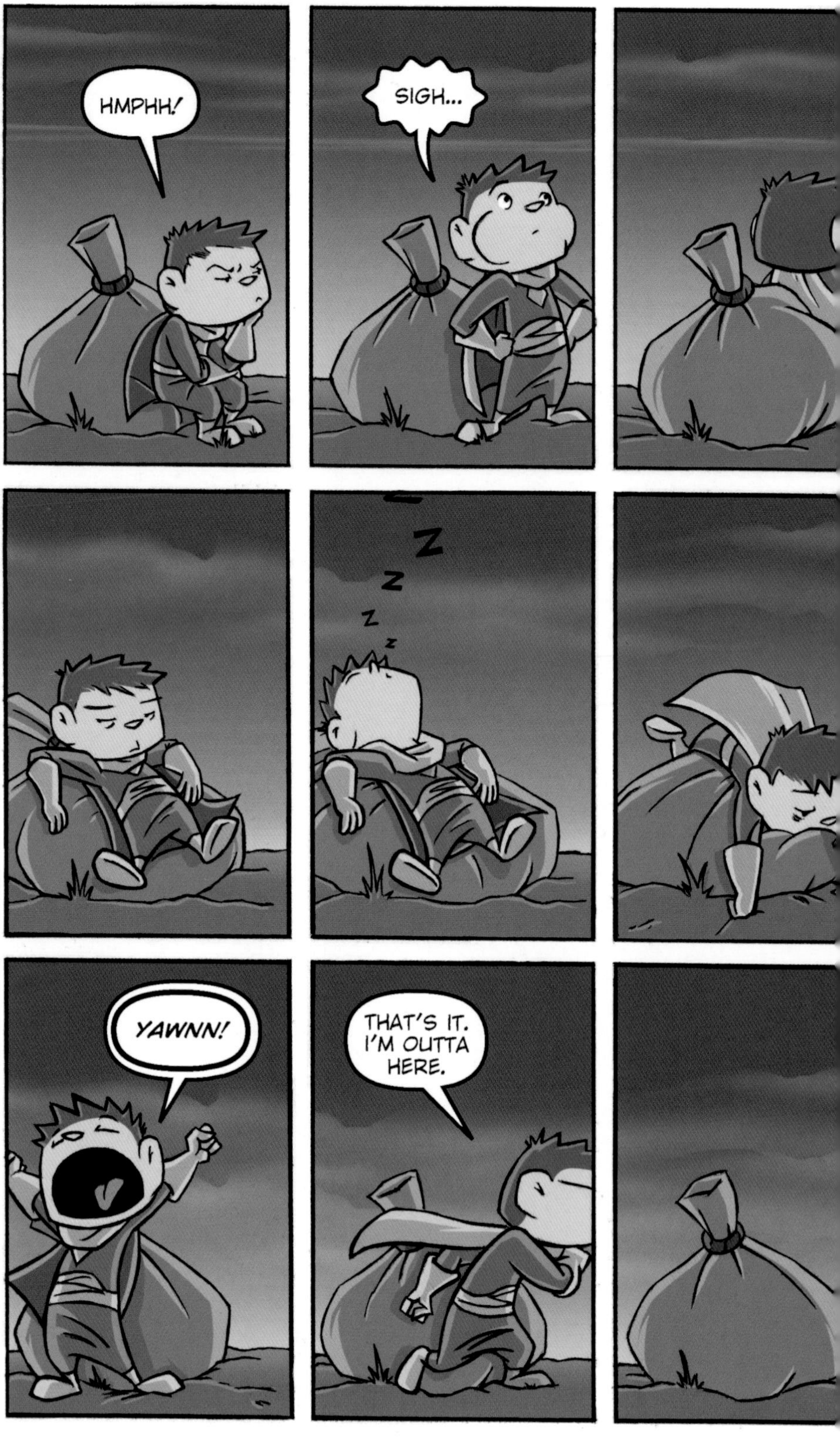
HMPHH!
SIGH...
Z
Z
Z
z
YAWNN!
THAT'S IT.
I'M OUTTA
HERE.

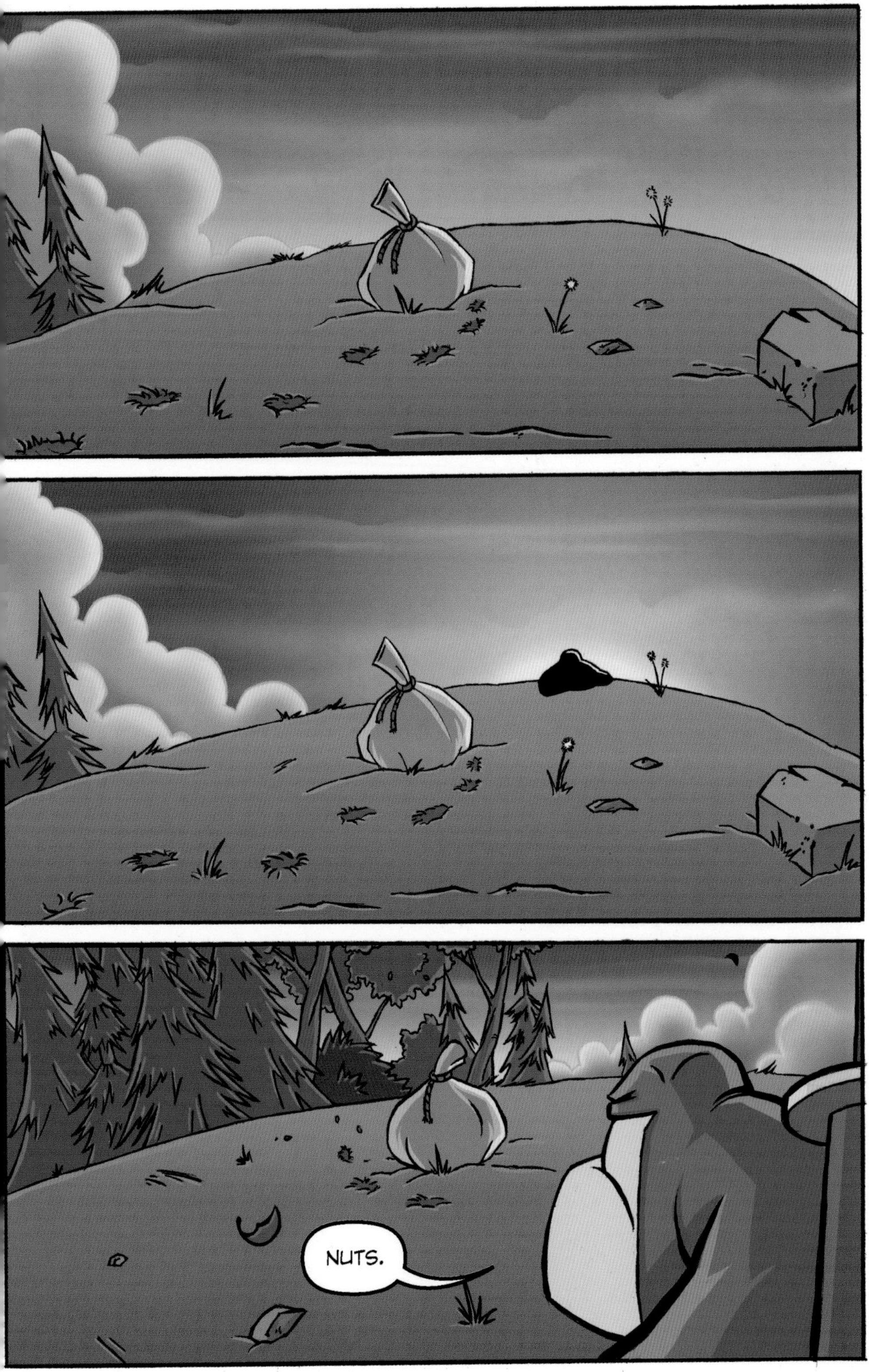
NUTS.

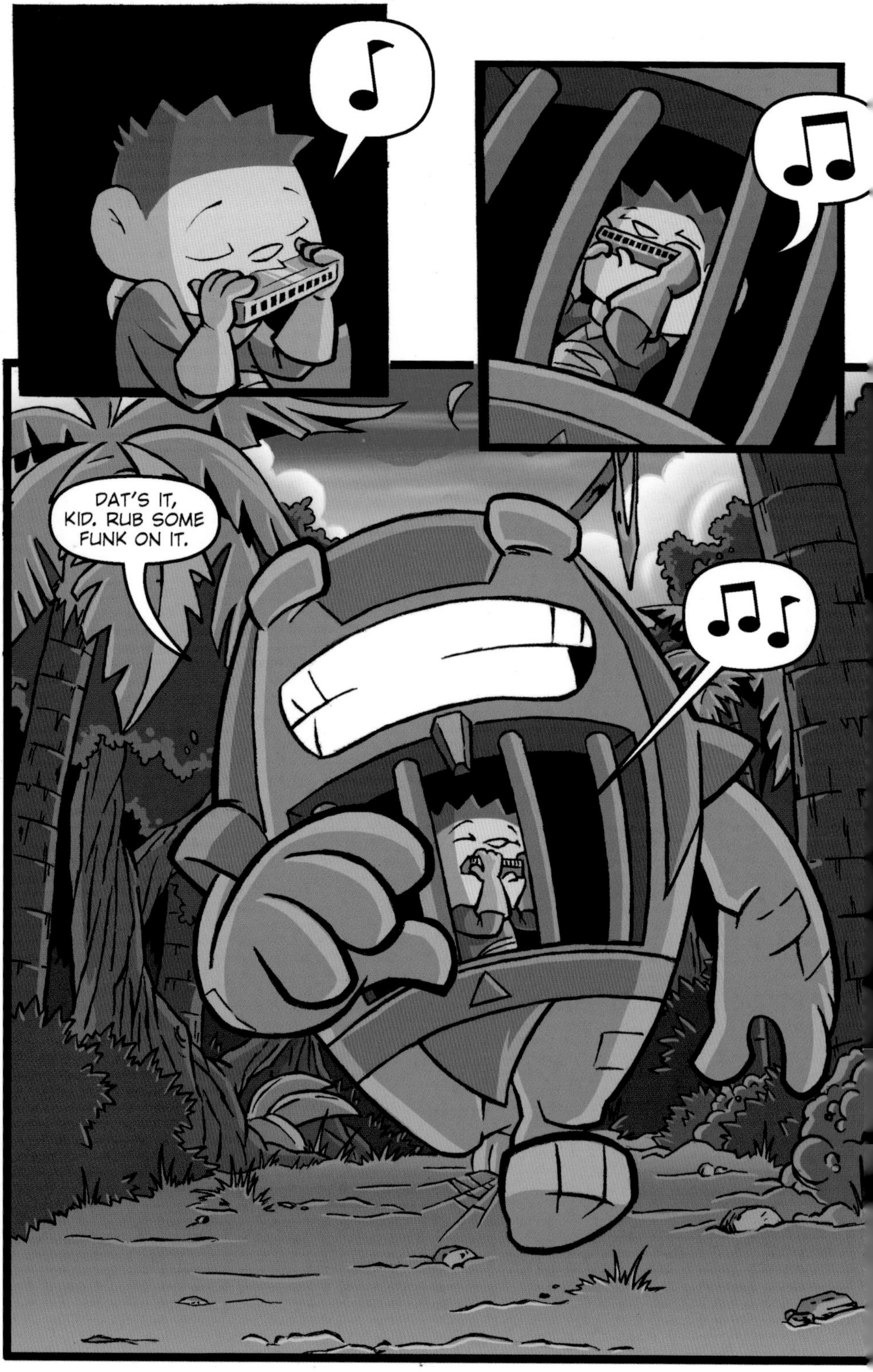
♪
♫
DAT'S IT, KID. RUB SOME FUNK ON IT.
♫♪

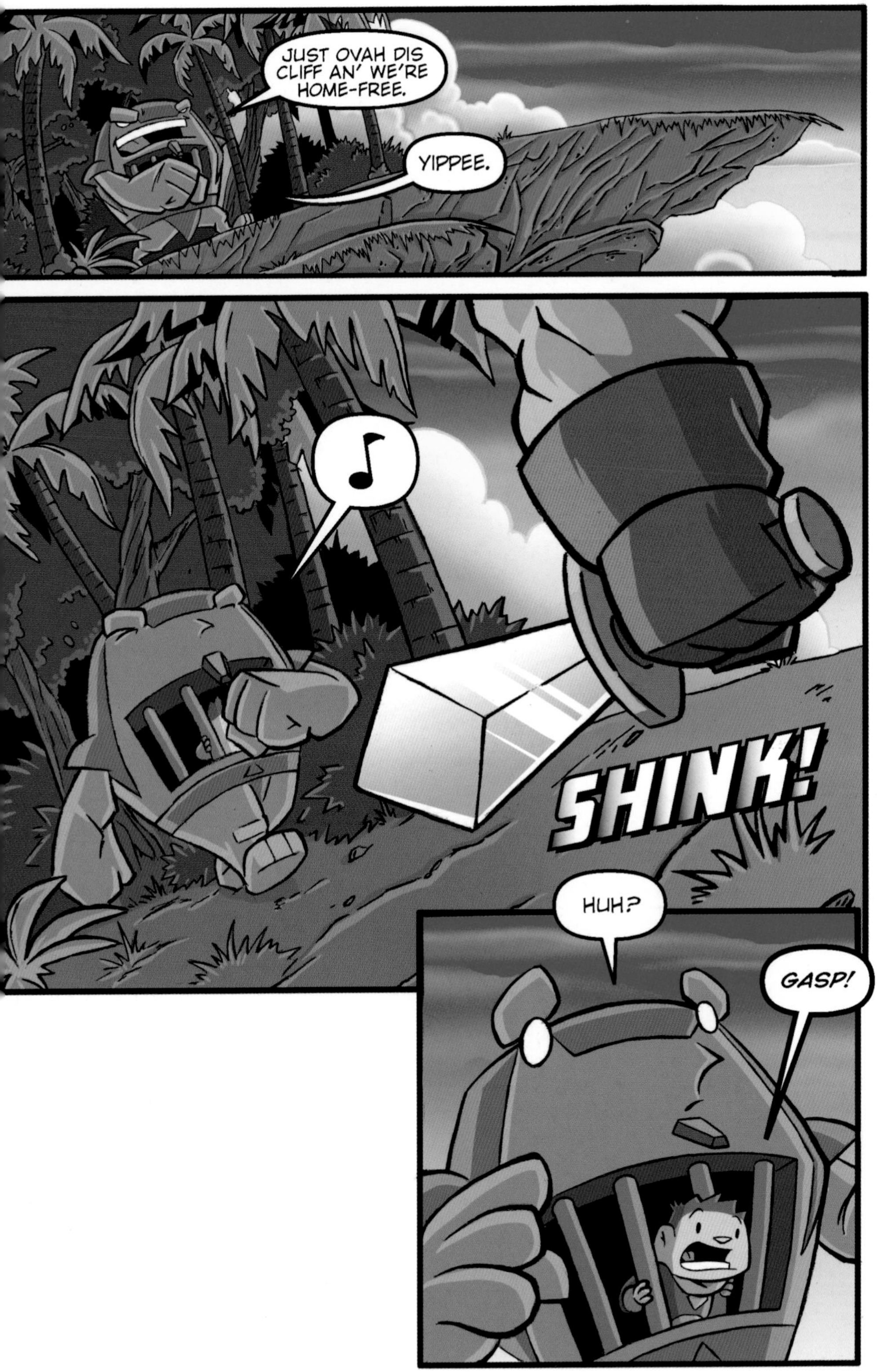
JUST OVAH DIS CLIFF AN' WE'RE HOME-FREE.
YIPPEE.
♪
SHINK!
HUH?
GASP!

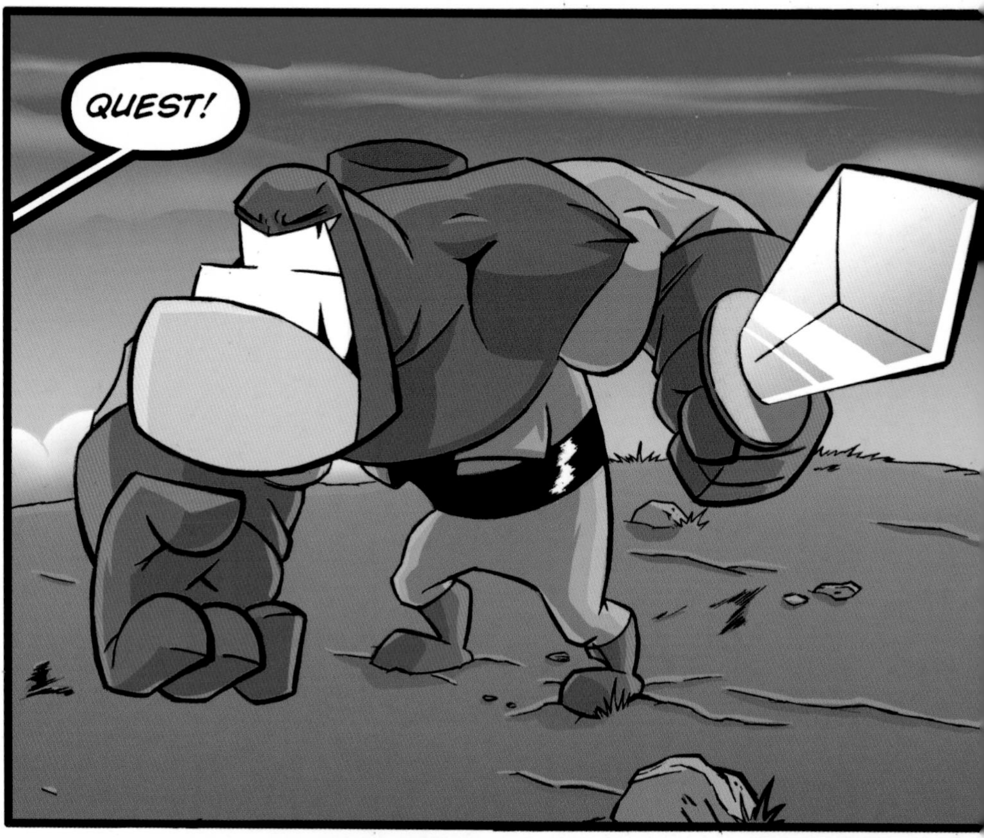
QUEST!

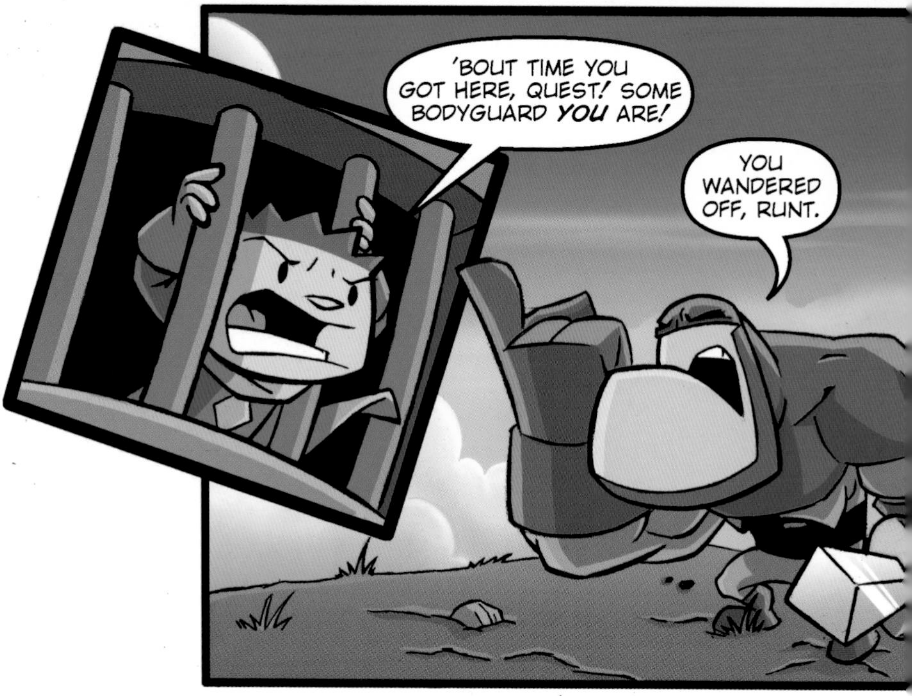
'BOUT TIME YOU GOT HERE, QUEST! SOME BODYGUARD YOU ARE!
YOU WANDERED OFF, RUNT.

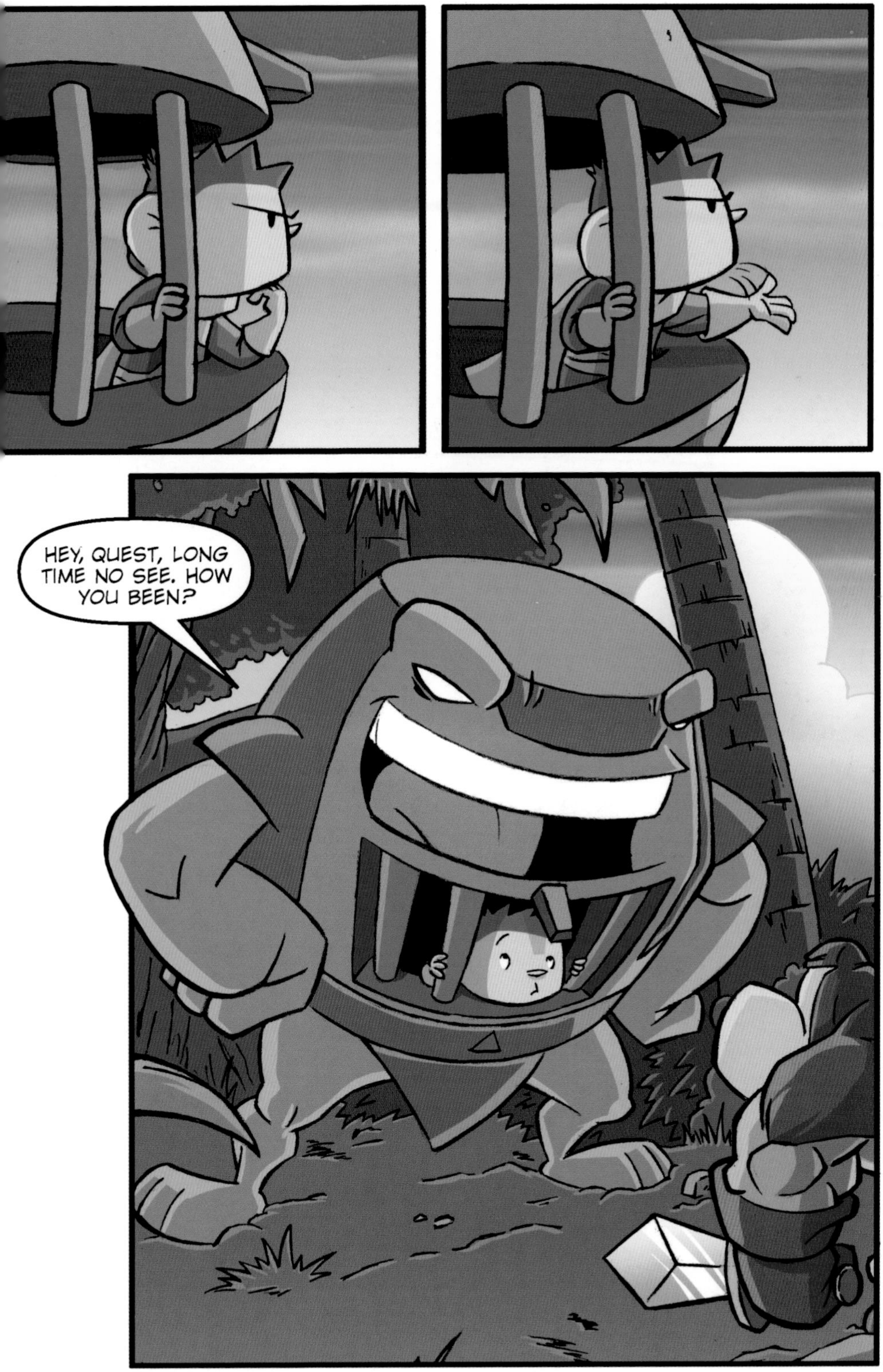
HEY, QUEST, LONG TIME NO SEE. HOW YOU BEEN?

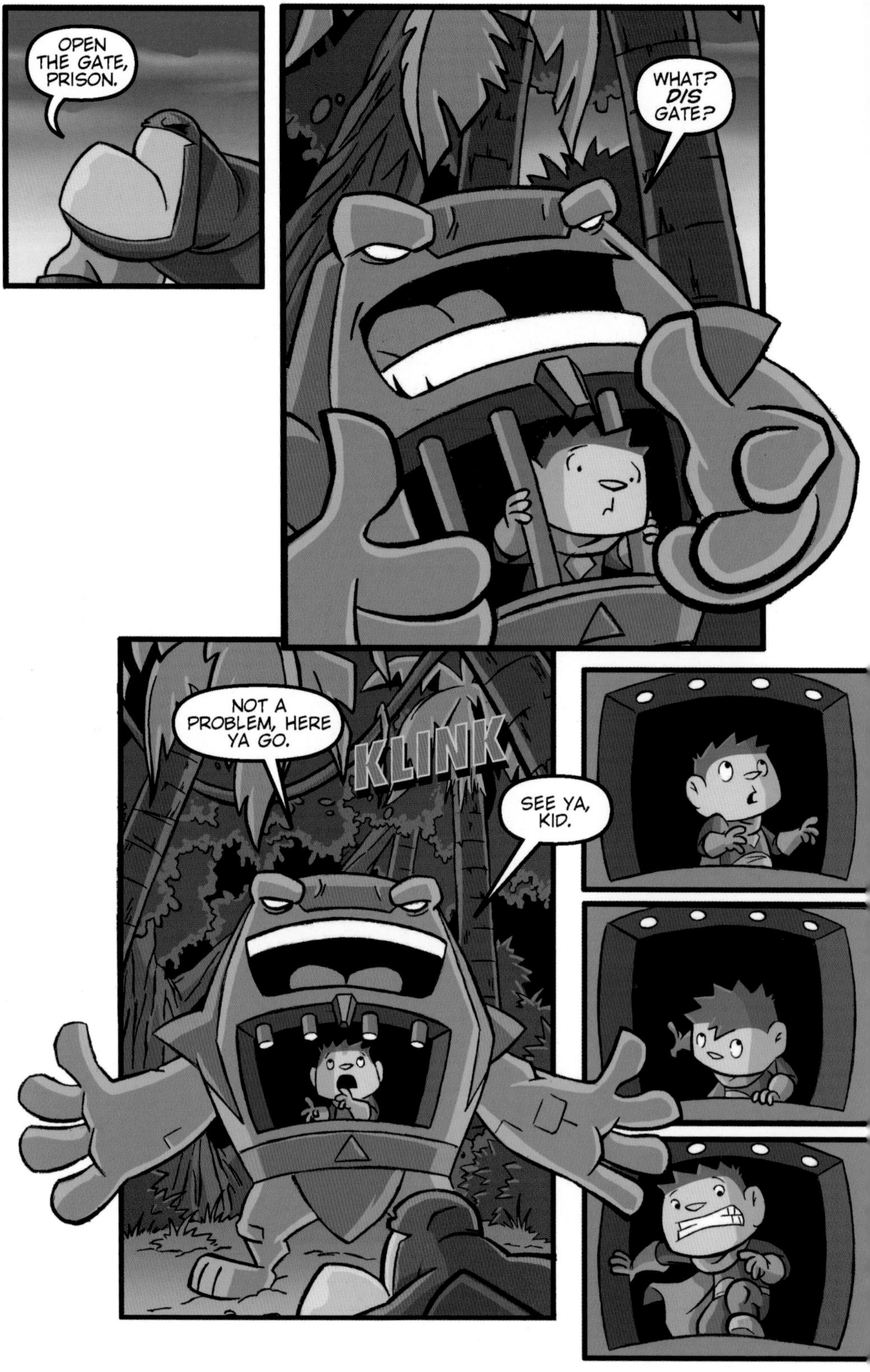
OPEN THE GATE, PRISON.
WHAT? DIS GATE?
NOT A PROBLEM, HERE YA GO.
KLINK
SEE YA, KID.

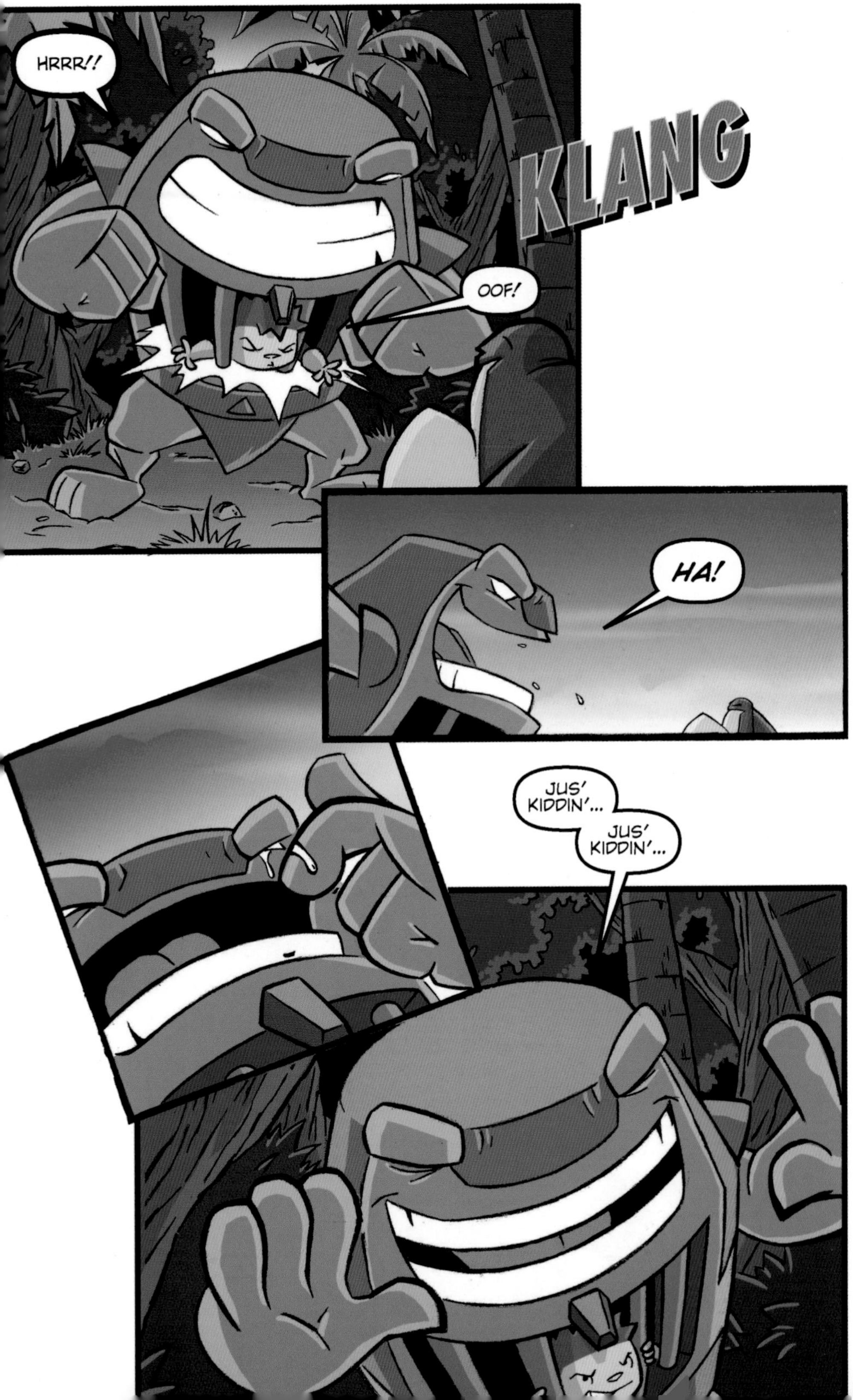
HRRR!!
KLANG
OOF!
HA!
JUS' KIDDIN'...
JUS' KIDDIN'...

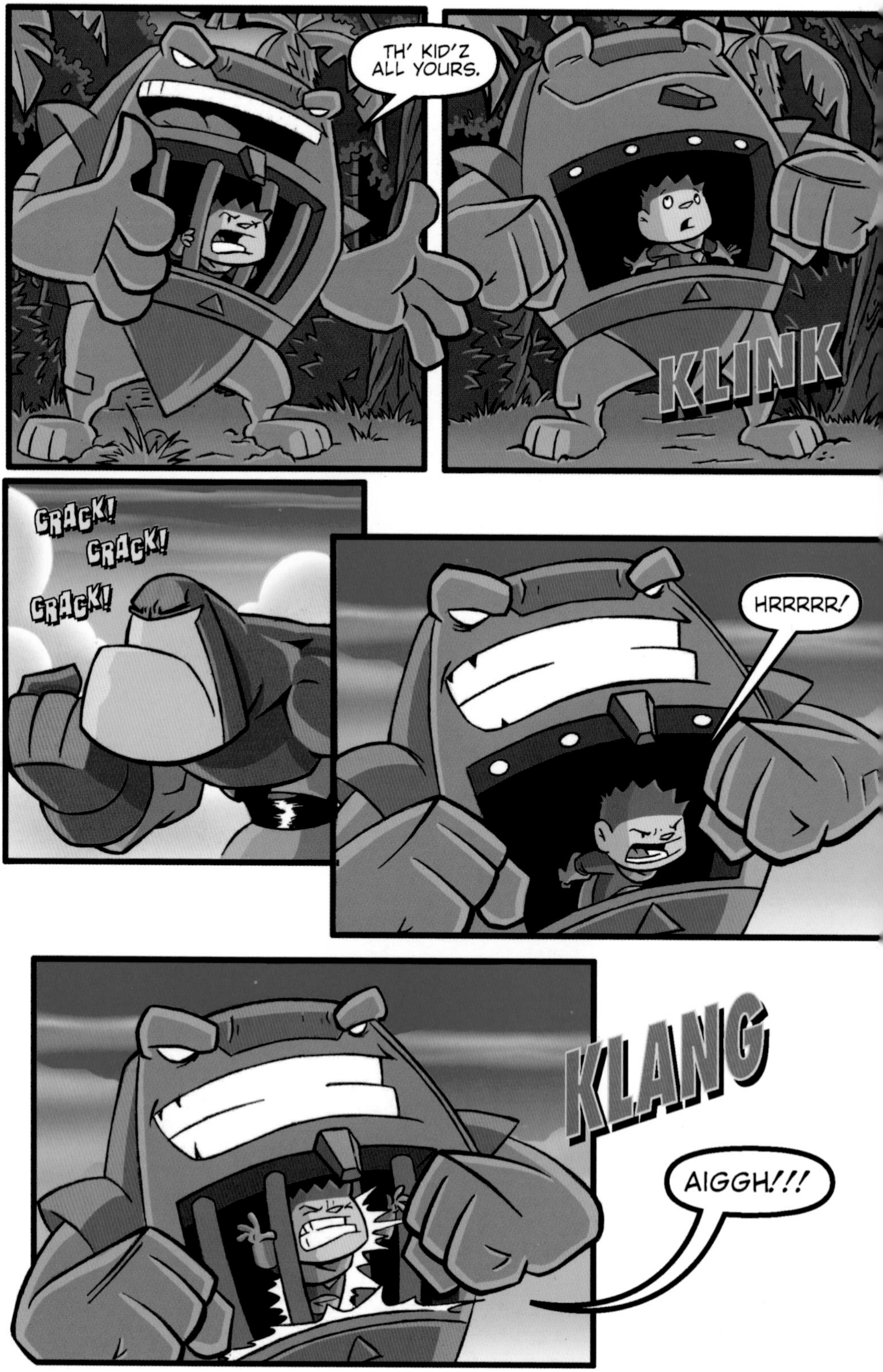
TH' KID'Z ALL YOURS.
KLINK
CRACK!
CRACK!
CRACK!
HRRRRR!
KLANG
AIGGH!!!

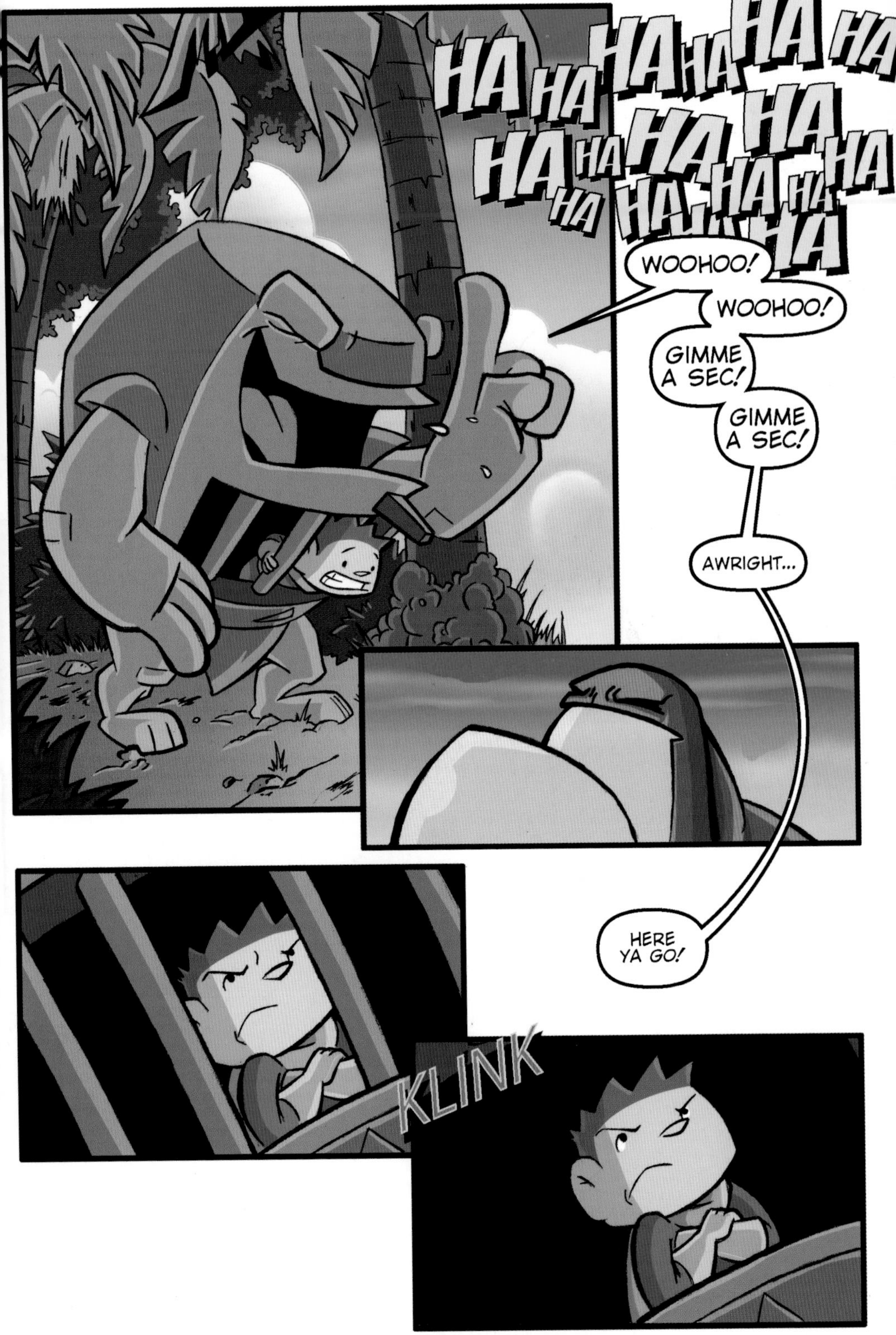
HA HA HA HA HA HA
HA HA HA HA HA
HA HA HA HA HA HA HA
WOOHOO!
WOOHOO!
GIMME A SEC!
GIMME A SEC!
AWRIGHT...
HERE YA GO!
KLINK

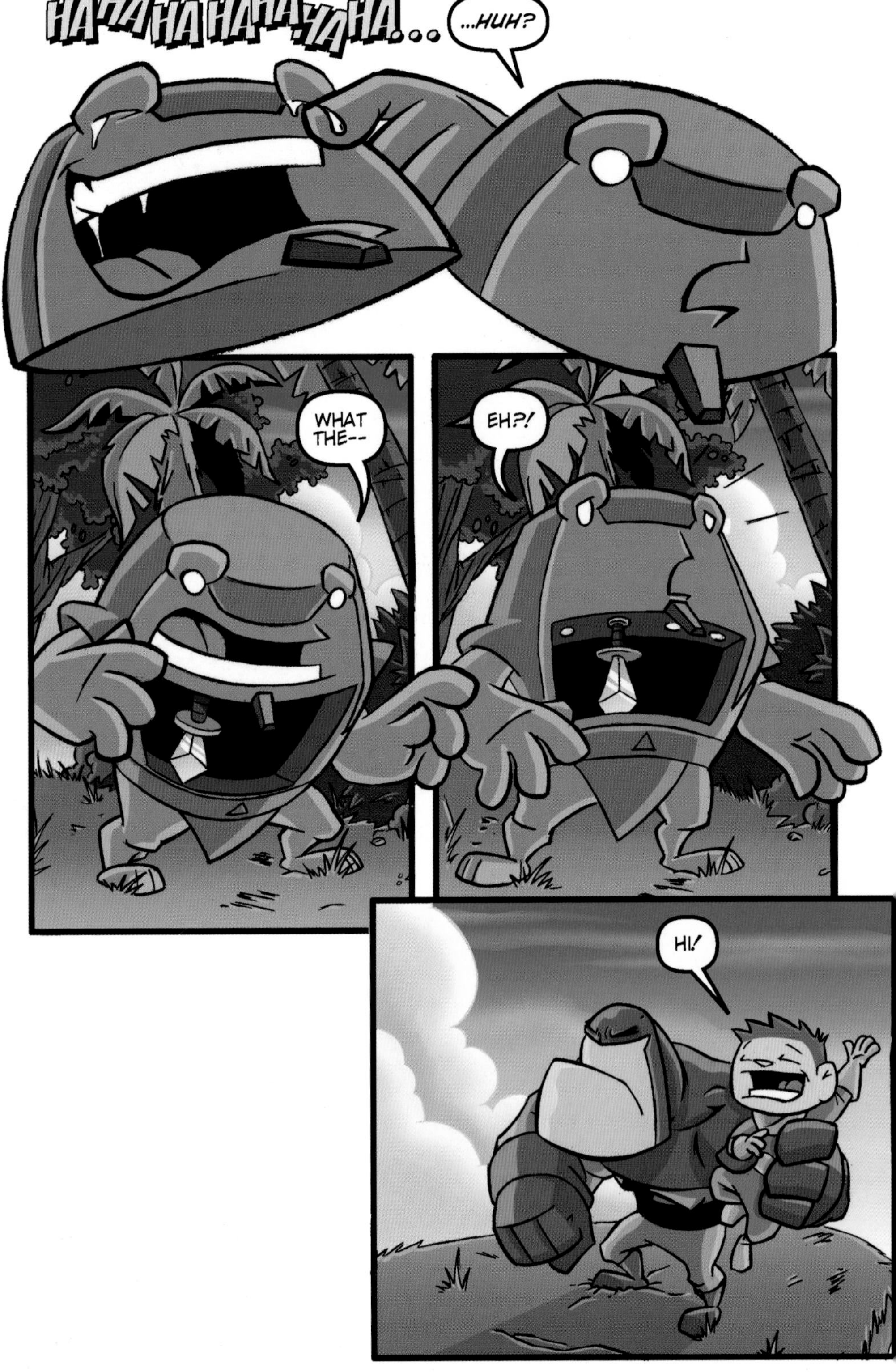
HAHAHA HAHAYAHA...
...HUH?
WHAT THE--
EH?!
HI!

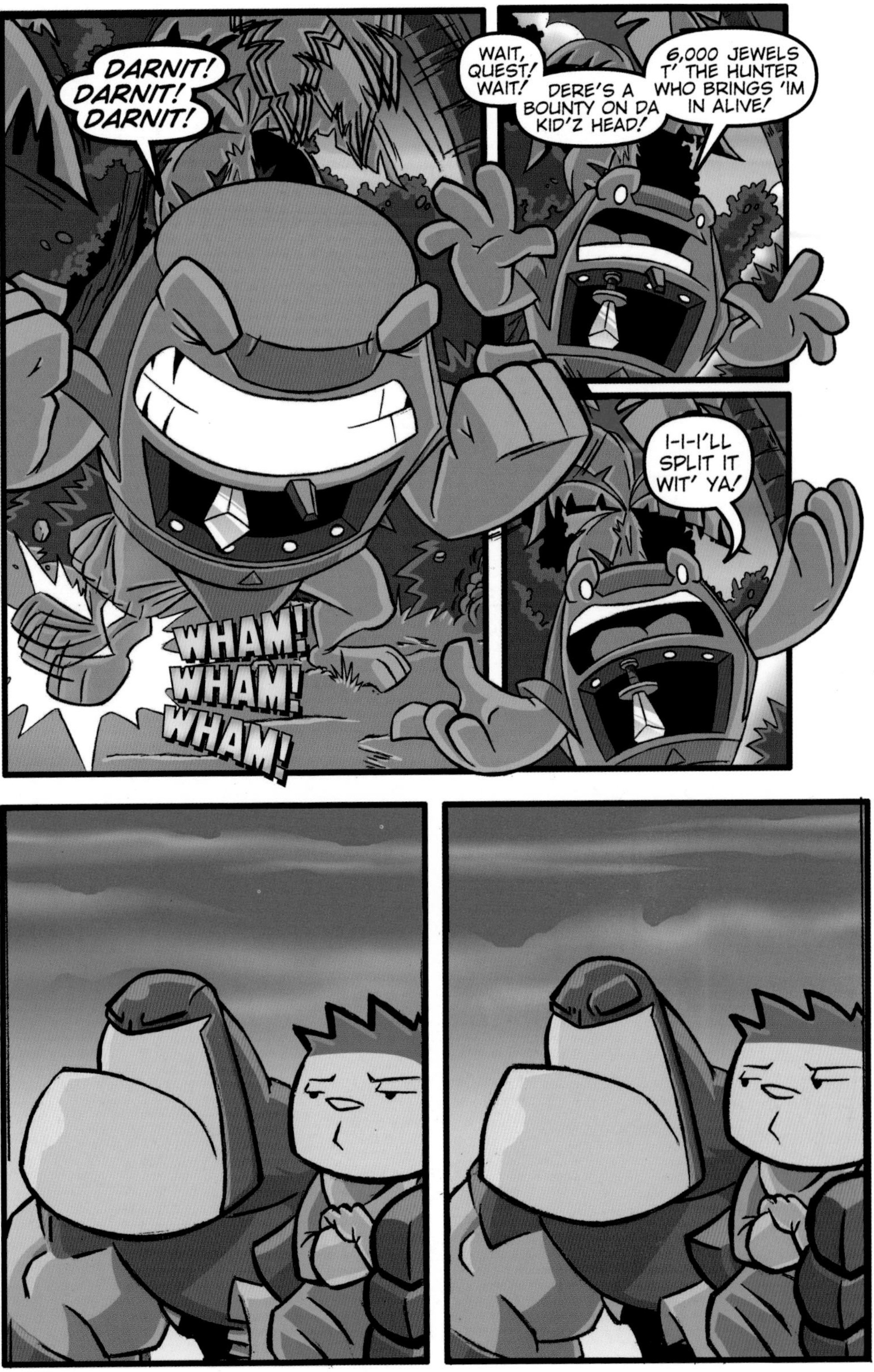
DARNIT! DARNIT! DARNIT!
WHAM! WHAM! WHAM!
WAIT, QUEST! WAIT!
DERE'S A BOUNTY ON DA KID'Z HEAD!
6,000 JEWELS T' THE HUNTER WHO BRINGS 'IM IN ALIVE!
I-I-I'LL SPLIT IT WIT' YA!

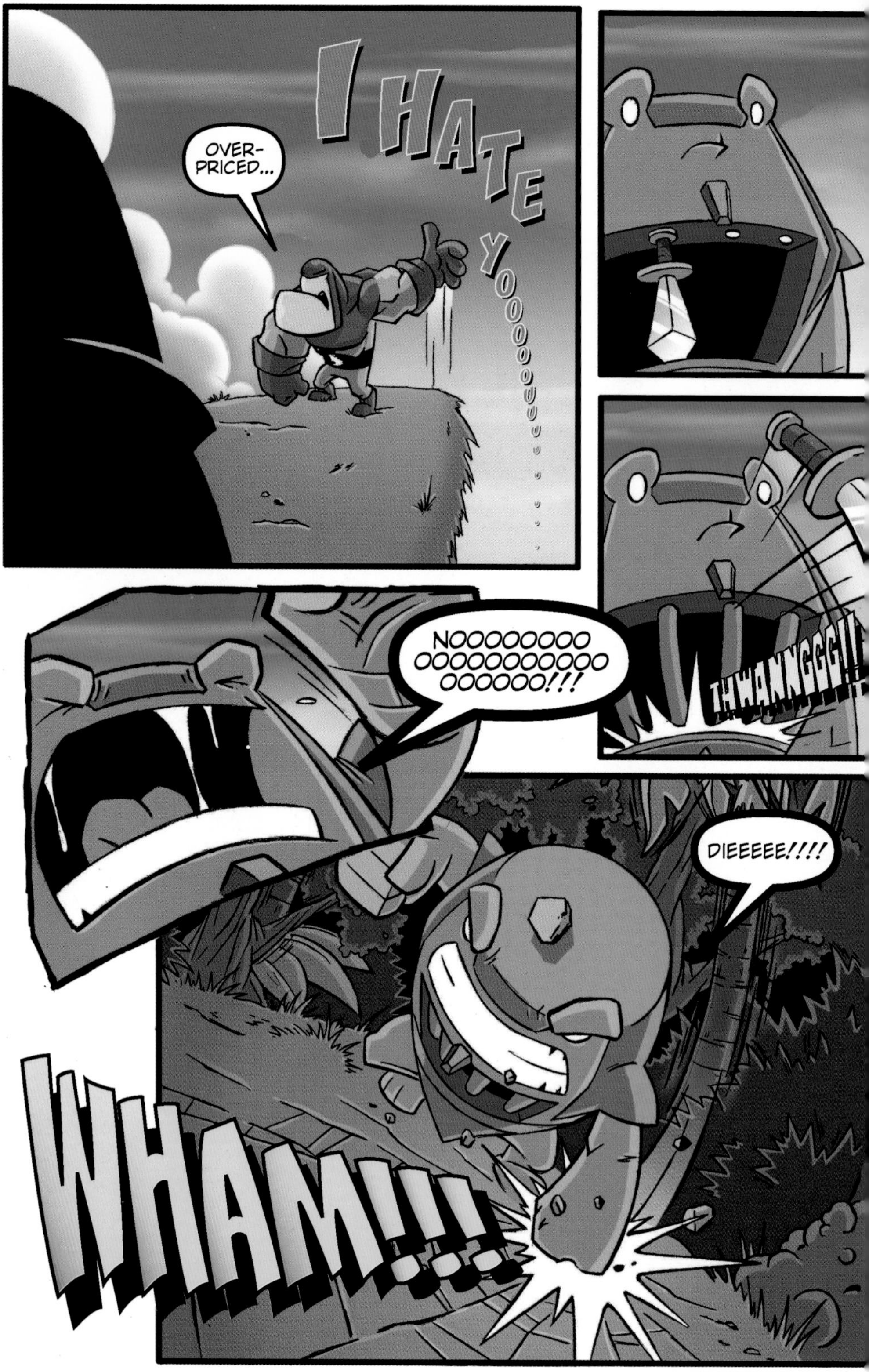
I HATE
OVER-PRICED...
YOOOOOOUUUUUUU
NOOOOOOOOO OOOOOOOOOOO OOOOOO!!!
THWANNGGG!!
DIEEEEE!!!!
WHAM!!!

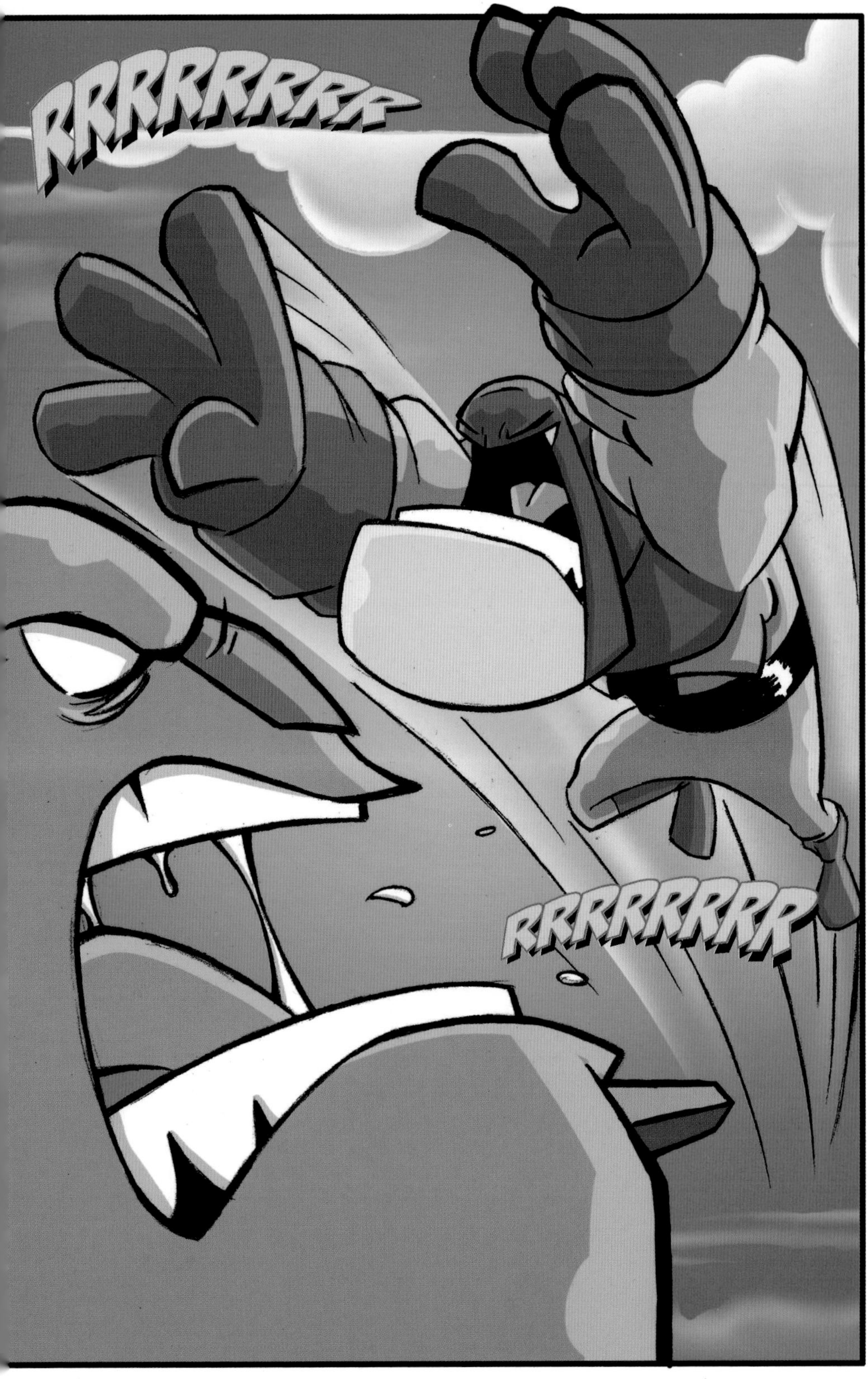
RRRRRRRR
RRRRRRRR

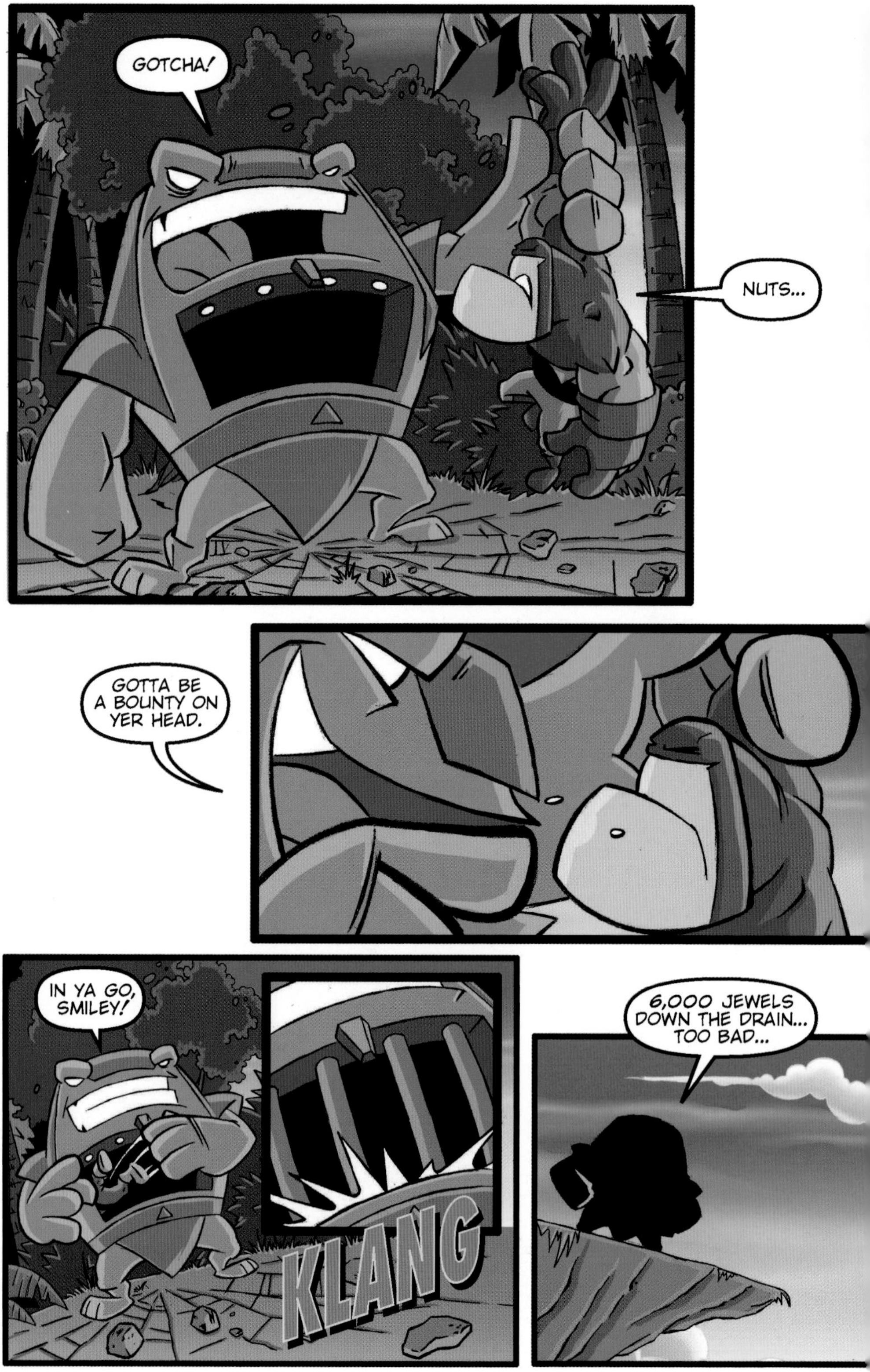
GOTCHA!
NUTS...
GOTTA BE A BOUNTY ON YER HEAD.
IN YA GO, SMILEY!
KLANG
6,000 JEWELS DOWN THE DRAIN... TOO BAD...

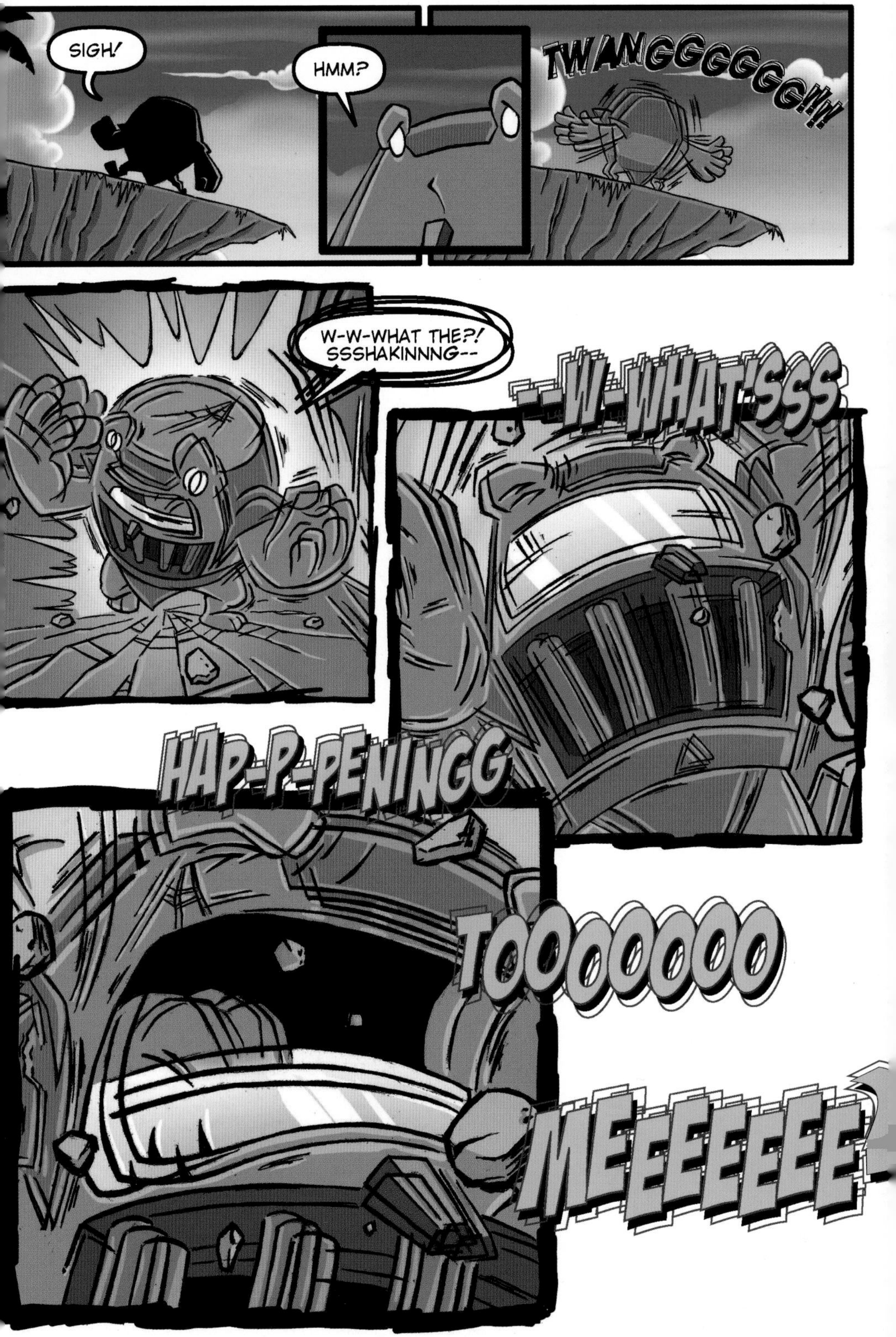
SIGH!
HMM?
TWANGGGGGGG!!!!
W-W-WHAT THE?! SSSHAKINNNG--
--W-WHAT'SSS
HAP-P-PENINGG
TOOOOOOO
MEEEEEEE

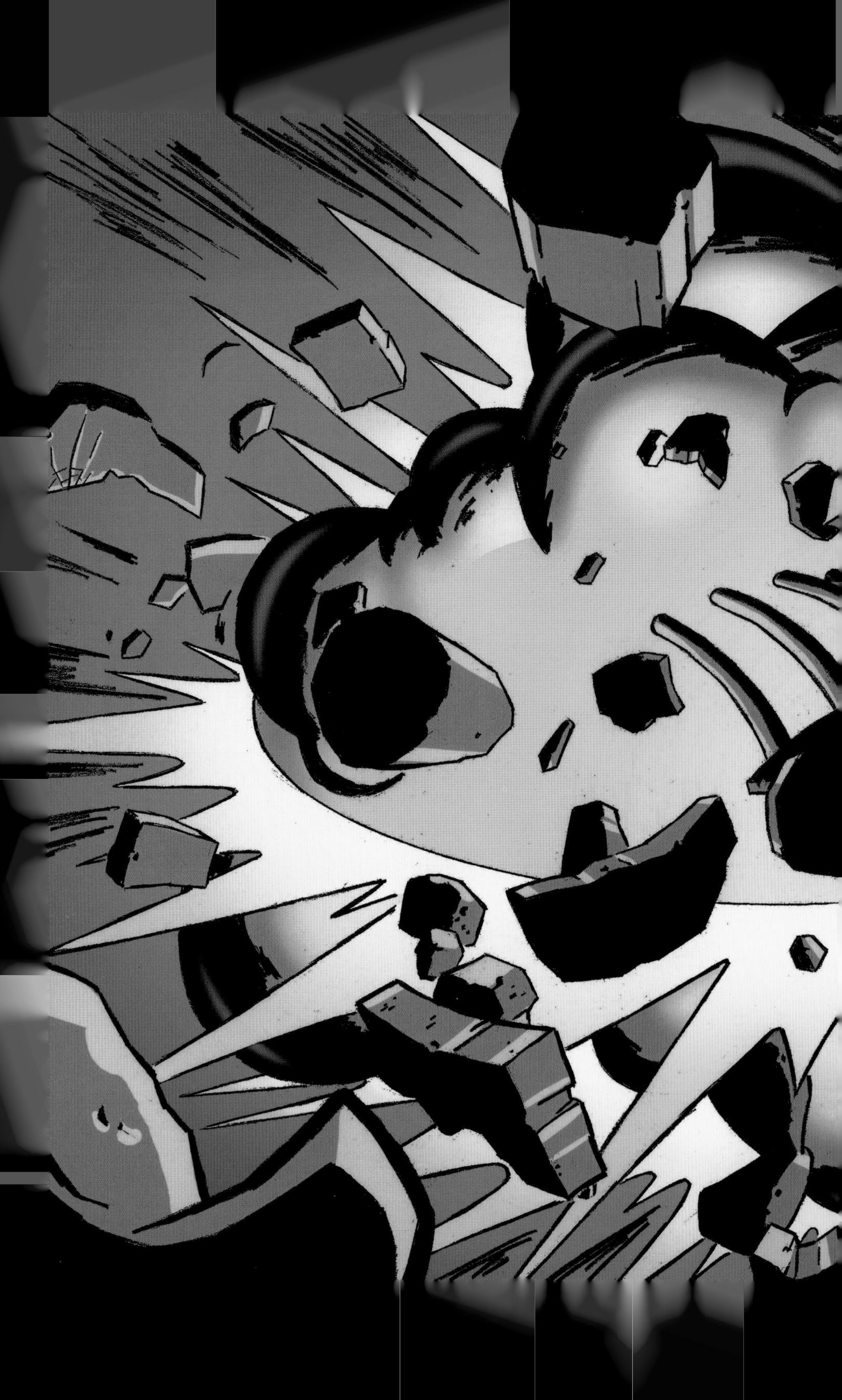

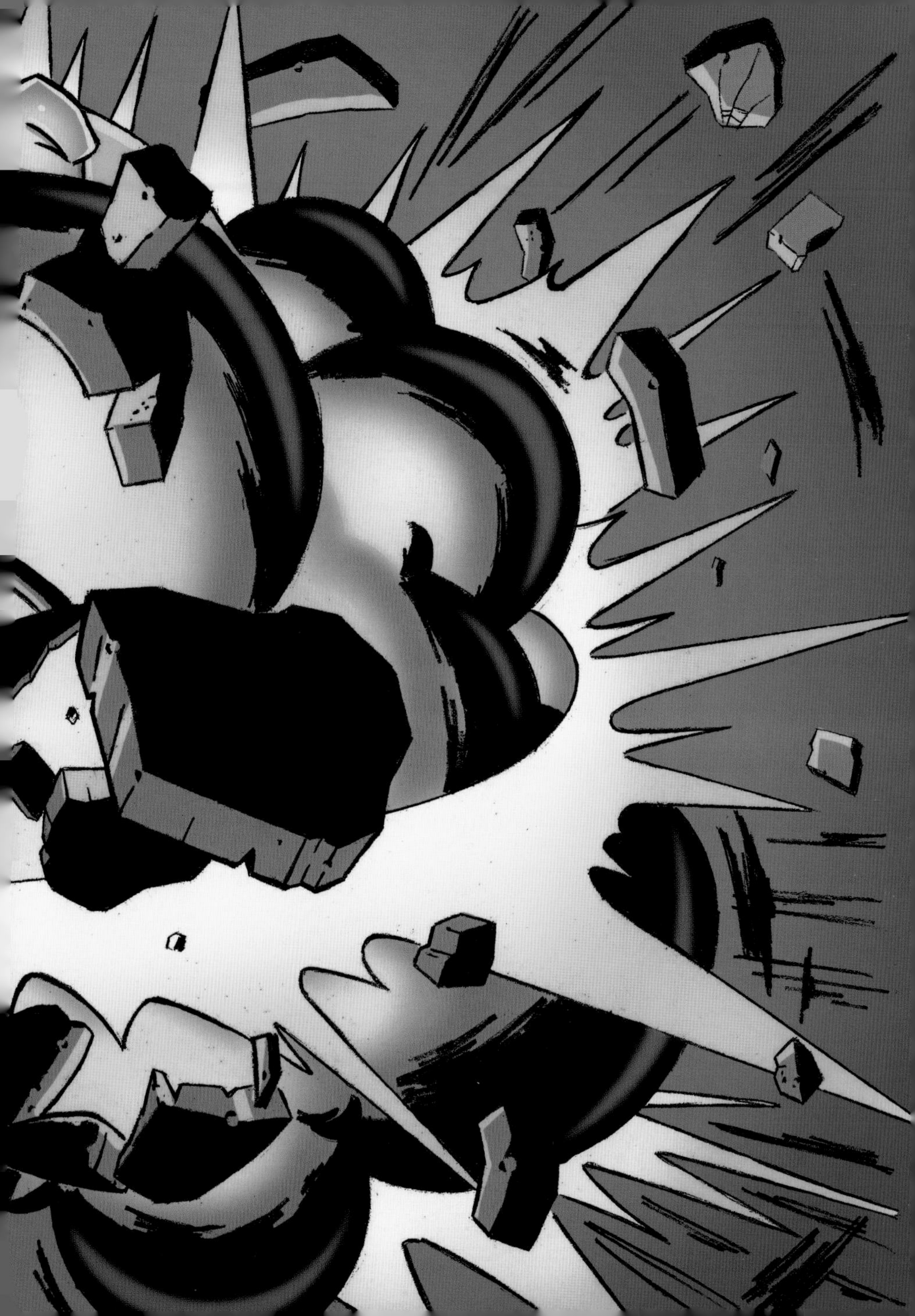

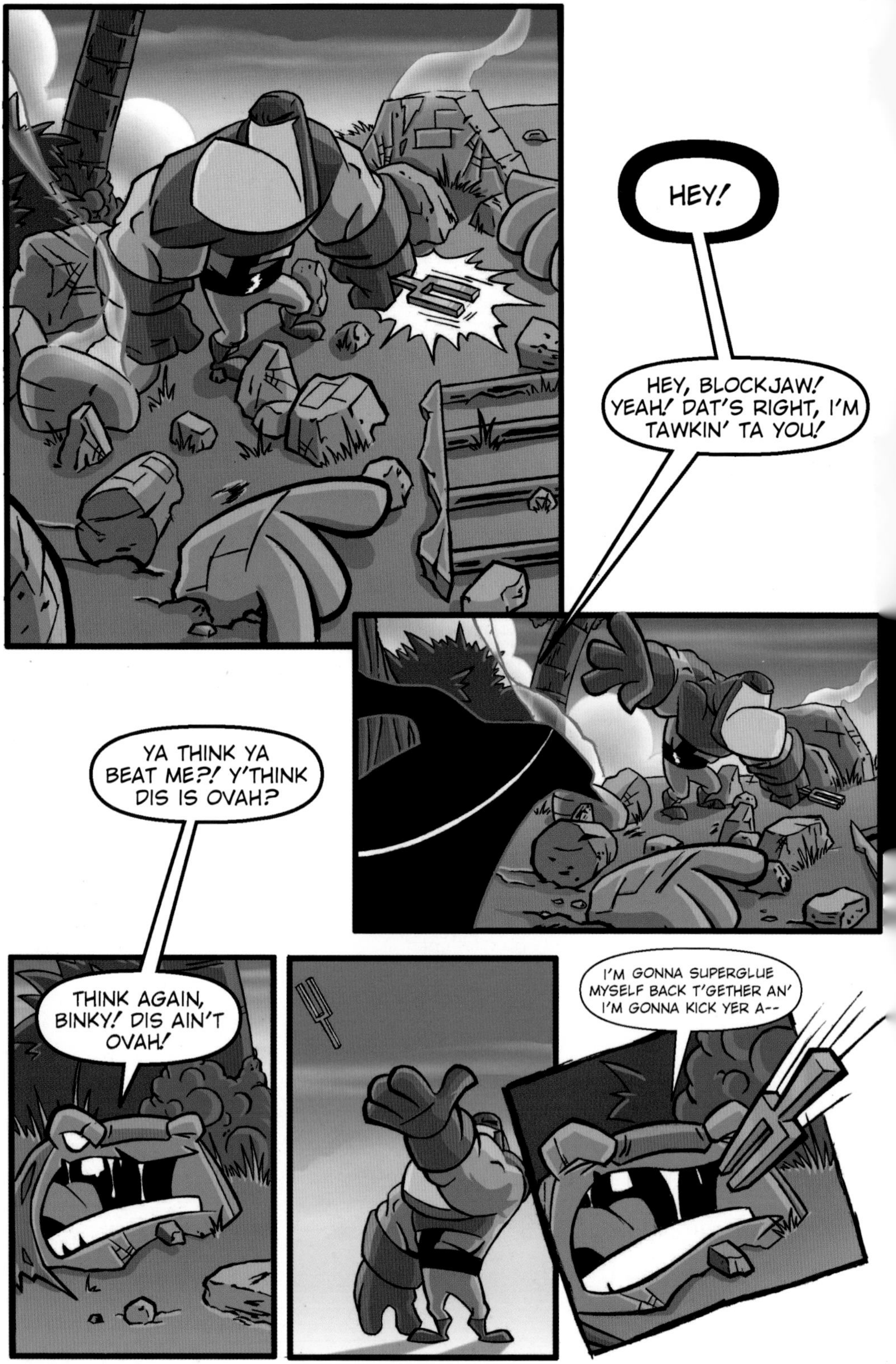
HEY!
HEY, BLOCKJAW! YEAH! DAT'S RIGHT, I'M TAWKIN' TA YOU!
YA THINK YA BEAT ME?! Y'THINK DIS IS OVAH?
THINK AGAIN, BINKY! DIS AIN'T OVAH!
I'M GONNA SUPERGLUE MYSELF BACK T'GETHER AN' I'M GONNA KICK YER A--

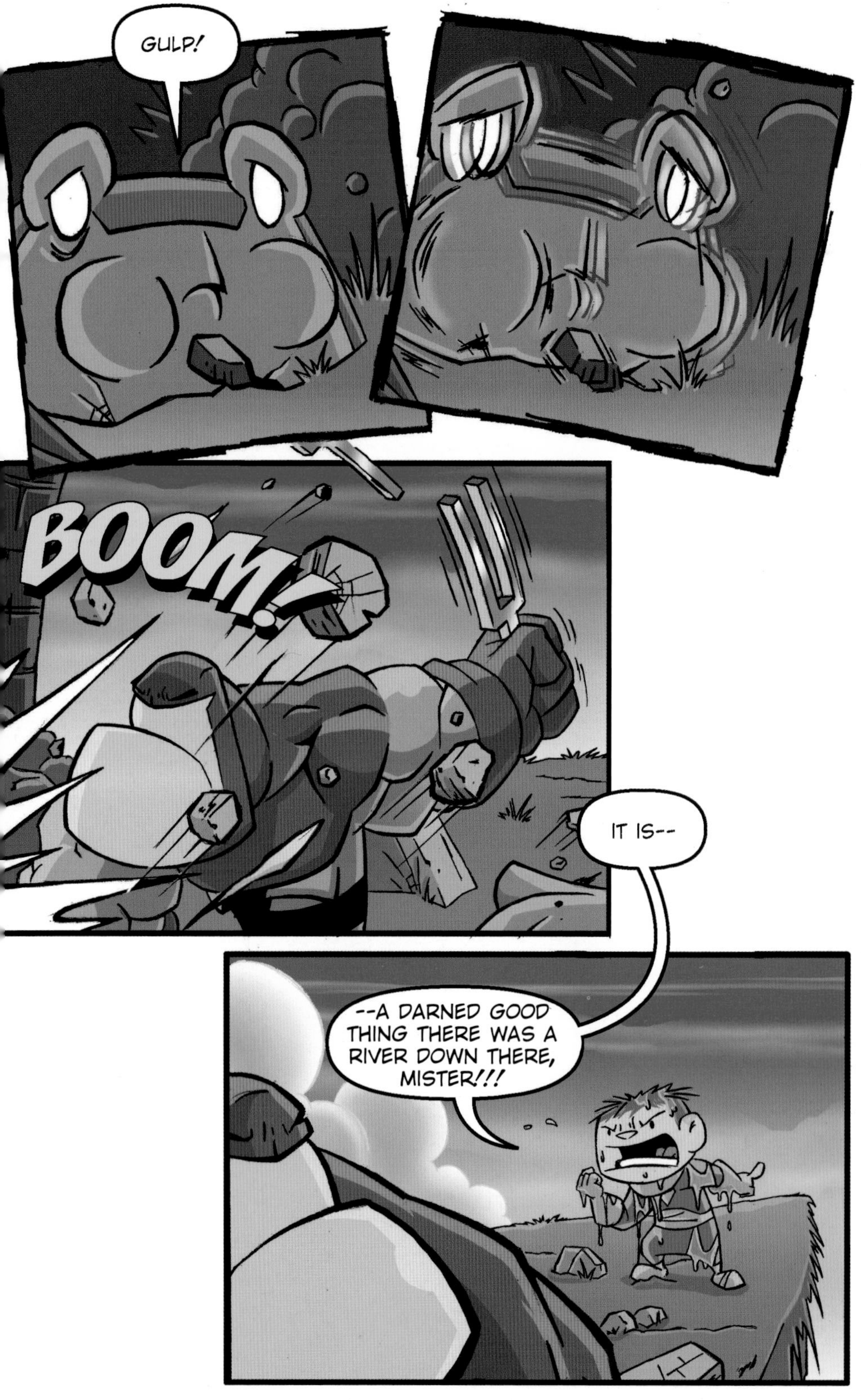
GULP!
BOOM!
IT IS--
--A DARNED GOOD THING THERE WAS A RIVER DOWN THERE, MISTER!!!

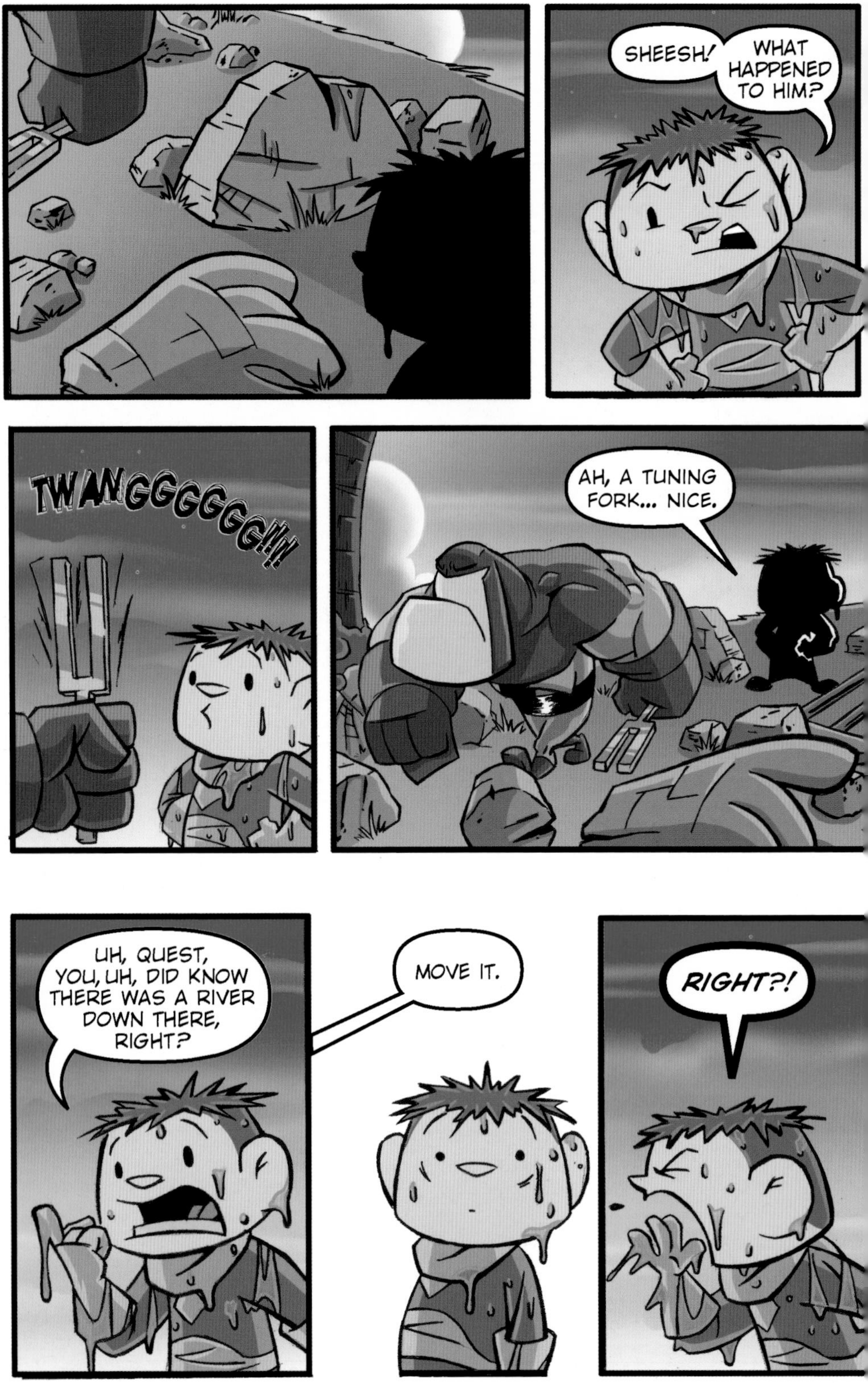
SHEESH!
WHAT HAPPENED TO HIM?
TWANGGGGGGG!!!!
AH, A TUNING FORK... NICE.
UH, QUEST, YOU, UH, DID KNOW THERE WAS A RIVER DOWN THERE, RIGHT?
MOVE IT.
RIGHT?!

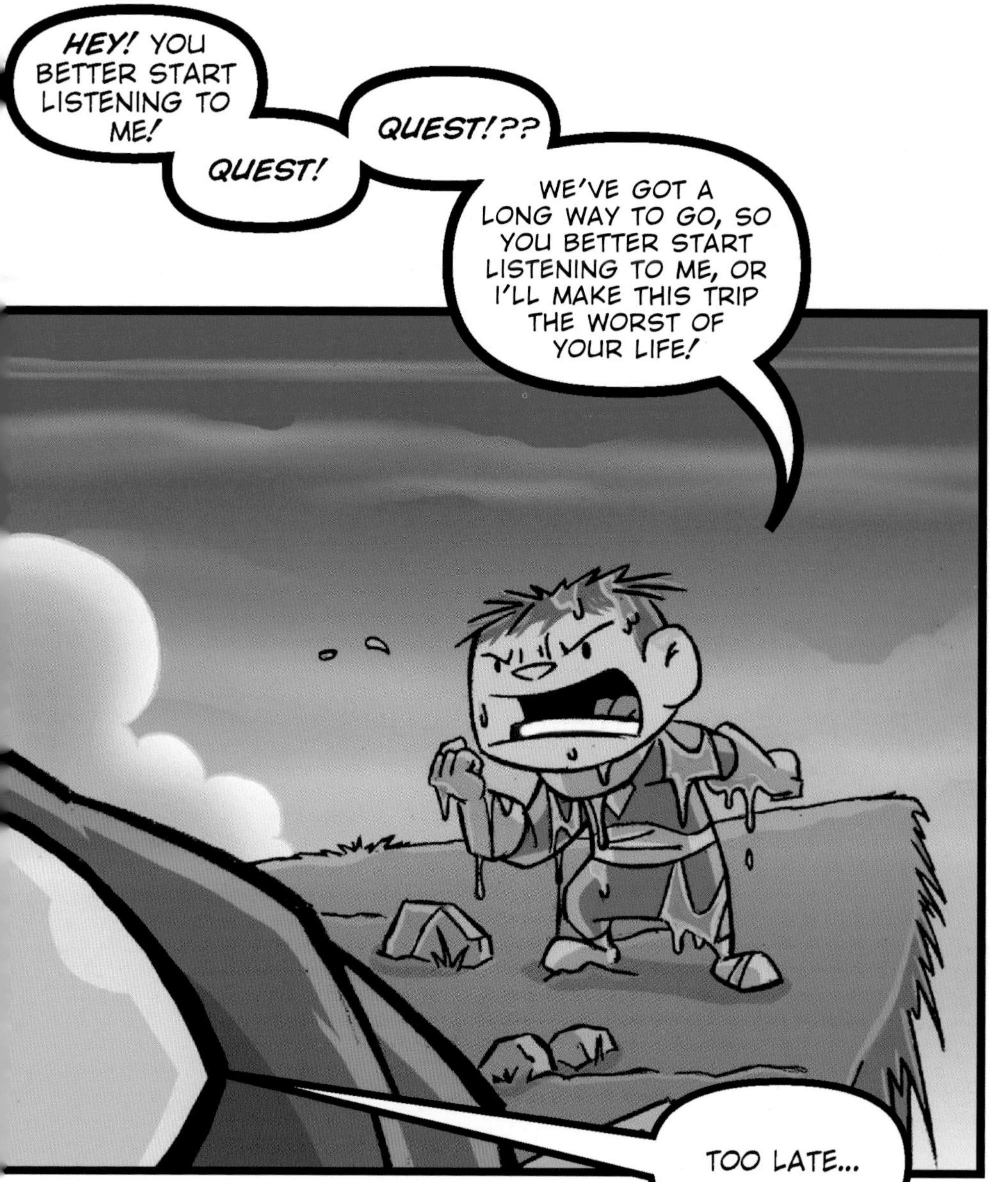
HEY! YOU BETTER START LISTENING TO ME!
QUEST!
QUEST!??
WE'VE GOT A LONG WAY TO GO, SO YOU BETTER START LISTENING TO ME, OR I'LL MAKE THIS TRIP THE WORST OF YOUR LIFE!
TOO LATE...

JUST THE BEGINNING...!

THE INHABITANTS OF ODYSSIA...

THIS IS YOUR GUIDE TO THE CHARACTERS AND CREATURES THAT LIVE IN NESTOR AND QUEST'S WORLD.

HERE YOU'LL FIND MORE INFORMATION ABOUT THE CHARACTERS IN THIS BOOK AND A SNEAK PEEK AT SOME UPCOMING CHARACTERS FROM FUTURE VOLUMES!

PRINCE NESTOR

NESTOR IS THE SPOILED SON OF **KING PANNING** AND **QUEEN KEIRAINE.** HE HAS BEEN CHARGED WITH PROTECTING THE **DAGGER OF THE WAY,** AS WELL AS FINDING THE LEGENDARY **"FIVE SWORDS"** WHICH ARE SAID TO BE THE KEY TO ULTIMATE POWER. BUT **LORD SPITE** WANTS THE SWORDS AS WELL. **NESTOR** ENLISTS **QUEST'S** HELP IN ORDER TO GET TO THE SWORDS FIRST. WITH **QUEST** AS HIS BODYGUARD HE SHOULD HAVE NO PROBLEM. . .

. . .AS LONG AS THEY DON'T KILL EACH OTHER FIRST!

QUEST

QUEST IS A MYSTERIOUS FORMER HERO OF THE LAND OF **ODYSSIA**. IT IS SAID HE APPEARED **25** YEARS AGO IN A MYSTERIOUS FLASH OF LIGHT WITH NO MEMORY OF WHO HE WAS OR WHERE HE CAME FROM. IT WAS **QUEST**, ALONG WITH HIS TEAM OF SPECIALISTS, **"THE ROUSTERS,"** WHO HELPED WIN THE WAR AGAINST THE EVIL **SHADOWSEED.** BUT DURING THE FINAL BATTLE, SOMETHING HAPPENED WHICH RESULTED IN **QUEST'S** BANISHMENT BY HIS TEAMMATES.

NOW **PRINCE NESTOR**, SON OF **QUEEN KEIRAINE**, HAS RECRUITED HIM TO AID IN THE EFFORT AGAINST A NEW MENACE TO THE LAND, **LORD SPITE.**

LORD SPITE

LORD SPITE IS THE NEW HEIR TO ***SHADOWSEED'S*** EVIL LEGACY. NO ONE KNOWS WHERE HE CAME FROM OR WHO HE REALLY IS. ***SPITE*** IS EXTREMELY POWERFUL DUE TO HIS CONNECTION TO ***THE SEED OF SHADOWS,*** WHICH IS THE SOURCE OF ALL EVIL MAGIC IN THE WORLD. ***SPITE*** HAS NUMEROUS MAGICAL POWERS INCLUDING THE ABILITY TO "CORRUPT" THE WEAK-MINDED AND CREATE EVIL NEW CREATURES, AND HE'S NEARLY INVULNERABLE TO ATTACK. HE TENDS TO EXHIBIT A CERTAIN LEVEL OF INSANITY; HE IS ANGRY ONE MINUTE, HAPPY AND FLAMBOYANTLY EVIL THE NEXT. . . PROBABLY DUE TO HIS EXPOSURE TO ***THE SEED.*** ANOTHER MYSTERY ABOUT ***SPITE*** IS HIS CONNECTION TO ***QUEST***. . .

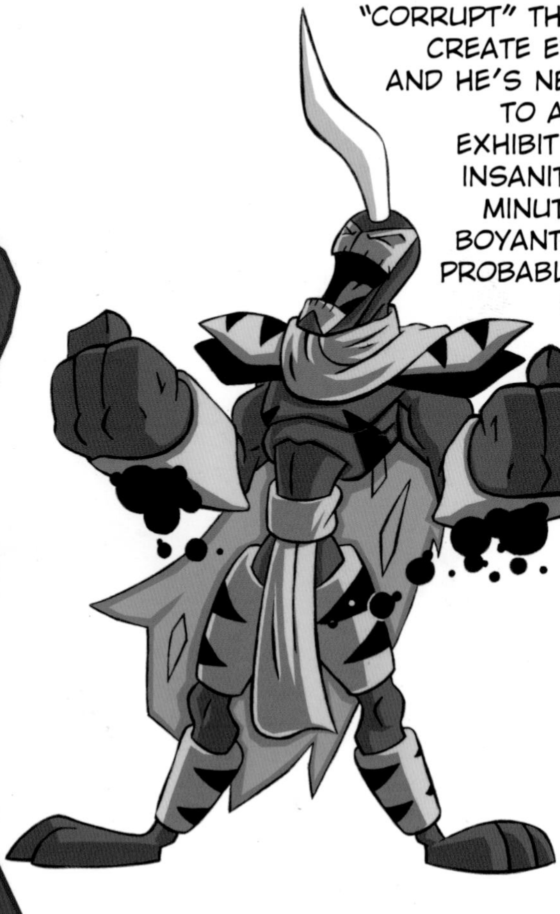

GENERAL OGUN

GENERAL OGUN WAS THE LEADER OF **KEIRAINE'S** ARMY DURING THE FIRST WAR. HE ULTIMATELY DEFECTED TO **SHADOWSEED'S** SIDE IN EXCHANGE FOR POWER AND THE ABILITY TO DESTROY **QUEST,** OF WHOM HE WAS EXTREMELY JEALOUS. **SHADOWSEED** (BEING THE DEVIL HE WAS) DUPED **OGUN** AND TOOK AWAY HIS EMOTIONS. THIS GAVE HIM THE POWER TO DEFEAT **QUEST** BUT ROBBED HIM OF THE SATISFACTION OF BEATING HIS ENEMY. TO THIS DAY, **OGUN** STILL DESIRES TO DESTROY THE FORMER HERO **QUEST** AND IS NOW **LORD SPITE'S** RIGHT-HAND MAN.

KATASTROPHE BROTHERS

KHAOS IS THE OLDEST OF THE **KATASTROPHE BROTHERS**, AND HE RESEMBLES A BULL. **KHAOS** IS HOT-HEADED AND THE STRONGEST OF THE THREE.

KONFUSION IS THE DUMBEST OF THE THREE, WHICH IS REALLY SAYING SOMETHING. HE RESEMBLES A "FRILLED" LIZARD.

KALAMITY IS THE PSEUDOINTELLECTUAL OF THE **KATASTROPHE BROTHERS.** HE RESEMBLES A VULTURE.

THE ***KATASTROPHE BROTHERS*** ARE THREE WATER DEMONS CREATED BY ***SHADOWSEED*** IN A MOMENT OF BOREDOM. SEPARATELY, THEY POSE LITTLE TO NO THREAT. BUT WHEN THEY ARE DOUSED WITH WATER, THEY COMBINE INTO ONE DEADLY, GIANT MONSTER KNOWN AS ***KATASTROPHE.*** HIS POWERS INCLUDE USING SPIT AS A CONCUSSIVE WEAPON, TRAPPING HIS ENEMIES WITH IT, AND FORGING THE SPIT INTO ANY SHAPE OR WEAPON HE WISHES.

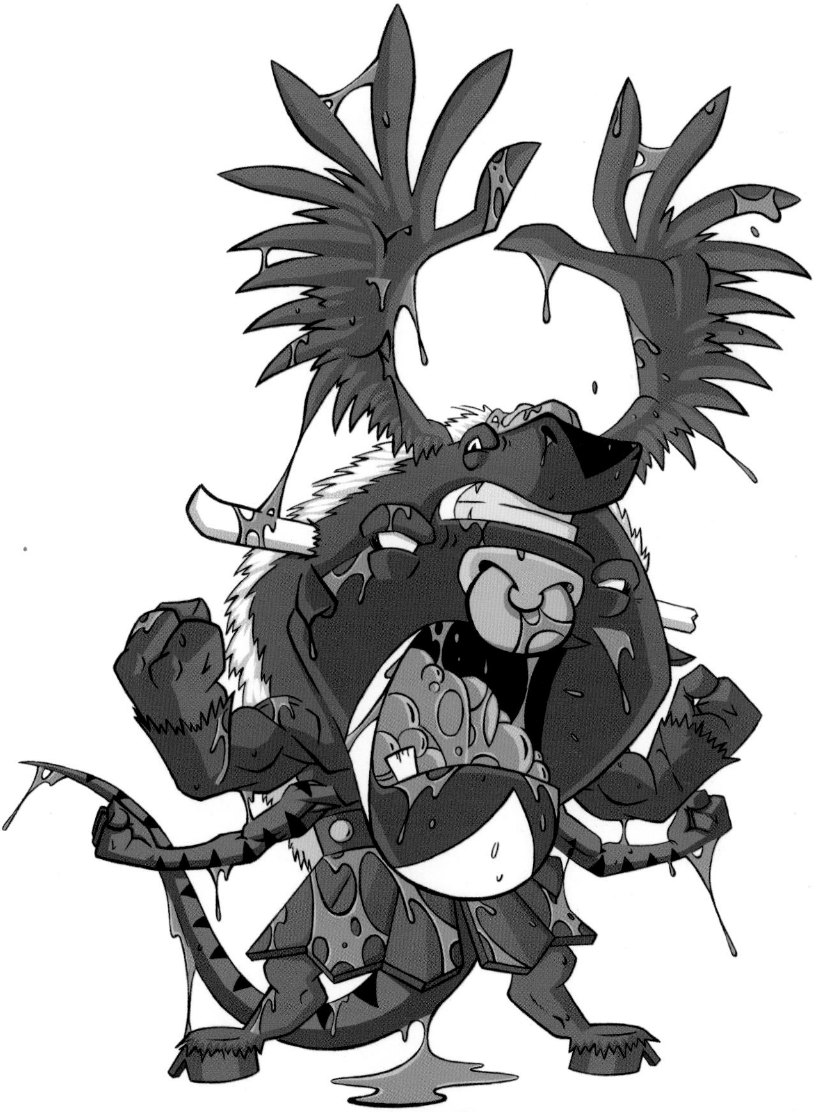

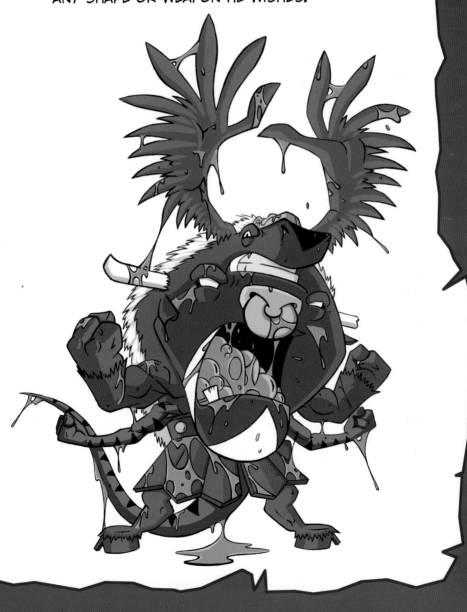

GATLING

GATLING IS ONE OF **QUEST'S** OLD **ROUSTER** BUDDIES. AS A CHILD, HE HAD A TERRIBLE CASE OF CAVITIES, SO HIS PARENTS TOOK HIM TO A BUMBLING WIZARD (UNBEKNOWNST TO THEM). THE WIZARD FIXED HIS JAW A LITTLE TOO WELL. . . **GATLING** CAN NOW CHEW UP ANYTHING AND SPIT IT OUT RAPID-FIRE. IN FACT, HIS ENTIRE SUIT OF ARMOR IS MADE UP OF METAL THAT HE CAN RIP OFF AND CHEW UP. **GATLING** AND **QUEST** SHARE A STRONG DISLIKE FOR ONE ANOTHER EVER SINCE AN INCIDENT DURING THE FINAL BATTLE WITH **SHADOWSEED** OVER 20 YEARS AGO.

ANNA MAHT

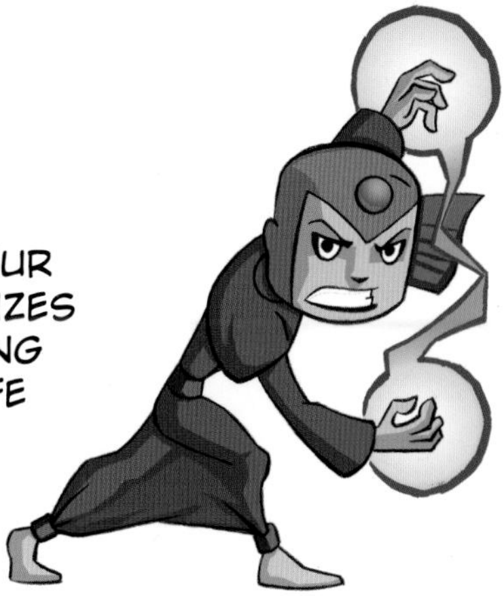

ANNA MAHT IS AN AMATEUR SORCERESS WHO SPECIALIZES IN ***ANIMANCY,*** OR BRINGING INANIMATE OBJECTS TO LIFE FOR A SHORT PERIOD OF TIME. SHE IS EAGER BUT INEXPERIENCED, AND HER SPELLS TEND TO MISFIRE. ***NESTOR*** RECRUITS HER AFTER SEEING HER SKILLS IN ACTION AT A WIZARD'S SCHOOL TOURNAMENT.

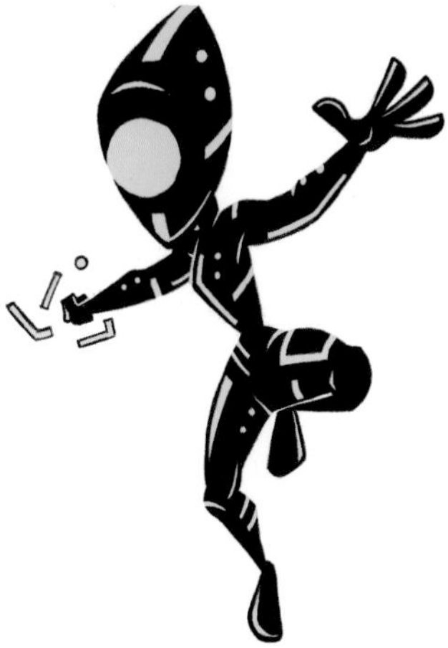

WAY

WAY IS A STRANGE AND MYSTERIOUS CREATURE. . .

THAT'S ALL WE CAN SAY FOR NOW!

DECEIT

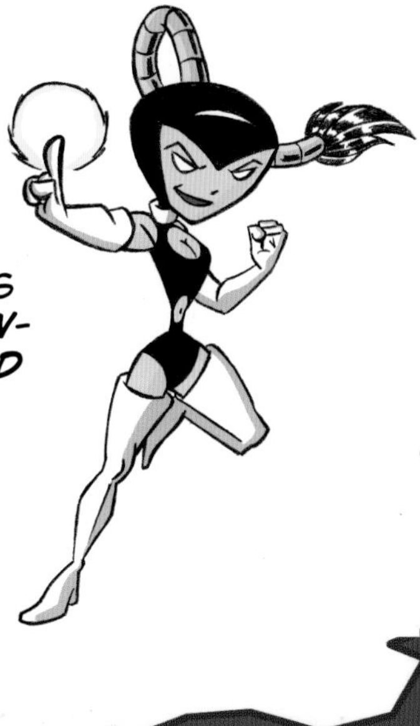

DECEIT IS AN EVIL, CONNIVING, EXTREMELY POWERFUL SORCERESS WHO FIRST WORKED FOR ***SHADOW-SEED*** AND NOW WORKS FOR ***LORD SPITE.*** HER FOREMOST ABILITY IS TO DISGUISE OTHERS, CAUSING CONFUSION ON THE BATTLEFIELD. MANY TIMES ALLIES HAVE FOUGHT AGAINST EACH OTHER BECAUSE ***DECEIT*** MADE THEM APPEAR AS THEIR ENEMIES.

SNARLS

CREATED BY ***SHADOWSEED*** AS THE FIRST LINE OF ATTACK IN HIS VAST ARMY, ***SNARLS*** REMAIN THE MAIN ARM OF ***LORD SPITE'S*** ARMY. UTTERLY VICIOUS KILLERS WITH RAZOR-SHARP TEETH, THEY ARE MERCILESS AND TOUGH BUT NOT VERY BRIGHT. ONE ODD QUIRK ABOUT ***SNARLS*** IS THAT THEY TAKE GREAT PRIDE IN THEIR HAIR. THEY HAVE THE ABILITY TO KNOCK A GROWN MAN DOWN AND EVEN BREAK SOME BONES WITH THEIR SNARLS. IN LARGE GROUPS, ***SNARLS*** HAVE BEEN KNOWN TO DECIMATE ENTIRE CITIES. THEY ARE RESISTANT (BUT NOT IMPERVIOUS) TO MAGIC, WHICH MADE DEFEATING THEM DURING THE WAR EXTREMELY DIFFICULT.

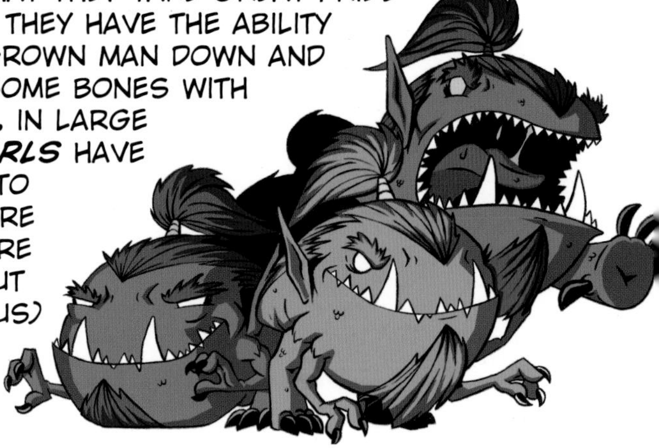

GRAER

GRAER IS A WILY, THIEVING GRIFFIN WHO LIVES FOR PARTYING, STEALING, AND OTHER FORMS OF DEBAUCHERY. DURING THE FIRST WAR, HE OFTEN SERVED AS ***QUEST'S*** BATTLE STEED BEFORE HE WAS KICKED OUT OF THE ***ROUSTERS*** FOR STEALING AND SELLING THEIR ARMOR ON THE BLACK MARKET.

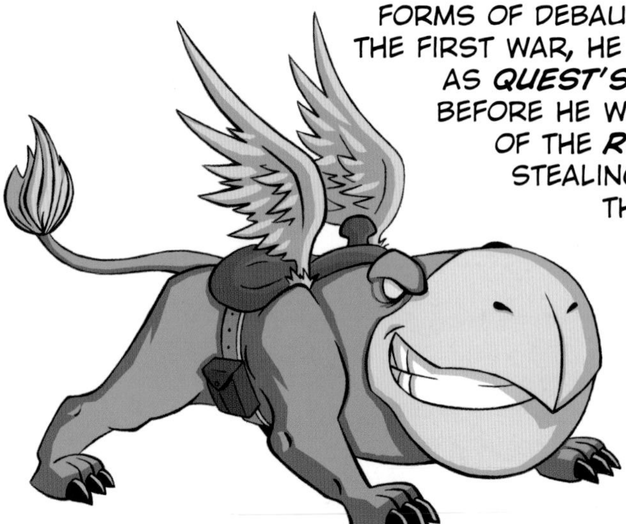

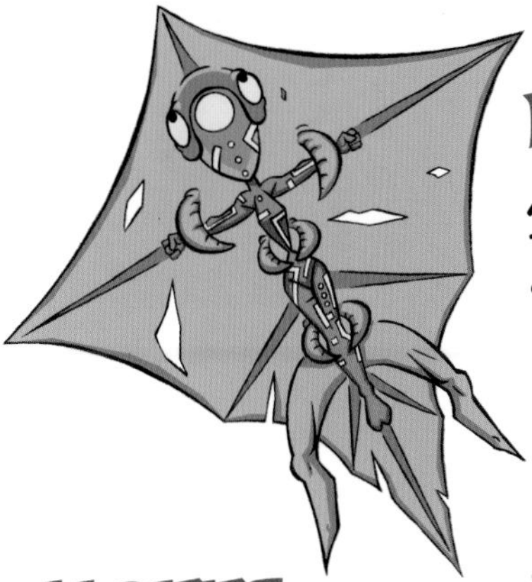

KITES

KITES ARE CREATURES THAT CAN BE STRAPPED TO SOMEONE'S BACK AND USED TO GLIDE AROUND THE SKIES. ***KITES*** FEED OFF THE SWEAT OF THE USER.

HOPPS

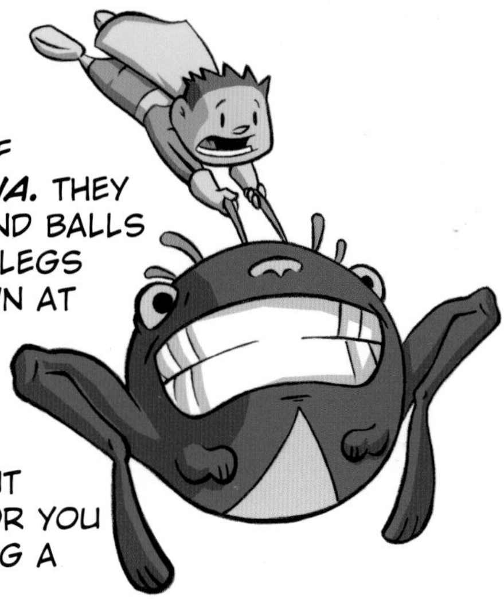

HOPPS ARE ONE OF THE PRIMARY MEANS OF TRANSPORT IN ***ODYSSIA.*** THEY ARE ESSENTIALLY ROUND BALLS WITH GIANT, FROGLIKE LEGS THAT HOP UP AND DOWN AT GREAT SPEEDS FOR GREAT DISTANCES. THEY ARE DIMWITTED BUT VERY FRIENDLY CREATURES. WATCH OUT FOR THEIR TONGUES, OR YOU MIGHT WIND UP GETTING A REALLY GROSS BATH!

ALBERT / BASTIONITES

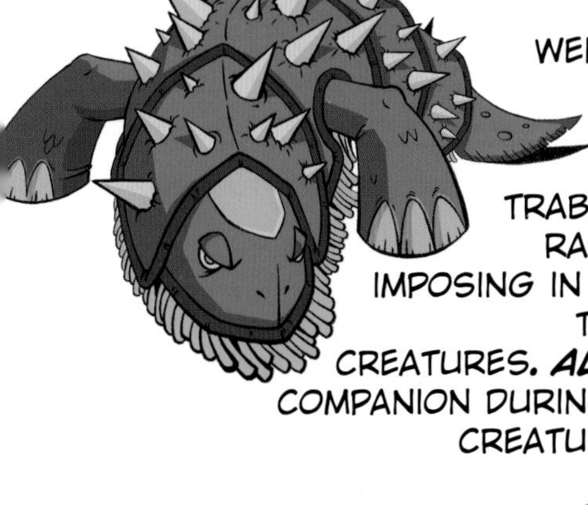

ALBERT IS A ***BASTIONITE,*** A RACE OF RARE, HUGE, LIVING FORTRESSES. THEIR INTERIORS ARE USED TO STORE WEAPONRY AND ARMOR, AS WELL AS FOR SLEEPING QUARTERS. A ***BASTIONITE'S*** SHELL IS EXTREMELY TOUGH (NEARLY IMPENETRABLE), AND IT IS COVERED WITH RAZOR-SHARP SPIKES. THOUGH IMPOSING IN APPEARANCE, ***BASTIONITES*** TEND TO BE GENTLE, DOGLIKE CREATURES. ***ALBERT*** WAS ***QUEST'S*** LOYAL COMPANION DURING THE WAR AND IS THE ONLY CREATURE ***QUEST*** SEEMS TO "LIKE."

HERE'S WHAT PEOPLE ARE SAYING ABOUT QUEST!

"It's an utterly charming book that grabs you from the start and doesn't let go."

—Augie De Blick, Comic Book Resources

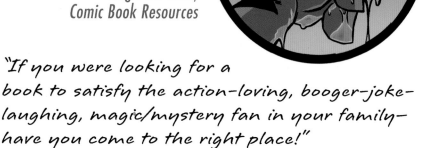

"If you were looking for a book to satisfy the action-loving, booger-joke-laughing, magic/mystery fan in your family—have you come to the right place!"

—ComicsintheClassroom.net

"There is a distinct sense of childlike whimsy to this comic, a playful feeling that anything goes as the creator's imagination practically bleeds onto the page."

—Eric Lindberg, Broken Frontier

"Fun, imaginative, and frequently twisted, *The World of Quest* smacks the traditional hero genre firmly in the jaw. Enjoy!"
—Tom Pugsley, writer/editor, TEEN TITANS, THE BATMAN, BEN 10

"What a read! I haven't been this intrigued and entertained since I read the first [trade paperback] for *Bone*. 4.5 stars out of 5!"
—Luis Pagan, *SilverBulletComics.com*

"*Quest* rocks! Fantastic adventure. Beautiful artwork and writing! A must-read!"
—Tommy Castillo, artist, DETECTIVE COMICS, GREEN ARROW

"FUN!"
"FANTASTIC!"
"A MUST-READ!"
"TWISTED!"

"Check it out. It's smart, funny, and definitely worth it . . . plus there's mucus, lots and lots of mucus!"
—Michael Ryan, artist, NEW X-MEN, EXCALIBUR, SPIDER-MAN

"I'm Scott Lobdell and I support this book!"
—Scott Lobdell, two-time Wizard Award® winning writer, X-MEN

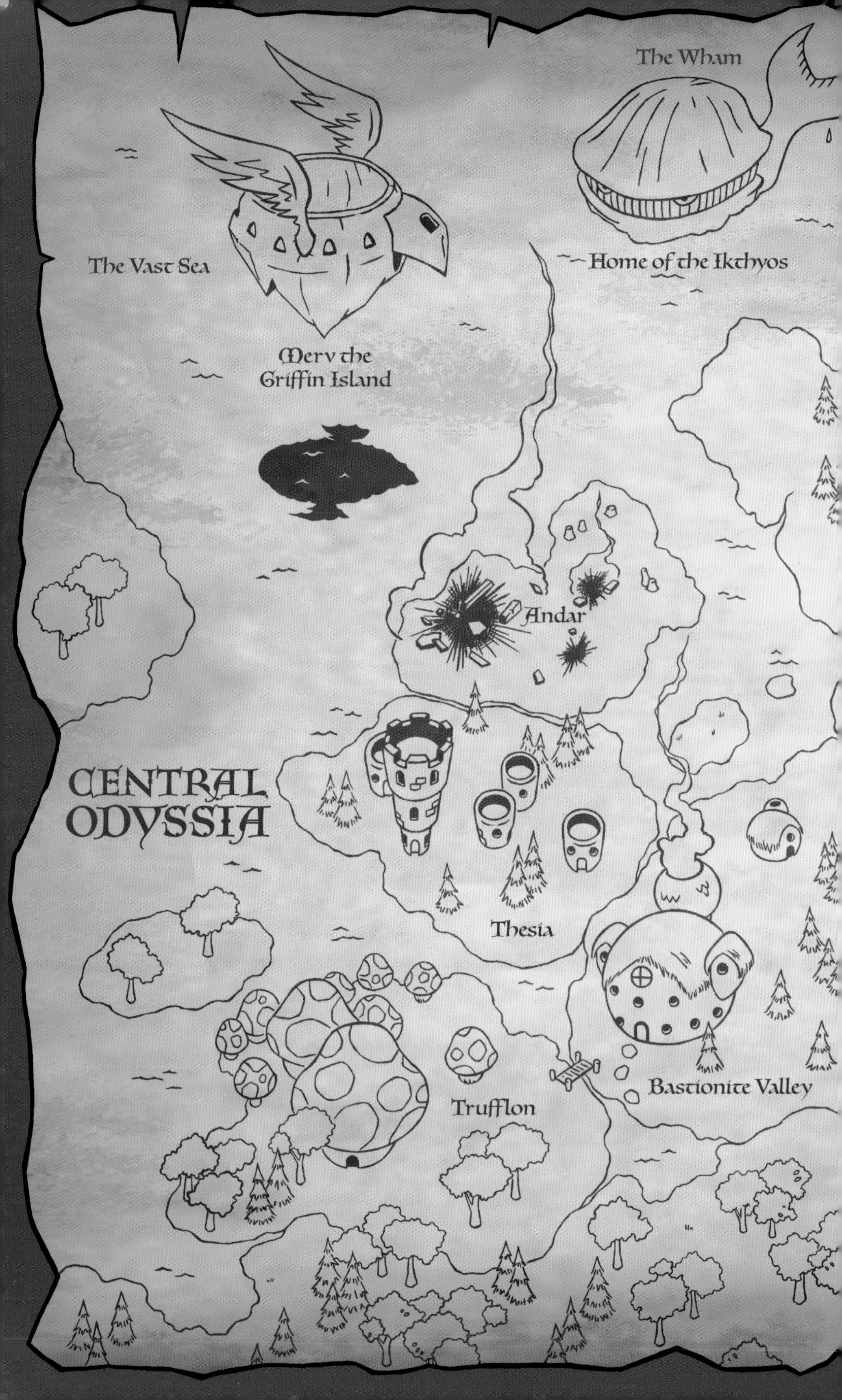

The Wham
The Vast Sea
Home of the Ikthyos
Merv the
Griffin Island
Andar
CENTRAL
ODYSSIA
Thesia
Bastionite Valley
Trufflon

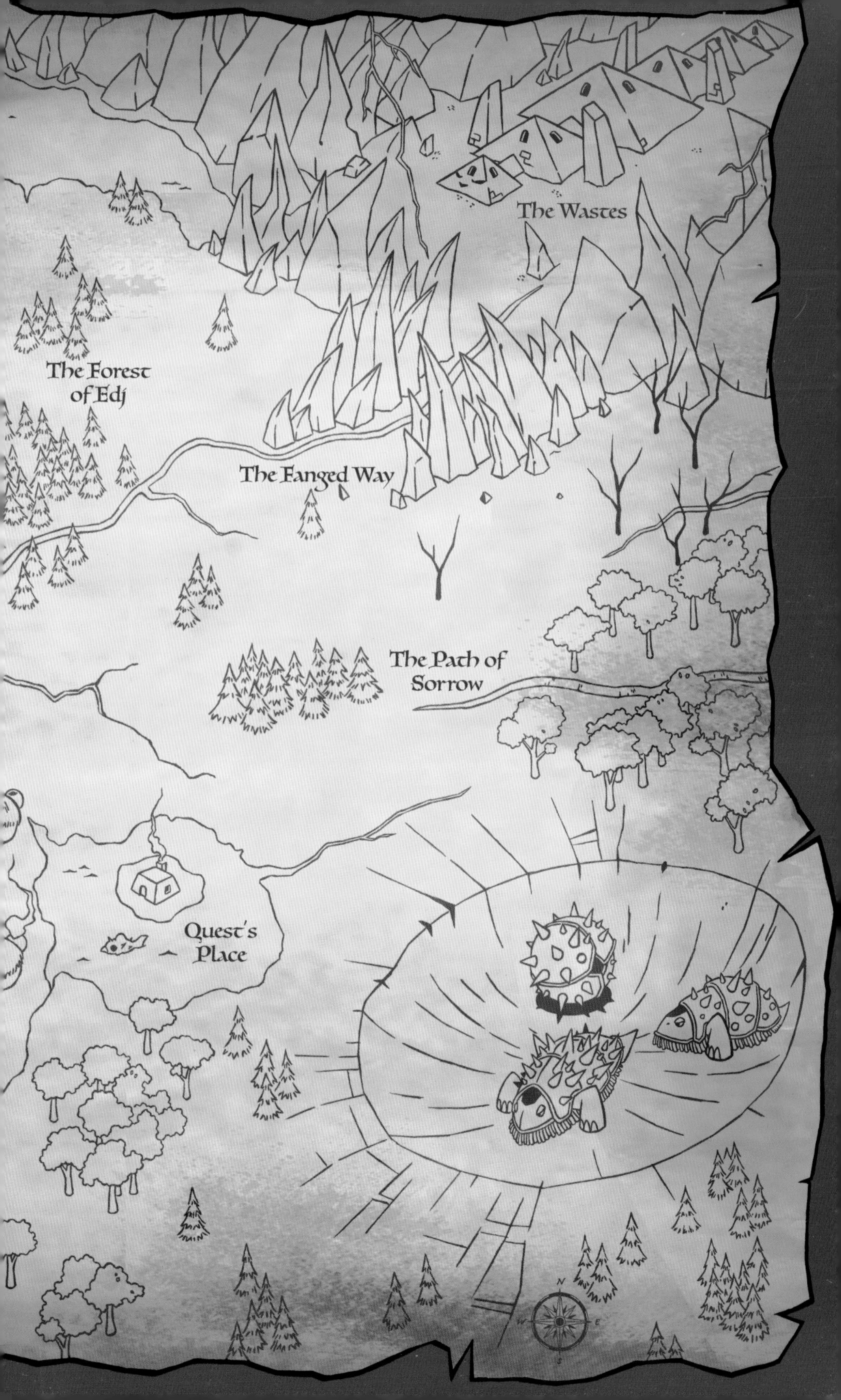
The Wastes
The Forest of Edj
The Fanged Way
The Path of Sorrow
Quest's Place

YEN PRESS
HACHETTE BOOK GROUP USA
237 PARK AVENUE, NEW YORK, NY 10017

VISIT US ON THE WEB AT WWW.YENPRESS.COM
AND WWW.HACHETTEBOOKGROUPUSA.COM.

YEN PRESS IS AN IMPRINT OF *HACHETTE BOOK GROUP USA,*
INC. THE *YEN PRESS* NAME AND LOGO IS A TRADEMARK OF
HACHETTE BOOK GROUP USA, INC.

FIRST EDITION: NOVEMBER 2007

ISBN-13: 978-0-7595-2402-6
ISBN-10: 0-7595-2402-5

10   9   8   7   6   5   4   3   2   1

MDA

PRINTED IN CHINA